on the Market!

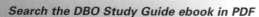

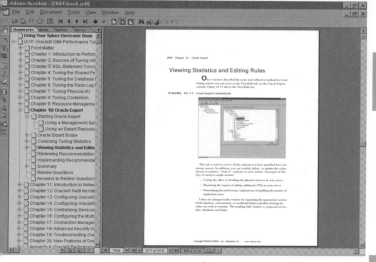

Search the DBO Study Guide ebook in PDF

- Access the entire *OCP: Oracle8i DBO Study Guide*, complete with figures and tables, in electronic format.

- Use Adobe Acrobat Reader (included on the CD-ROM) to view the electronic book.

- Search chapters to find information on any topic in seconds.

Oracle8i Evaluation Version

- Preview Oracle8i in this downloadable evaluation version.

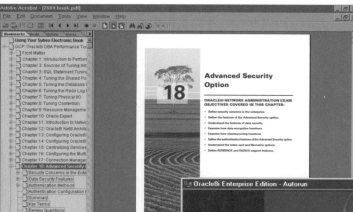

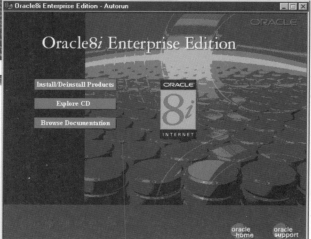

SYBEX

OCP:
Oracle8i DBO
Study Guide

OCP:
Oracle8i™ DBO
Study Guide

Lance Mortensen

San Francisco • Paris • Düsseldorf • Soest • London

SYBEX®

Associate Publisher: Richard Mills
Contracts and Licensing Manager: Kristine O'Callaghan
Acquisitions and Developmental Editor: Kim Goodfriend
Editor: Julie Sakaue
Production Editor: Leslie E.H. Light
Technical Editors: Dax Mickelson and Ashok Hanumanth
Book Designer: Bill Gibson
Graphic Illustrator: Tony Jonick
Electronic Publishing Specialist: Susie Hendrickson
Proofreaders: Laurie O'Connell, Jennifer Campbell, and Molly Glover
Indexer: Ann Rogers
CD Coordinator: Kara Eve Schwartz
CD Technician: Kevin Ly
Cover Designer: Archer Design
Cover Photograph: Photo Researchers

Library of Congress Card Number: 00-108230

ISBN: 0-7821-2686-3

SYBEX and the SYBEX logo are either registered trademarks or trademarks of SYBEX Inc. in the United States and/or other countries.

Screen reproductions produced with FullShot 99. FullShot 99 © 1991-1999 Inbit Incorporated. All rights reserved. FullShot is a trademark of Inbit Incorporated.

The CD interface was created using Macromedia Director, © 1994, 1997-1999 Macromedia Inc. For more information on Macromedia and Macromedia Director, visit http://www.macromedia.com.

Internet screen shot(s) using Microsoft Internet Explorer 5.5 reprinted by permission from Microsoft Corporation.

SYBEX is an independent entity from Oracle Corporation and is not affiliated with Oracle Corporation in any manner. This publication may be used in assisting students to prepare for an Oracle Certified Professional exam. Neither Oracle Corporation nor SYBEX warrants that use of this publication will ensure passing the relevant exam. Oracle is either a registered trademark or a trademark of Oracle Corporation in the United States and/or other countries.

TRADEMARKS: SYBEX has attempted throughout this book to distinguish proprietary trademarks from descriptive terms by following the capitalization style used by the manufacturer.

The author and publisher have made their best efforts to prepare this book, and the content is based upon final release software whenever possible. Portions of the manuscript may be based upon pre-release versions supplied by software manufacturer(s). The author and the publisher make no representation or warranties of any kind with regard to the completeness or accuracy of the contents herein and accept no liability of any kind including but not limited to performance, merchantability, fitness for any particular purpose, or any losses or damages of any kind caused or alleged to be caused directly or indirectly from this book.

Manufactured in the United States of America

10 9 8 7 6 5 4 3 2 1

Software License Agreement: Terms and Conditions

This book is dedicated to the many health professionals who spend countless hours and energy patching people up. Hopefully Oracle databases can make your job just a bit easier.

Acknowledgments

I would like to thank all the many people at Sybex who stuck through this project. We faced a few stumbling blocks (including a head-on crash that involved my entire family), but managed to get through it. Many thanks go to Kim for starting the book, Julie for being a great editor, Leslie for keeping things going, and Susie, Tony, Laurie, Jennifer, and Molly for turning the words and images into a book. As always, thanks to Neil for being a good friend and publisher, and Richard for stepping in and seeing this project to the end. Thanks also go to Dax for checking the technical content and Temsha for helping with the installation chapter.

I would also like to thank Dr. Vader and Dr. Kabins for taking care of my kids. There's nothing like seeing your two oldest in intensive care to help you keep your priorities straight. I would also like to thank Dr. Bronstein and Dr. Schwartsman for fixing me up. I asked for bionic parts, but since the insurance wouldn't cover it, they got stuck with making my old parts work again.

As always, thanks go to my wife and kids for just being themselves. Bryce now plays D&D and computer games with me, Jessany is growing up too fast, Devin plays robots and spaceships with me, and Logan is definitely a two year old. Luann more than once has wondered if she is the only grownup around, especially when we have our "Iron Chef" dessert battles.

Contents at a Glance

Introduction   *xxi*

Assessment Test   **xxxi**

Chapter   1   Introduction to Oracle and Relational Databases   1

Chapter   2   Installing and Configuring Oracle8i   31

Chapter   3   Oracle8i Enterprise Manager and Other Tools   81

Chapter   4   Introduction to SQL and PL/SQL   123

Chapter   5   Creating and Managing Databases   159

Chapter   6   Oracle Users and Security   197

Chapter   7   Installing and Managing Applications   227

Chapter   8   Importing and Exporting Data   259

Chapter   9   Proactive Management of an Oracle Server   291

Chapter   10   Backups and Restorations   323

Chapter   11   Introduction to WebDB   353

Appendix   A   Practice Exam   393

Appendix   B   Performance and Tuning   409

Glossary   441

Index   *447*

Contents

Introduction   *xxi*

Assessment Test   **xxxi**

Chapter   1   Introduction to Oracle and Relational Databases   1

Responsibilities of the Database Operator   2
  Installing Oracle8i   3
  Creating Databases   3
  Importing and Exporting Data   3
  Implementing Tablespaces   3
  Managing the Databases and Server   4
Responsibilities of the Database Administrator   5
Responsibilities of the Application Developer   6
Oracle Basics   7
  Networks and Oracle8i   7
  Types of Databases   10
  Oracle Instances   13
  Communicating with Oracle8i   16
Database Components   17
  Physical Objects   17
  Logical Objects   18
Warehousing versus Transaction Processing   20
Summary   21
  Key Terms   22
Review Questions   23
Answers to Review Questions   28

Chapter   2   Installing and Configuring Oracle8i   31

Oracle8i Directory Structure   32
  Initialization Parameter Files (INIT.ORA)   34
  Password Files (PWD.ORA)   34
  General Client Preferences (SQLNET.ORA)   35

Installing Oracle8i on Linux   35

   Hardware and Software Installation Requirements   36

   Tasks to Be Performed as User Root   37

   Tasks to Be Performed as User Oracle   39

   Installing Oracle 8.1.6 on Linux   40

   Post-Installation Tasks   45

Installing Oracle8i on Windows NT   49

   Installation Requirements   49

   Tasks to Do Before Installing Oracle   49

   Installing Oracle 8.1.6 on Windows NT   50

Installing Oracle8i on Novell NetWare   55

   Installation Requirements   55

   Tasks to Do Before Installing Oracle   55

Managing Oracle Trace Files   57

Using Server Manager to Start Up and Shut Down Oracle Databases   57

   Starting Oracle   57

   Stopping Oracle   59

Listener Configuration (LISTENER.ORA)   60

   Starting and Stopping the Listener   61

Client Installation   63

Net8 Configuration (TNSNAMES.ORA)   70

Summary   71

   Key Terms   72

Review Questions   73

Answers to Review Questions   78

Chapter   3   Oracle8i Enterprise Manager and Other Tools   81

Installing Enterprise Manager   83

Oracle Enterprise Manager   91

   Discovering Databases   93

   Configuring Preferences   95

   Adding Administrators to the Management Server   97

   Creating Groups   98

   Creating Jobs and Events   99

   Using the Enterprise Manager Configuration Assistant   100

Managing Instances with Instance Manager 100
SQL Commands and SQLPlus Worksheet 109
SQL Commands and SQL*Plus 110
Server Manager 112
Storage Manager 112
Schema Manager 113
Security Manager 113
Backup Manager 113
Diagnostics Pack 114
Tuning Pack 114
Summary 115
   Key Terms 115
Review Questions 117
Answers to Review Questions 121

Chapter	4	**Introduction to SQL and PL/SQL**	**123**

PL/SQL Tools 126
   Starting SQLPlus Worksheet 127
   Starting Server Manager 128
   Starting SQL*Plus 129
The SELECT Statement 130
   Renaming Columns 134
   Selecting Tables from Other Schemas 134
   Arithmetic Functions 135
   Character Functions 137
   NULL Values 138
   Logical Operators 139
   Summarizing Data 139
   UNION Operator 140
   Joining Tables 142
   Adding Comments to SQL Code 145
Updating Rows 146
Inserting Rows 146
Procedures 147

Summary	148
Key Terms	149
Review Questions	150
Answers to Review Questions	156

Chapter 5   Creating and Managing Databases   159

Performance and Placement of Database Files	160
Planning for Fault Tolerance and Reliability	161
Planning for Speed	166
Planning for Growth	167
Where to Put the Database	167
Understanding Database Files and SIDs	168
System IDs (SIDs)	168
Physical Components of a Database	169
Creating Databases	172
Checking Prerequisites	172
Creating the Password File	173
Creating the Parameter File	173
Starting and Restarting the Instance	173
Creating the Database Using PL/SQL	173
Creating the Database Using Database Configuration Assistant	175
Managing Database Files	184
Storage Manager	184
Logical Components of a Database	187
Summary	187
Key Terms	188
Review Questions	189
Answers to Review Questions	194

Chapter 6   Oracle Users and Security   197

Understanding Object Security and Ownership	198
Default Users	199
Creating New Users	200
Database Roles	207

System Privileges 212

Object Permissions 213

Profiles 214

NetWare and Oracle Integration 216

NT and Oracle Integration 218

Unix and Oracle Integration 218

Summary 218

Key Terms 219

Review Questions 220

Answers to Review Questions 225

Chapter 7 Installing and Managing Applications 227

Designing or Acquiring a Database Design 229

Logical Database Design 229

Instance Parameters 232

Physical Database Design 233

Ensuring Adequate Resources 233

Creating and Managing a Tablespace 234

Creating a Schema Account 237

Database Accounts and Schemas 237

Creating and Managing Schema Accounts 238

Creating and Managing Database Objects 240

Creating Schemas Using SQL Syntax and Schema Manager 240

Planning, Implementing, and Managing Database Security 250

Ensuring Adequate Tablespace Sizing 250

Summary 250

Key Terms 251

Review Questions 252

Answers to Review Questions 257

Chapter 8 Importing and Exporting Data 259

The INSERT Statement 260

Data Management Tools 264

Exporting Oracle Data 264

		Importing Data	269
		Loading Non-Oracle Data	274
		Scheduling Data Jobs	282
		Summary	282
		Key Terms	283
		Review Questions	284
		Answers to Review Questions	289
Chapter	**9**	**Proactive Management of an Oracle Server**	**291**
		Common Problems in Oracle	292
		Detecting Problems	293
		Responding to Problems	294
		Oracle Intelligent Agent	295
		Loading the Windows NT Agent	296
		Loading the NetWare Agent	300
		Loading the UNIX Agent	302
		Oracle Events	302
		Creating Events	303
		Modifying Events	305
		Oracle Jobs	307
		Creating Jobs	307
		Modifying and Running Jobs Manually	312
		Viewing Job Details, Output, and History	313
		Deleting Jobs	315
		Summary	316
		Key Terms	316
		Review Questions	317
		Answers to Review Questions	321
Chapter	**10**	**Backups and Restorations**	**323**
		Why Backup	324
		Developing a Backup Plan	325
		How Often Will the Backups Occur?	325
		To What Medium Will the Backups Be Made?	325

Who Is Responsible for the Backups?   326
How Will the Backups Be Verified?   326
Protecting Your Data with Various OS Options   326
Backup and Recovery Scenarios   327
Instance Failures versus Media Failures   327
Cold versus Warm Backups   328
NOARCHIVELOG Mode versus ARCHIVELOG Mode   328
Backing Up in NOARCHIVELOG Mode   329
Converting a Database to ARCHIVELOG Mode   330
Creating Backup Jobs   335
Backing Up the Database Immediately   338
Restoring Databases   343
Restoring Data from a Cold Backup   343
Restoring Data from a Full Backup   343
Summary   345
Key Terms   346
Review Questions   347
Answers to Review Questions   351

Chapter 11   **Introduction to WebDB**   **353**

Key Features of WebDB   354
Installing WebDB   355
Connecting to WebDB   361
Browsing Database Objects   362
Building Database Objects   367
Administering Users, Privileges, and Roles   373
User Manager   373
Grant Manager   373
Role Manager   374
Changing Your Password   375
Reporting WebDB Privileges   375
Configuring WebDB Activity Logs   377
Configuring Listener Settings   378
Changing Listener Settings   379

Monitoring WebDB		382
Building a Site		383
Summary		385
	Key Terms	386
Review Questions		387
Answers to Review Questions		391
Appendix A	**Practice Exam**	**393**
	Answers to Practice Exam	404
Appendix B	**Performance and Tuning**	**409**
	Analyzing Database Usage	410
	Locking Issues	411
	Rollback Segment Issues	412
	Redo Log File Issues	414
	Parameter File Issues	415
	Performance Issues	416
	The Diagnostics Pack	417
	Installing the Diagnostics Pack	417
	Running the Diagnostics Pack	420
	The Tuning Pack	429
	Oracle Expert	429
	Index Tuning Expert	436
	SQL Analyze	439
	Tablespace Manager	439
	Summary	439
Glossary		**441**
Index		*447*

Table of Exercises

Exercise	**2.1**	Installing Oracle on a Linux Server.	40
Exercise	**2.2**	Installing Oracle on a Windows NT Server	50
Exercise	**2.3**	Installing Oracle on NetWare	56
Exercise	**2.4**	Installing the Oracle Client	63
Exercise	**3.1**	Installing Enterprise Manager and the Diagnostics and Tuning Packs	83
Exercise	**3.2**	Discovering Databases.	93
Exercise	**3.3**	Configuring Preferences	96
Exercise	**3.4**	Adding Enterprise Manager Administrators	97
Exercise	**3.5**	Using Instance Manager to Start and Stop an Instance	101
Exercise	**3.6**	Using SQLPlus Worksheet to Run SQL Commands	109
Exercise	**3.7**	Using SQL*Plus to Run SQL Commands	111
Exercise	**5.1**	Creating Databases Using the Database Configuration Assistant	175
Exercise	**6.1**	Creating New Users	201
Exercise	**6.2**	Changing Tablespace Assignments of a User	204
Exercise	**6.3**	Setting Quotas on Users	206
Exercise	**6.4**	Creating Oracle Database Roles	208
Exercise	**6.5**	Granting Privileges and Roles to Roles	209
Exercise	**6.6**	Assigning Users to Roles.	211
Exercise	**6.7**	Creating and Editing Profiles	214
Exercise	**6.8**	Assigning Profiles to Users	216
Exercise	**7.1**	Creating New Tablespaces	234
Exercise	**7.2**	Creating a Schema Account	238
Exercise	**7.3**	Creating Tables.	241
Exercise	**7.4**	Creating Indexes	244
Exercise	**7.5**	Creating Views	246
Exercise	**7.6**	Creating Procedures.	247
Exercise	**7.7**	Creating Synonyms	249
Exercise	**8.1**	Using the INSERT Statement	262
Exercise	**8.2**	Exporting Oracle Data	265

Exercise 8.3   Importing Oracle Data 269

Exercise 8.4   Disabling and Enabling Constraints. 275

Exercise 8.5   Loading Non-Oracle Data 277

Exercise 9.1   Configuring and Loading the Windows NT Agent 298

Exercise 9.2   Loading the NetWare Agent 301

Exercise 9.3   Loading the UNIX Agent 302

Exercise 9.4   Creating Events 303

Exercise 9.5   Modifying Events 305

Exercise 9.6   Creating an Operating System Job 308

Exercise 9.7   Creating a SQL Job 310

Exercise 9.8   Viewing Job Details, Output, and History 313

Exercise 10.1   Performing a Full Database Backup in NOARCHIVELOG Mode. 330

Exercise 10.2   Editing the INIT.ORA File to Support Automatic Archiving 331

Exercise 10.3   Converting a Database to ARCHIVELOG Mode Using Instance Manager. . . 332

Exercise 10.4   Creating a Backup Job 335

Exercise 10.5   Backing Up the Database Immediately 339

Exercise 10.6   Restoring a Database Using A Full Backup 343

Exercise 11.1   Installing WebDB 355

Exercise 11.2   Browsing Objects with WebDB Administrator 363

Exercise 11.3   Building and Running Database and Internet Objects 367

Exercise B.1   Creating Rollback Segments. 414

Exercise B.2   Installing the Diagnostics Pack 417

Exercise B.3   Oracle Expert and Tuning Sessions 429

Exercise B.4   The Index Tuning Expert 436

Introduction

There is high demand and competition for professionals in the Information Technology (IT) industry, and the Oracle Certified Professional (OCP) certification is the hottest credential in the database realm. You have made the right decision to pursue certification. Being an OCP will give you a distinct advantage in this highly competitive market.

Many readers may already be familiar with Oracle Corporation and its products and services. For those who aren't familiar with the company, Oracle Corporation, founded in 1977, is the world's leading database company and second largest independent software company, with revenues of more than $10.1 billion and clients in more than 145 countries. Oracle's CEO, Lawrence J. Ellison, saw the future of information technology in Internet computing, and the Oracle8i database was created to meet the needs of this technological evolution.

This book is intended to help you continue on your exciting new path toward obtaining the Oracle8i certified database operator certification. The book will give you the necessary knowledge of the Oracle Server architecture and the hands-on skills you need to pass Exams 1Z0-411.

Why Become an Oracle Certified Professional?

The number one reason to become an Oracle Certified Professional is to gain more visibility and greater access to the industry's most challenging opportunities. The OCP program is Oracle's commitment to provide top-quality resources for technical professionals who want to become Oracle specialists in specific job roles. The certification tests are scenario based, which is the most effective way to access your hands-on expertise and critical problem-solving skills.

Certification is proof of your knowledge and shows that you have the skills required to support Oracle's core products according to the standards established by Oracle. The OCP program can help a company identify proven performers who have demonstrated their skills to support the company's investment in Oracle technology. It demonstrates that you have a solid understanding of your job role and the Oracle products used in that role.

So, whether you are beginning a career, changing careers, securing your present position, or seeking to refine and promote your position, this book is for you!

Oracle Certifications

Oracle has several certification tracks designed to meet different skill levels. Each track consists of several tests that can be taken in any order. The following tracks are available:

- Oracle Database Administrator
- Oracle Application Developer
- Oracle Database Operator
- Oracle Java Developer
- Oracle Financial Applications Consultant

Oracle Database Administrator (DBA)

The role of Database Administrator (DBA) has become a key to success in today's highly complex database systems. The best DBAs work behind the scenes, but are in the spotlight when critical issues arise. They plan, create, and maintain databases to ensure that the databases meet the data management needs of the business. DBAs also monitor the databases for performance issues and work to prevent unscheduled downtime. Being an effective DBA requires a broad understanding of the architecture of Oracle databases and expertise in solving system-related problems. The Oracle8i certified administrator track consists of the following five tests:

- 1Z0-001: Introduction to Oracle—SQL and PL/SQL
- 1Z0-023: Oracle8i—Architecture and Administration
- 1Z0-024: Oracle8i—Performance Tuning
- 1Z0-025: Oracle8i—Backup and Recovery
- 1Z0-026: Oracle8i—Network Administration

Oracle Application Developer

This track tests your skills in client-server and Web-based application development using Oracle application development tools such as Developer/2000, SQL, PL/SQL, and SQL*Plus. The following four tests compose this track:

- 1Z0-001: Introduction to Oracle—SQL and PL/SQL
- 1Z0-101: Develop PL/SQL Program Units

- 1Z0-131: Build Internet Applications I
- 1Z0-132: Build Internet Applications II

Oracle Database Operator (DBO)

A Database Operator (DBO) performs simple operational tasks on Oracle databases in a support role to the DBA. DBOs need an introductory knowledge of the commands and utilities associated with managing a database. DBOs also install and set up databases, create users, and perform routine backups. You need take the following test to be certified as a Database Operator:

- 1Z0-411: Internet Database Operator

Oracle Java Developer

This certification track is part of the Certification Initiative for Enterprise Development, a multi-vendor collaboration with Sun Microsystems, IBM, Novell, and the Sun-Netscape Alliance to establish standards for knowledge and skill levels for enterprise developers in the Java technology. The Initiative recognizes three levels of certification requiring five tests. At each skill level, a certificate is awarded to candidates who successfully pass the required exams in that level.

- **Level 1: Sun Certified Programmer for the Java Platform**
  - 1Z0-501: Sun Certified Programmer for the Java 2 Platform
- **Level 2: Oracle Certified Solution Developer—JDeveloper**
  - 1Z0-502: Oracle JDeveloper: Develop Database Applications with Java (JDeveloper, Release 2)

    or

    1Z0-512: Oracle JDeveloper: Develop Database Applications with Java (JDeveloper, Release 3)

    and

  - 1Z0-503 or 1Z0-513: Object-Oriented Analysis and Design with UML
- **Level 3: Oracle Certified Enterprise Developer—Oracle Internet Platform**
  - 1Z0-504: Enterprise Connectivity with Java Technology
  - 1Z0-505: Enterprise Development on the Oracle Internet Platform

Oracle Financial Applications Consultant

This certification tests your expertise in Oracle Financial applications. These exams are designed to test your knowledge of the business processes incorporated into the Oracle Financial applications software. You must take the following first two and then take either the Procurement or Order Fulfillment exam, depending upon what you would like to specialize in.

- 1Z0-210: Oracle Financial Applications: Financial Management R11
- 1Z0-220: Oracle Applications: Applied Technology R11

and

- 1Z0-230: Oracle Financial Applications: Procurement R11

or

- 1Z0-240: Oracle Financial Applications: Order Fulfillment R11

More Information

The most current information about Oracle certification can be found at http://education.oracle.com. Follow the Certification Home Page link, and choose the track you are interested in. Read the Candidate Guide for the test objectives and test contents, and keep in mind that they can change at any time without notice.

OCP: Database Operator Track

The Oracle8i Internet Database Operator certification consists of a single test, which this Sybex study guide covers. Table F.1 lists the exam for the DBO track, its scoring, and the Sybex study guide that will help you pass the exam.

TABLE F.1   OCP Database Operator Test and Passing Score

Exam #	Title	Total Questions	Questions Correct	Passing %	Sybex Study Guide
1Z0-411	**Oracle Internet Database Operator**	70	47	67%	*OCP: Oracle8i™ DBO Study Guide*

Skills Required for DBO Certification

- Understanding RDBMS concepts
- Writing queries and manipulating data
- Creating and managing users and database objects
- Understanding Oracle Server architecture—Database and Instance
- Understanding completely physical and logical database storage concepts
- Managing data—storage, loading, and reorganization
- Managing roles, privileges, passwords, and resources
- Understanding backup and recovery options
- Configuring Net8 on the server side and client side
- Understanding graphical and character mode backup, recovery, and administration utilities

Tips for Taking OCP Exams

- Each OCP test contains about 60–80 questions to be completed in about 90 minutes. Answer the questions you know first, so that you do not run out of time.

- Many questions on the exam have answer choices that at first glance look identical. Read the questions carefully. Don't just jump to conclusions. Make sure that you are clear about exactly what each question asks.

- Many of the test questions are scenario based. Some of the scenarios contain non-essential information and exhibits. You need to be able to identify what's important and what's not.

- Do not leave any questions unanswered. There is no negative scoring. You can mark a difficult question or a question you are unsure about and come back to it later.

- When answering questions that you are not sure about, use a process of elimination to get rid of the obviously incorrect answers first. Doing this greatly improves your odds if you need to make an educated guess.

- Many questions will ask you to place a marker on the appropriate location. This is where experience with the product is critical. Don't just read this book—install Oracle and go through at least some of the exercises to get hands-on experience.

What Does This Book Cover?

Think of this book as your guide to Oracle8i DBO certification. It begins by covering the most basic of SQL databases and Oracle concepts, including an introduction to Oracle8i, its platforms, and its version of the SQL language (Procedural SQL or PL/SQL). The following chapters cover the topics you need to know for the exam and in your day-to-day work as a database operator:

- SQL database and Oracle8i basics
- Installing and configuring Oracle8i on the server
- Installing and configuring Oracle clients
- Starting and stopping an Oracle instance
- Using the Oracle utilities to administer your system
- PL/SQL basic commands and syntax
- Creating and managing databases
- Setting up database security for users
- Backing up and restoring databases
- Automating maintenance tasks
- Managing, copying, and moving data
- Installing and managing WebDB
- Tuning Oracle 8i performance

Throughout each chapter, you will find hands-on exercises that take you step by step through the various tasks. At the end of each chapter, there are review questions to test your knowledge of the topics covered in that chapter.

Oracle8i and Operating Systems

The Oracle 8i DBO test is operating system–independent, which means that it shouldn't matter if you are running Windows NT, NetWare, Unix (all three of which are covered in this book), or any other operating system. I have included detailed instructions for all three operating systems where they differ from each other. For example, Chapter 2, "Installing and Configuring Oracle8i," has details on installing Oracle on Windows NT, NetWare, and Unix.

To stay consistent, this book uses Windows NT and 2000, NetWare 5, and Linux (Red Hat version 6) for the operating systems in this book, although Oracle8i has been successfully installed on other versions of these operating systems.

Although detailed questions on the various operating systems should not be on the test, I hope the instructions tailored for each operating system will be of use.

Where Do You Take the Exam?

You may take the exam at any of the more than 800 Sylvan Prometric Authorized Testing Centers around the world. For the location of a testing center near you, call 1-800-891-3926. Outside of the United States and Canada, contact your local Sylvan Prometric Registration Center.

To register for an Oracle Certified Professional exam:

- Determine the number of the exam you want to take.

- Register with the nearest Sylvan Prometric Registration Center. At this point, you will be asked to pay in advance for the exam. At the time of this writing, the exams are $125 each and must be taken within one year of payment. You can schedule exams up to six weeks in advance or as soon as one working day prior to the day you wish to take it. If something comes up and you need to cancel or reschedule your exam appointment, contact Sylvan Prometric at least 24 hours in advance.

- When you schedule the exam, you'll get instructions regarding all appointment and cancellation procedures, the ID requirements, and information about the testing-center location.

You can also register for the test online at `http://www.2test.com/register/frameset.htm`. If you live outside the United States, register online at `http://www.2test.com/register/testcenterlocator/ERN_intl_IT&FAA.htm`.

How to Use This Book

This book can provide a solid foundation for the serious effort of preparing for the Oracle Certified Professional Oracle Internet Database Operator exam. To best benefit from this book, use the following study method:

1. Take the Assessment Test immediately following this introduction. (The answers are at the end of the test.) Carefully read over the explanations for any questions you get wrong, and note which chapters the material comes from. This information should help you plan your study strategy.

2. Study each chapter carefully, making sure that you fully understand the information and the test objectives listed at the beginning of each chapter. Pay extra close attention to any chapter for which you missed questions in the Assessment Test.

3. Closely examine the sample queries that are used throughout the book. You may find it helpful to type in the samples and compare the results shown in the book to those on your system. Once you're comfortable with the content in the chapter, answer the review questions related to that chapter. (The answers appear at the end of the chapter, after the review questions.)

When typing in examples from the book, do not type the line numbers that appear in the sample output; the Oracle query tools automatically number lines for you.

4. Note the questions that confuse you, and study those sections of the book again.

5. Take the Practice Exam in this book. You'll find it in Appendix A. The answers appear at the end of the exam.

6. Before taking the exam, try your hand at the bonus exam that is included on the CD that comes with this book. The questions in this exam appear only on the CD. This will give you a complete overview of what you can expect to see on the real thing.

7. Remember to use the products on the CD that is included with this book. The electronic flashcards and the EdgeTest exam preparation software have all been specifically picked to help you study for and pass your exams. Oracle also offers sample exams on their certification Web site: `http://education.oracle.com/certification/`. The electronic flashcards can be used on your Windows computer or on your Palm device.

To learn all the material covered in this book, you'll have to apply yourself regularly and with discipline. Try to set aside the same time period every day to study, and select a comfortable and quiet place to do so. If you work hard, you will be surprised at how quickly you learn this material. All the best!

What's on the CD?

Sybex and I worked hard to provide some really great tools to help you with your certification process. All of the following tools should be loaded on your workstation when studying for the test.

The EdgeTest for Oracle Certified DBO Preparation Software

Provided by EdgeTek Learning Systems, this test preparation software prepares you to successfully pass the OCP: Oracle Internet Database Operator exam. In this test engine, you will find all of the questions from the book, plus an additional Practice Exam that appears exclusively on the CD. You can take the Assessment Test, test yourself by chapter, take the practice exams that appear in the book or on the CD, or take an exam randomly generated from any of the questions.

Electronic Flashcards for PC and Palm Devices

After you read the book, read the review questions at the end of each chapter, and study the practice exams included in the book and on the CD. But wait, there's more! Test yourself with the flashcards included on the CD. If you can get through these difficult questions, and understand the answers, you'll know you're ready for the OCP: Oracle Internet Database Operator exam.

The flashcards include 150 questions specifically written to hit you hard and make sure you are ready for the exam. Between the review questions, Practice Exam, and flashcards, you'll be more than prepared for the exam.

OCP: Oracle8i DBO Study Guide Ebook

Sybex is now offering the Oracle Certification books on CD, so you can read them on your PC or laptop. They are in Adobe Acrobat format. Acrobat Reader 4 is also included on the CD.

This will be extremely helpful to readers who fly and don't want to carry a book, as well as to readers who find it more comfortable reading from their computer.

How to Contact the Author

You can e-mail Lance Mortensen at LMSQL@aol.com.

About the Author

Lance Mortensen is an Oracle Certified Professional with more than ten years of database experience. Lance is a certified trainer and has been consulting on and teaching various databases and Oracle all over the country. Lance is the co-author of many study guides including the best-selling *MCSE: Windows 95 Study Guide*, *MCSE: Windows 98 Study Guide*, and *MCSE: SQL Server 7 Administration Study Guide* all from Sybex.

Assessment Test

1. Oracle8i supports flat-file databases. True or False?

2. Where do these commands belong?

```
log_archive_start = true
log_archive_dest_1 = "location=d:
      \Oracle\oradata\<SID>\archive"
log_archive_format = "%%<SID>%%T%TS%S.ARC"
```

   A. In the parameter file for the database

   B. You run them once for each database from SQLPlus Worksheet

   C. You run them from Instance Manager

   D. You run them from Enterprise Manager

3. There is a tornado coming toward your building. You need to shut down the server and get out. Which of these would you use?

   A. SHUTDOWN ABORT

   B. SHUTDOWN NORMAL

   C. SHUTDOWN TRANSACTIONAL

   D. SHUTDOWN IMMEDIATE

4. Which of the following tools is used to create a new view?

   A. Object Manager

   B. Enterprise Manager

   C. SQLPlus Worksheet

   D. Schema Manager

5. What is the default quota size when quotas on tablespaces are assigned?

   A. None

   B. Unlimited

   C. One-half of the total tablespace

   D. One-half of the available tablespace

6. Which utility can be used to create new users?

   A. Security Manager

   B. User Manager

   C. Schema Manager

   D. Enterprise Manager

7. What command prompt program do you run on the Oracle server that allows you to start and stop the instance?

   A. Server Manager

   B. SQLPlus Worksheet

   C. SQL*Plus

   D. SQL Manager

8. By default, what is shown in the upper-right pane of Enterprise Manager?

   A. Jobs

   B. Events

   C. Groups

   D. Databases, Listeners, and Nodes

9. The ORDER BY clause in an SQL SELECT statement is used to do what?

   A. Force the SELECT to use a certain index

   B. Order the columns

   C. Order the result set

   D. Specify that a join should be done

10. What is the default folder for database files?

   A. \data

   B. \database

   C. \oradata

   D. \oracle

11. In order to edit events, they must be what?

    A. Created with the Edit option

    B. Stored in the Event Library

    C. Tagged with Administrator rights

    D. Named names that start with SYS_

12. When running in ARCHIVELOG mode, which of these can be backed up on a live database? (Choose all that apply.)

    A. The full database

    B. Tablespaces

    C. Datafiles

    D. Archive logs

13. What would be the path to a site called SITE1 on a server called SERVER1?

    A. `http://SERVER1/SITE1`

    B. `http://SERVER1/WEBDB/SITE1`

    C. `http://SERVER1/SITE1s`

    D. `http://SERVER1/WEBDB/SITE1s`

14. Which of the following is the correct SQL syntax to create a new index?

    A.
```
BUILD INDEX "SALES_OWNER"."INDEX_NAMES"
ON "SALES_OWNER"."CUSTOMERS"
("LNAME", "FNAME") TABLESPACE "SALES_APP";
```

    B.
```
CREATE INDEX "SALES_OWNER"."INDEX_NAMES"
AT "SALES_OWNER"."CUSTOMERS"
("LNAME", "FNAME") TABLESPACE "SALES_APP";
```

    C.
```
BUILD INDEX "SALES_OWNER"."INDEX_NAMES"
AT "SALES_OWNER"."CUSTOMERS"
("LNAME", "FNAME") TABLESPACE "SALES_APP";
```

    D.
```
CREATE INDEX "SALES_OWNER"."INDEX_NAMES"
ON "SALES_OWNER"."CUSTOMERS"
("LNAME", "FNAME") TABLESPACE "SALES_APP";
```

15. Which utility allows you to create new roles in the database?

   A. Schema Manager

   B. Security Manager

   C. Enterprise Manager

   D. Instance Manager

16. When can you delete an Oracle trace file?

   A. When the instance is stopped

   B. When the instance is running in RESTRICT mode

   C. When the instance is in NOMOUNT mode

   D. At any time

17. Which of these is a valid INSERT statement?

   A. `INSERT emp (7986,'MASTERS','Clerk',`
   `7902,sysdate,900,NULL,20);`

   B. `INSERT into emp values (7986,MASTERS,Clerk,`
   `7902,sysdate,900,NULL,20);`

   C. `INSERT into emp values (7986,'MASTERS','Clerk',`
   `7902,sysdate,900,NULL,20);`

   D. `INSERT into emp values (7986,'MASTERS','Clerk',`
   `7902,sysdate,900,NULL,20)`

18. Which operating systems does Oracle8i run on? (Choose all that apply.)

   A. NetWare

   B. Windows NT Server

   C. Unix

   D. MS-DOS

19. What command stops the Oracle Intelligent Agent in Unix?

   A. `lsnrctl dbsnmp_stop`

   B. `lsnrctl dbsnmp_start`

   C. `lsnrctl dbsnmp_status`

   D. `lsnrctl agent_stop`

20. How do you restore a database that was backed up "cold."

A. Create a restore job from within Enterprise Manager.

B. Use the Database Creation Wizard.

C. Copy the database files back to their original location, and restart the instance.

D. Use Storage Manager to bring back the files and database.

21. You have a damaged datafile. What mode should you open the database in?

A. OPEN

B. NOMOUNT

C. MOUNT

D. RESTRICT

22. In the INIT file, the `remote_login_passwordfile` parameter must be set to what in order to assign additional users to the Sysdba role?

A. Shared

B. User

C. Additional

D. Exclusive

23. The Build menu of WebDB Administrator allows you to do which of the following? (Choose all that apply.)

A. Create new objects

B. See existing objects

C. Change the security of objects

D. Monitor the usage of objects

24. Which type of Data Manager activity requires constraints to be disabled?

A. Export

B. Import

C. Conventional load

D. Direct load

25. Which command lets you get subtotal summary information?

    A. ORDER BY

    B. GROUP BY

    C. SORT BY

    D. TOTAL BY

26. Which keyword, when used, will leave existing rows alone when loading new rows?

    A. Insert

    B. Replace

    C. Truncate

    D. Append

27. Which of these is NOT a database object?

    A. Table

    B. Index

    C. View

    D. Control File

28. When should users be allowed to place their data on system tablespaces?

    A. Never

    B. Always

    C. Indexes only

    D. Views only

Answers to Assessment Test

1. False.   Oracle8i supports relational databases. See Chapter 1 for more details.

2. A.   These commands go in the parameter file. See Chapter 10 for more details.

3. A.   SHUTDOWN ABORT immediately shuts down the instance and disconnects all users, and all transactions that were in progress are thrown out. SHUTDOWN ABORT is the fastest way to stop the instance. See Chapter 2 for more details.

4. B, C, D.   There is no such thing as Object Manager, and the other tools can all be used to create and manage objects. See Chapter 7 for more details.

5. A.   The default quota size is none, which means that users cannot use any space on any tablespace. See Chapter 6 for more details.

6. A.   Security Manager is used to create new users. See Chapter 6 for more details.

7. A.   Server Manager is the command prompt utility that is run from the Oracle server and used to start and stop the instance. See Chapter 3 for more details.

8. C.   Groups are shown in the upper-right pane of Enterprise Manager. See Chapter 3 for more details.

9. C.   The ORDER BY clause selects which field to sort on. See Chapter 4 for more details.

10. C.   The \oradata folder, located under the <Oracle Root> directory, is the default folder for database files. See Chapter 5 for more details.

11. B.   Events have to be in the library before they can be edited. See Chapter 9 for more details.

12. A, B, C, D.   All of these can be backed up on live databases when running in ARCHIVELOG mode. See Chapter 10 for more details.

13. A. The path to a site is //<server>/<site name>. See Chapter 11 for more details.

14. D. The CREATE INDEX...ON command creates a new index. See Chapter 7 for more details.

15. B. Security Manager is used to create users and roles. See Chapters 3 and 6 for more details.

16. D. Trace files can be deleted at any time. See Chapter 2 for more details.

17. C. Option A is missing INTO and VALUES. Option B is missing the '' around character data, and option D is missing the ending semicolon. See Chapter 8 for more details.

18. A, B, C. Oracle runs on NetWare, Windows NT, and Unix, but not MS-DOS. See Chapter 1 for more details.

19. A. The lsnrctl dbsnmp_stop command stops the Oracle Intelligent Agent in Unix. See Chapter 9 for more details.

20. C. A cold backup implies that you stopped the instance and copied all of the database files to a safe location. To restore them, simply stop the instance and copy the files back to their original location. See Chapter 10 for more details.

21. C. MOUNT mode starts the instance and opens the control file but does not open any datafiles, which is what you want when fixing damaged datafiles. See Chapter 2 for more details.

22. D. The remote_login_passwordfile parameter must be set to Exclusive to add additional users to the Sysdba role. See Chapter 6 for more details.

23. A. The Build option allows you to create objects. See Chapter 11 for more details.

24. D. Direct loads need constraints disabled. See Chapter 8 for more details.

25. B. The GROUP BY command allows you to get subtotal summary information. See Chapter 4 for more details.

26. D. The Append keyword is needed when a data load should leave existing data in place. See Chapter 8 for more details.

27. D. A control file is not a database object. See Chapter 1 for more details.

28. A. Users should have tablespaces created for them, so they won't have any data on system tablespaces. See Chapter 5 for more details on assigning tablespaces to users.

Chapter 1

Introduction to Oracle and Relational Databases

ORACLE8i DBO EXAM OBJECTIVES OFFERED IN THIS CHAPTER:

✓ **What are the Duties of an Oracle Database Operator?**

- List the main job tasks of the Oracle Database Operator
- Define the appropriate tool for performing each task

✓ **Define an Oracle Database**

- Explain the difference between a database management system and a flat file system
- List the tasks of the relational database management system (RDBMS)
- Define the components of an Oracle database
- Distinguish the logical and physical structure of an Oracle database
- List the most common terms used in a relational database

Exam objectives are subject to change at any time without prior notice and at Oracle's sole discretion. Please visit Oracle's Training and Certification Web site (http://education .oracle.com/certification/index.html) for the most current exam objectives listing.

Before we launch into Oracle8i, it's important to be familiar with the various duties of the database operator and others involved with the database. The basics of Oracle, Oracle databases, and databases in general will be covered. In particular, this chapter explains the differences between flat file and relational databases. Coverage of Oracle database basics will also include the types of objects found in a database.

Responsibilities of the Database Operator

An Oracle database operator (DBO) is usually responsible for the day-to-day administration of the database. The operator takes over where the programmer leaves off.

In this book, I will use the terms System DBO or Sysop to refer to a user that does day-to-day administration tasks and System DBA or Sysdba to refer to someone with advanced knowledge and experience in working with Oracle who may be called in to perform complex setups, configurations, and/or troubleshooting. Oracle Corporation also uses these terms in this way.

In many companies, the lines between operator and developer may become quite blurred, as the same person may be doing tasks related to both roles. The operator's duties can be summarized according to the following categories.

Installing Oracle8i

Installing Oracle8i sometimes falls under the responsibility of the database operator, especially if the network server operator doesn't know anything about databases. The installation and configuration of the software can be broken down into the following four major steps:

- Install the Oracle8i software on the server.
- Install the Oracle8i client software on the workstation.
- Configure the server.
- Configure the workstation.

Installing and configuring both servers and workstations for NetWare, Windows NT, and Linux is covered in Chapter 2, "Installing and Configuring Oracle8i."

Creating Databases

After Oracle is installed, a new database will have to be created if it isn't automatically done during the installation of a third-party application. In any event, an (empty) database needs to be created before any tables and data can be loaded into the database. You may wish to create the sample database when you install Oracle8i to make it easier to test the initial installation of Oracle. You can use the Database Assistant to assist you in creating a new database. Creating databases is covered in Chapter 5, "Creating and Managing Databases."

Importing and Exporting Data

Populating a new database, creating temporary tables, and exporting data are all common tasks that a database operator does. Data can be imported and exported using Schema Manager, Storage Manager, or Enterprise Manager. Importing and exporting data are covered in Chapter 8, "Importing and Exporting Data."

Implementing Tablespaces

Tablespaces are a way of organizing tables in a database based on an application or owner. There may be many different tablespaces in a single database. Tablespaces can be created and managed using Storage Manager or Enterprise Manager. Creating and managing tablespaces is covered in Chapter 7, "Installing and Managing Applications."

Managing the Databases and Server

Managing the databases and server can encompass a large variety of tasks including importing or exporting data, managing users and security, and ensuring that the database is backed up. Other tasks include monitoring redo logs and archive logs and tuning a database using procedures, indexes, and synonyms. Managing the server consists of integrating it effectively with the operating system and setting up proactive management of the server. A database operator will probably spend the majority of time managing existing databases. Managing the database is the subject of the majority of this book, especially Chapters 6 through 10.

Backing Up the Databases

Probably the most critical task of any operator is to successfully back up the system they are in charge of. Backups are not as glamorous as many aspects of administration, but they need to be done correctly 100 percent of the time. If the database needs to be restored but the backup is worthless, it doesn't matter how cleverly you named your users and roles—you are in a big mess. Backups can be done using Backup Manager and are covered in Chapter 10, "Backups and Restorations."

Restoring the Databases When Necessary

You don't just back up the database for fun—there may be a time when you need to restore something. Restorations go a lot smoother if you have practiced them long before the need arises. Restorations are covered in Chapter 10, "Backups and Restorations."

Setting Up and Managing Users for the Oracle8i Database

User accounts can be created that exist only in Oracle, or user accounts from the operating system can be linked into Oracle. For example, if a user account Linda with a password of Oct7 existed only in Oracle, you could connect to the database instance using Linda/Oct7. If your user account from NetWare or Windows NT was Sue and your account was linked to Oracle8i, you could log in to the network and connect to Oracle without having to revalidate (reenter your account and password). User accounts are managed with Security Manager and are covered in Chapter 6, "Oracle Users and Security."

Managing Security for Database Objects

Although many systems operate on the "Security by Ignorance" rule (which is where users don't realize the trouble they could cause because of excessive rights), one of the best ways to prevent problems from happening is to grant users only the minimum rights needed by them. Securing database objects is done using Security Manager and is covered in Chapter 6, "Oracle Users and Security," and Chapter 7, "Installing and Managing Applications."

Installing and Tuning Applications

Usually, Oracle8i is installed to support a third-party application. Successfully installing the application involves setting up the correct database, tablespace, users, security, and instance. Installing applications in Oracle8i is covered in Chapter 7, "Installing and Managing Applications."

Tuning Oracle for Optimal Performance

Tuning databases for optimal performance can be accomplished in Oracle by installing and using various Experts. Tuning a database involves looking at indexes, file placement, table placement, and server configuration. Tuning Oracle8i is covered in Appendix B, "Performance and Tuning." The Diagnostics Pack and Tuning Expert can be used to troubleshoot and tune the database.

Troubleshooting Problems

Troubleshooting Oracle8i installations and databases is an ongoing process for a database operator. Some keys to successful troubleshooting include finding what changed on the system, changing only one thing at a time, and documenting the solution. Troubleshooting topics are covered in each chapter.

Responsibilities of the Database Administrator

While the database operator can handle day-to-day operations, complex or mission critical operations may dictate that someone who is an expert in Oracle assist the operator. Oracle Corporation defines such a person as a database administrator or DBA. The database administrator will ideally have more experience and training than the database operators, and the DBA should be a valuable resource for operators, who might have network duties beside caring for the Oracle database.

Sybex publishes a complete series of books for the Oracle database administrator, which go much deeper into administration topics and examples than this book is able to. Go to www.sybex.com for more information on this series.

Responsibilities of the Application Developer

An Oracle application developer is responsible for designing, programming, and populating the database.

Because the focus of this book is the operation of an Oracle database (and not the design, creation, etc.) the duties of the developer are not covered in detail.

The developer's responsibilities can be summarized as follows:

- They analyze the business situation to see what type of system is required. Is it a new system or an upgrade? Is it a small company at one location or a big corporation with multiple locations?

- They design the database, tables, and all objects. In the design process, the developer identifies objects and relationships and how they all fit together as logical entities, which are then translated into physical tables (normalized). The developer must then plan for the application design, including reports and queries, as well as other pieces such as access to Web pages.

- They design and implement the initial security for the database.

- They design any data-replication scenarios.

- They program the database, tables, and all objects.

- They design the user interface, reports, and update screens. This is the front-end of the system and will probably have the most impact on the users.

- They test the design, interface, reports, and update screens.

- They populate the database with live data from legacy systems and prepare the database to receive new data.

- They hand the project over to the operator with appropriate documentation and training.

A good developer and a well-planned and -implemented application will do much to ease the burden of the database operator. Conversely, a poorly designed or implemented database solution will be a constant headache for the database operator and administrator.

Oracle Basics

Oracle Corporation is the second largest software company in the world, supplying database and project management software to 70 percent of Fortune 500 companies and 64 percent of Fortune 100 companies. Oracle programs and sells many different products and, in fiscal year 2000, had sales of over 10 billion dollars. The company operates in 145 countries. Oracle database software powers some of the most sophisticated and mission critical databases, including many popular commerce Web sites such as CDNOW.com, ONSALE.com, Netflix.com, CBS.com, and many others.

For many companies, data is one of the critical components of the company, and Oracle database software is widely known as the premier database product. The most current version of their main database program is Oracle8i, with Oracle9i due out in 2001.

One of the major advantages of Oracle 8i is that it can run on a variety of servers, including Windows NT, Unix, NetWare, Linux, and others. Basically, whatever servers a company is using can be installed as Oracle database servers.

Networks and Oracle8i

Oracle8i can run on a variety of network operating systems, including the following:

- Novell NetWare
- Windows NT Server
- Unix (including HP-UX, Linux, Solaris, and others)

This book will cover Oracle8i on NetWare, Windows NT, and Unix for a couple of reasons. First, the Oracle8i DBO test is operating system–independent, which means that the test will not cover operating system–specific information or commands. The other reason is that once the server is installed, the administration tools are basically the same for whatever version you are running on.

NetWare 5 ships with a five-user version of Oracle8i. Additional client licenses should be purchased to cover all clients that will use Oracle. Previous versions of NetWare also support Oracle, although Oracle must be purchased and installed separately with these versions.

Windows NT Server supports Oracle8i, although you must purchase Oracle8i separately. Windows NT workstations are common Oracle8i clients, although Windows 95/98 workstations can also be Oracle clients.

There are various versions of Oracle for the various versions of Unix, including Sun Solaris versions, HP-UX versions, and Linux versions. You will need to purchase Oracle8i separately for the version of Unix you are using.

Demo versions of the Oracle software can be downloaded or ordered from www.oracle.com.

Client/Server Architecture

An Oracle database server is a client/server application. Client/server can be defined as an application that is split into at least two parts: one part runs on a server, and the other part runs on client computers or workstations. The server side of the application provides security, fault-tolerance, performance, concurrency, and reliable backups. The client side provides the user interface and may contain items such as empty reports, queries, and forms.

In older, non-client/server database systems, the work is not shared between the server and workstation machines. For example, suppose that you have a 10MB database stored on your network server. When a client runs a non-client/server application and accesses the data, all 10MB are downloaded to the client, and then the data is processed by the client computer. See Figure 1.1.

FIGURE 1.1 A non-client/server database application storing data on the server

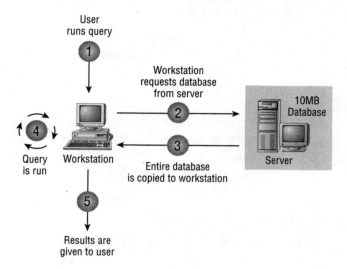

In contrast, when a query is run on a client/server system, the server searches the database and then sends back to the client just those rows that match the search conditions, as shown in Figure 1.2. This not only saves bandwidth on your network, but is often faster than having the workstations do all of the work (as long as the server is a powerful enough machine).

FIGURE 1.2 A client/server database application storing data on the server

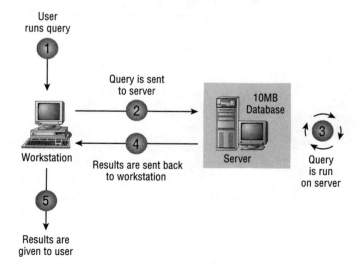

Types of Databases

A *database* can generally be thought of as a collection of related data. However, that data can be organized in various ways, and the database can be designed to store historical data or changing data. Although there are several different ways to store data, we are most interested in relational databases, as that is the type of database that Oracle8i supports. Flat-file databases are of interest because of their historical use and because many Oracle administrators will be familiar with flat-file terms. Oracle8i can also be thought of as an object-oriented database, because items beside data can easily be stored in the database, although items like JAVA code are beyond the scope of this book.

Flat-File Databases

In earlier database products, a database was usually one file—something like `payroll.dbf` for a payroll-related file or `patients.dbf` for a doctor's office. When all of the database's information is stored in a single file and accessed sequentially, the database is considered a flat-file database. A flat-file database resembles a spreadsheet, because it is all contained in one "page" or file (see Figure 1.3). Figure 1.3 represents a simple database designed to track books on loan from a personal library.

FIGURE 1.3   A flat-file database

First_Name	Last_Name	Book_Title	Book_Author	Book_Subject	Date_Out	Date_In

dBASE, Access, and other personal computer databases are examples of flat-file databases. Although flat-file databases are relatively easy to set up, they become more difficult to maintain when holding complex data.

Flat-file databases have many disadvantages. Two of the most serious involve redundant data and inconsistent data. In Figure 1.3, for example, you need to enter the first name and last name for a person whenever they check a book out. If a person checks out multiple books, you need to enter their first and last names multiple times, thus generating a lot of redundant data. If a person changes their last name and has five books checked out, you would have to change their last name in all five rows. If you missed one change, you would have inconsistent data.

Another disadvantage of flat-file databases is that the logical schema is tied to the physical structure of the file. For instance, if you modify a column by changing its width or name, you may impact other columns. Users also usually need to know the physical name and location of the file in order to use it. Moving the database file to a different computer or even drive could impact users of the database.

Relational Databases

A relational database is composed of tables, which contain related data. The process of organizing data into tables in a consistent and complete format is referred to as normalizing the database.

NOTE

Normalization of relational designs is a complex topic, which won't be addressed in this book. You can refer to other books that are devoted to this topic. However, before you implement your database design, you should start with a fully normalized view of your database.

In a relational database management system (RDBMS), such as Oracle8i, a database is not necessarily tied to a file; it is more of a logical concept that is based on a collection of related objects. A database in Oracle8i not only contains the raw data, it also contains the structure of the database, the security of the database, and any views or stored procedures related to that particular database.

Figure 1.4 shows the same book loan database we used in the flat-file example, but it's organized into a relational database with separate tables for people, books, and on-loan status.

FIGURE 1.4 A book loan relational database

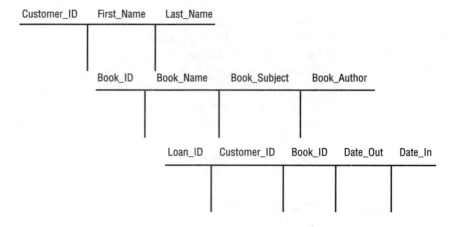

Relational databases hide the physical structure from users. You can easily add, modify, and delete columns without impacting applications that use the database. You can also make your physical location of the database as simple or as complex as you need without impacting users, as users only need to know the name of the database and the objects within it.

In relational databases, there is one row per entity, and relationships between entities are tracked in a link table. For example, if a person called John Hanson wanted to check out two books, there would be only one entry for John in the People table, one entry for each book in the Books table, and one entry for each book checked out in the Out table. See Figure 1.5.

FIGURE 1.5 Entries for relational data

Customer_ID	First_Name	Last_Name
1	John	Hanson

Book_ID	Book_Name	Book_Subject	Book_Author
1	SQL Primer	SQL	Sawtell
2	Win2K is OK	Win2K	Lee

Loan_ID	Customer_ID	Book_ID	Date_Out	Date_In
1	1	1	8/12	
2	1	2	8/12	

Oracle Instances

An Oracle *instance* consists of the shared code, memory space, and server processes used to open database files and make a database accessible to users. For example, if you had a database called SALES99 that you wanted to make available for users, you would start a database instance that would open the database. The instance would take some resources from the operating system for the base code for Oracle8i, the shared data cache, and resources for database access.

If the instance is not running, the database is not accessible to the users. Typically you would have only one or possibly two instances running on a particular computer (for performance reasons). An instance only opens a single database (unless you are using multi-server Oracle servers, which is beyond the scope of this book).

Starting and stopping an Oracle instance is covered in detail in Chapter 2, "Installing and Configuring Oracle8i." You can use Enterprise Manager, Instance Manager, or Server Manager to start and stop instances.

Components of an Instance

There are several components to an instance, including configuration files, shared pages (called the SGA or System Global Area), personal data areas (called the PGA or Program Global Area), and server processes. Figure 1.6 shows a graphical representation of an instance.

FIGURE 1.6 A graphical view of an instance

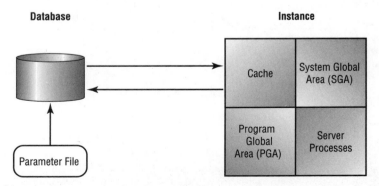

Configuration Files

Each instance will need a configuration file. The configuration file contains entries for items such as the location of the database control file(s), the database file(s), the redo log files, the size of the cache, and how the database will be backed up. The default file is called INITSEED.ORA and is located in the \Oracle_home\database folder. The file is ASCII, which makes it easy to edit, back up, and restore in case of loss or to revert to previous versions. When an instance is started, a configuration file will need to be specified. The configuration file can be stored on the server or the local administration workstation. A partial configuration file (for the default ORCL database) is shown in Figure 1.7.

FIGURE 1.7   An instance configuration file

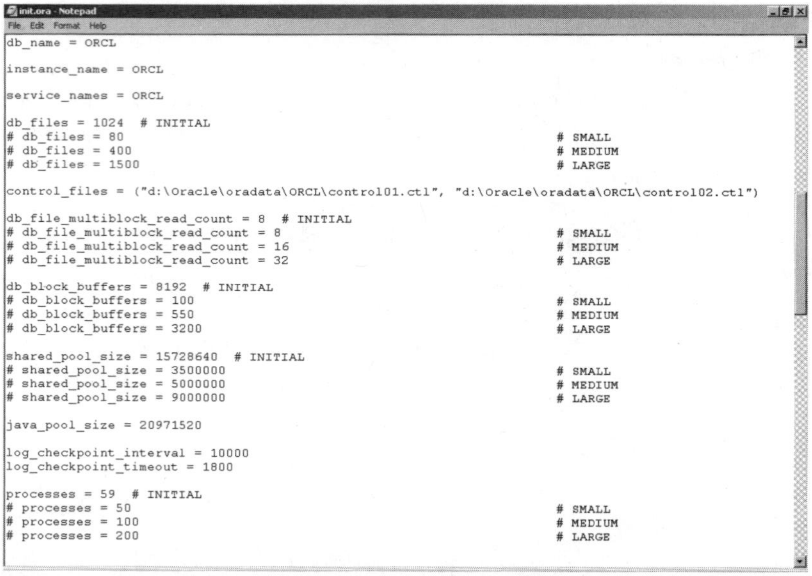

```
db_name = ORCL

instance_name = ORCL

service_names = ORCL

db_files = 1024  # INITIAL
# db_files = 80                                                  # SMALL
# db_files = 400                                                 # MEDIUM
# db_files = 1500                                                # LARGE

control_files = ("d:\Oracle\oradata\ORCL\control01.ctl", "d:\Oracle\oradata\ORCL\control02.ctl")

db_file_multiblock_read_count = 8  # INITIAL
# db_file_multiblock_read_count = 8                              # SMALL
# db_file_multiblock_read_count = 16                             # MEDIUM
# db_file_multiblock_read_count = 32                             # LARGE

db_block_buffers = 8192  # INITIAL
# db_block_buffers = 100                                         # SMALL
# db_block_buffers = 550                                         # MEDIUM
# db_block_buffers = 3200                                        # LARGE

shared_pool_size = 15728640  # INITIAL
# shared_pool_size = 3500000                                     # SMALL
# shared_pool_size = 5000000                                     # MEDIUM
# shared_pool_size = 9000000                                     # LARGE

java_pool_size = 20971520

log_checkpoint_interval = 10000
log_checkpoint_timeout = 1800

processes = 59  # INITIAL
# processes = 50                                                 # SMALL
# processes = 100                                                # MEDIUM
# processes = 200                                                # LARGE
```

SGA (System Global Area)

The SGA (System Global Area) consists of RAM allocated to the instance for the caching of data and procedures. The SGA is shared amongst all users and gains benefits from multiple users of the same data and code because frequently used data and code tend to stay in the cache and be quickly available for users. The SGA consists of the buffer cache, the shared pool, and the redo log buffer. The size of the SGA is controlled in the instance startup file with the shared_pool_size = x parameter.

BUFFER CACHE

The buffer cache is where data from the database is cached. The cache operates on a least recently used scheme, which means that data that is accessed more often is more likely to be in the cache, while data accessed infrequently has less chance of being in the cache.

Like most caching processes, the more RAM devoted to the cache, the greater chance of data being in the cache.

SHARED POOL

The shared pool consists of two areas, the library cache area and the dictionary cache area. The library cache is where SQL statements and execution plans are cached, while the dictionary cache is used for schema type information, such as table and column names and security information.

The shared pool is used by all users, thus making similar queries to the same tables and columns faster.

REDO LOG BUFFER

The redo log buffer is used to temporarily store changes to the data until the changes are flushed to the database. Changes are cached to provide performance increases, but can also be recovered by the administrator, in case of a crash, by restoring the redo logs.

PGA (Program Global Area)

The PGA (Program Global Area) is the part of Oracle that tracks individual session information such as variables, cursor information, and sort information. Each user will have their own PGA, as the PGA is not shared among users.

Server Processes

There are several server processes happening behind the scenes to make Oracle function smoothly and reliably. While most processes happen automatically, you do have control over the way some of them act. For most purposes, default values should be used unless you are configuring your server for performance and tuning issues and know exactly what you are doing. In Appendix B, "Performance and Tuning," I will cover some of the most commonly changed items. In the meantime, following are four of the most common processes.

DBWR (DATABASE WRITER)

The database writer process writes data from the buffer cache to disk. Data that has been changed is called dirty and is written out at least once every three seconds by the DBWR process.

LGWR (LOG WRITER)

The log writer process writes changes to the redo log files of a database.

CKPT (CHECKPOINT)

The checkpoint process starts the flushing of changed data to the database. The CKPT process can trigger the LGWR and DBWR processes.

SERVER PROCESS

A server process is needed for each client in order for them to access the database. Every single client can be assigned their own server process (for performance reasons) or can use a shared pool of server processes (to save server resources). The server process is used to get data when a SELECT statement is run or a WHERE clause is contained within a modification statement.

Communicating with Oracle8i

In order for clients to submit queries and get reports from an Oracle server, the client must first connect to the (running) server. Opening an Oracle database (and thus running the database software) is what you do when you start an Oracle instance, as was covered earlier. Oracle database servers operate on top of a network operating system just like other types of application servers, such as HTTP (WWW) servers, and can be compared to WWW servers for ease of understanding.

With WWW servers, you have the client (a browser), a protocol (TCP/IP), a connection type (HTTP), a database name lookup service (DNS), a management application (IIS Administrator, etc.), and a server (IIS, Apache, etc.) that listens for client requests. Oracle works very similarly in that you have various clients (SQL*Worksheet, custom applications, etc.), a protocol (TCP/IP, IPX, etc.), a connection type (Net8), a database lookup service (TNS Names service), a management application (Oracle Enterprise Manager), and a server (Oracle) that listens for client requests (*Listener*).

Net8

Net8 is the method of communication used between client and servers. It is the language that Oracle clients and servers communicate with. Of course, clients and servers must be using a common protocol that is configured correctly in order to make Net8 work.

Net8 is configured on the client by running the Net8 Assistant or the Easy Configuration program, while servers run just the Net8 Easy Configuration program. Note that NetWare servers run the EASYCFG.NLM.

Configuring Net8 consists of correctly specifying connection information in the TNSNAMES.ORA file, which the EASYCFG does for you. Net8 configuration is covered in more detail in Chapter 2, "Installing and Configuring Oracle8i."

The Listener

In order for the Oracle server to see incoming requests, the Listener must be correctly configured and started. Once the Listener hears an incoming connection, it will pass the connection to the appropriate server process. The Listener is also configured using the Easyconfig utility and is also covered in Chapter 2.

Of course, the database instance must first be started successfully before any clients can communicate with the database.

Database Components

A database operates on two levels, at the physical components level of the database and the logical objects level within the database. While database administrators and operators need to be very familiar with the physical implementation of the database, normal users only need to know the logical naming and relationships of objects in order to effectively use the database.

For example, database operators need to know where the physical files of the database are located in order to make sure they are getting backed up properly. Users need to know what a particular column is named so they can build a custom query to run a report (the logical objects).

Physical Objects

Oracle databases consist of the following three primary physical objects:

- Control file(s)
- Datafile(s)
- Redo Log Files

Every database needs at least one control file. Oracle highly recommends copying the control file to a separate volume, thus using at least two copies of the control file, in case one gets corrupted. The control file is a non-ASCII file that is constantly updated while the database is in use. A control file is initially created by Oracle as part of the database creation process. If the control file for a database is not available, the database cannot be opened. Multiple control files are separated by a ";" (semicolon) after the path for each one.

Control files are specified in the configuration file for the instance (usually called INIT<SID>.ORA) on a line that looks something like this:

```
control_files = c:\orant\DATABASE\ctl1ORCL.ora.
```

Datafiles are where the actual data resides. You must specify at least one database file per database, although you may want more for performance or organizational reasons. Datafiles are specified during the initial creation of the database and can be altered using the ALTER DATABASE command or the Storage Manager application (covered in Chapter 3, "Oracle8i Enterprise Manager and Other Tools").

Redo log files are used to track changes to the data. Redo log files are used by the system to ensure consistency while data is being modified and can be used by the backup process as well. You must have at least two redo log files for a database, as Oracle alternates between the files. Backups can take advantage of the alternating redo log files and can backup the file most recently closed.

NOTE

Creating databases is covered in more detail in Chapter 5, "Creating and Managing Databases." Backing up and recovering databases is covered in Chapter 10, "Backups and Restorations."

Logical Objects

An Oracle relational database is composed of many different types of objects. See Figure 1.8.

FIGURE 1.8   Common database objects

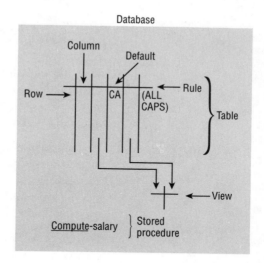

The following are some of the more common types of objects used in a database:

Object	Description
Table	The object that contains rows, columns, and the actual raw data.
Column	A part of the table; the object that holds the data.
Row	A row is not a separate object, but rather a complete set of columns within a single table. It is a logical construct, not a physically implemented object like the rest of the items discussed here.
Datatype	There are various datatypes that can be used in columns, such as character, numeric, and date. A column may only hold data of a single datatype.
Procedure	A set of PL-SQL statements combined together to perform a single task or set of tasks. This object is like a macro, in that SQL code can be written and stored under a name. By invoking the name, you actually run the code.

Object	Description
Trigger	This object is a stored procedure that activates when data is added, edited, or deleted from a table. Triggers are used to ensure that tables linked by keys stay internally consistent with each other. For example, an automobile dealer's database might include a trigger that makes sure that every time a car is added, the assigned salesperson actually exists.
Rule	This object is assigned to a column so that data being entered must conform to standards you set. For example, rules can be used to make sure that the state in a person's address is entered in uppercase letters and that phone numbers contain only numbers.
Default	This object is assigned to a column so that if no data is entered, the default value will be used. An example might be to set the state code to the state where most of your customers reside, so that the default can be accepted for most entries.
View	A view is much like a stored query—you don't need to rewrite the query every time you'd like to run it; you can use the view instead. A view appears very much like a table to most users. A view usually either excludes certain fields from a table or links two or more tables together.
Index	A storage structure designed for fast data retrieval.

Warehousing versus Transaction Processing

There are two general categories that databases fall into. They are as follows:

- Storage and querying of historical data, often referred to as data warehousing or DSS (decision support systems). Another common name is *OLAP* (online analytical processing). The main focus of data warehousing is the ability to quickly query existing data and perform complex analysis, usually looking for patterns or other relationships that are difficult to locate during day-to-day operations of a company. In other words, reading data is emphasized over writing data.

- Live, continually changing data. This type of database activity is referred to as *OLTP* (online transaction processing) or as a data mart. In this case, the flexibility to expand and edit the database is the main focus. In other words, writing data is emphasized over reading data.

Although these types of databases may appear to be the same at first glance, they are basically exact opposites. OLAP emphasizes reading the database with long-running transactions; OLTP emphasizes writing to the database with very quick transactions. Another way to look at it is that OLAP databases should have a lot of indexes because you do a lot of searches, while OLTP databases should not have a lot of indexes (because indexes are automatically maintained with data changes).

Oracle makes a great server for both OLTP and OLAP types of databases. However, if your company is using both OLTP and OLAP type applications on the same database (and especially on the same tables of a database), you may want to consider using two machines—one for each function—in order to get optimal performance.

Another related (and rapidly growing) use of databases is to put the data into a Web page and publish it either internally on an intranet or to the public on the Internet. Again, the same basic types of databases are used: data warehousing if the data on the Web page is for historical reporting purposes or OLTP if the customer can order from the Web page. Currently, most of the data is historical, or static, but that will change as the security and tools for transaction processing across the Internet improve. Oracle is a leading vendor of Internet commerce servers.

Summary

Oracle is the leading database vendor in the world and powers some of the most critical commerce sites on the Internet. Oracle8i is the latest version of Oracle Corporation's relational database engine.

As a database operator, you will probably be responsible for tasks such as installing Oracle; creating databases; managing data, users, and security; doing backups; and performing some tuning on the database.

A relational database is made up of various types of objects, including tables (which hold the data), views (which let you easily query the data), indexes (which speed up queries), and other objects.

An Oracle database consists of various data files, and an instance is the server processes and memory structures used to open a database.

Communicating with an Oracle instance requires the use of Net8, which is the language Oracle servers and clients understand. The Oracle server runs a listener process which continually looks for incoming requests from Oracle clients. The listener then hands the client connection to the server.

There are generally two types of databases, OLTP (online transactional processing) and OLAP (online analytical processing). OLTP databases emphasize many quick changes, while OLAP databases are mostly for reports, such as a data warehouse.

Key Terms

Before you take the exam, make sure you're familiar with the following terms:

database

index

instance

Listener

Net8

OLAP

OLTP

procedure

table

view

Review Questions

1. Which of the following options are physical components of an Oracle database? (Select all that apply.)

   A. Control file

   B. Tables

   C. Datafile

   D. Redo log files

2. Which of the following options are logical components of an Oracle database? (Select all that apply.)

   A. Tables

   B. Indexes

   C. Control files

   D. Views

3. An Oracle instance is which of the following options?

   A. A collection of databases

   B. The database files that make up a database

   C. The shared RAM in charge of database caching

   D. The shared RAM and processes that allow access to a database

4. A database warehouse would work best in which situation? Select two answers.

   A. A database with lots of indexes

   B. A database with few data modifications

   C. A database with few indexes

   D. A database with lots of data modifications

5. Which of these is a task of the database operator?

   A. Program the database, tables, and all objects.

   B. Design the user interface.

   C. Analyze the business situation.

   D. Back up the database.

6. In order to access a database, which is required? (Select all that apply.)

   A. Database

   B. Instance

   C. Operating system

   D. Connectivity

7. The physical structure of the database needs to be known by whom?

   A. Database users

   B. Database operators

   C. Database administrators

   D. Database programmers

8. The logical structure of the database needs to be known by whom?

   A. Database users

   B. Database operators

   C. Database administrators

   D. Database programmers

9. What tools can be used to start the database instance?

   A. Oracle Enterprise Manager

   B. Server Manager (command prompt)

   C. Instance Manager

   D. SQLPlus Worksheet

10. What tasks are critical to enabling users to use the database? (Select all that apply.)

    A. Creating the database

    B. Starting the instance

    C. Configuring Net8

    D. Configuring user security

11. Which object is used for fast data retrieval?

    A. Index

    B. Procedures

    C. Tables

    D. Columns

12. Which object is useful for repeated queries?

    A. Procedures

    B. Tables

    C. Columns

    D. Constraint

13. How many databases can an instance open?

    A. 1

    B. 2

    C. 4

    D. The number is limited by hardware.

14. Databases are opened by what process?

    A. Instance

    B. Installation

    C. DataManagement

    D. AccessDB

15. What happens if the control file for an existing database is unavailable?

   A. The control file will be re-created automatically.

   B. The control file must be re-created manually.

   C. The database will operate with default settings.

   D. The database will be unusable.

16. What is the minimum number of redo log files required for a database?

   A. 0

   B. 1

   C. 2

   D. 4

17. What is the minimum number of database files required for a database?

   A. 0

   B. 1

   C. 2

   D. 4

18. Which process watches for new clients attempting to connect to the Oracle server?

   A. DBWR

   B. Listener

   C. Server Process

   D. Connector

19. What program maintains the set of communication standards that allows clients to connect to Oracle servers?

   A. TCP/IP

   B. OR8

   C. Net8

   D. Conn8

20. Which of these tasks is normally NOT done by the operator?

    A. Install Oracle

    B. Manage security

    C. Design the database

    D. Import and export data

Answers to Review Questions

1. A, C, D. Databases are made up of control, data, and redo log files.

2. A, B, D. Tables, indexes, and views are logical components of a database.

3. D. An instance is shared RAM and processes that allow database files to be accessed by users.

4. A, B. A data warehouse implies historical data and large, ad hoc reports. Reporting is usually better with lots of indexes, and, to ensure consistency (and not impact the live data application), few data modifications.

5. D. Backing up the database is a common task of a database operator.

6. A, B, C, D. In order to access a database, you must have a database, an instance, an operating system, and connectivity to the instance.

7. B, C, D. Users do not need to know the physical structure in order to be able to use it, while administrators, operators, and programmers need to.

8. A, B, C, D. Users, operators, administrators, and programmers of the database all need to know the logical structure of the database.

9. A, B, C. Instances can be started by Enterprise Manager, Server Manager, and Instance Manager, but cannot be started by SQLPlus Worksheet.

10. A, B, C, D. All of these tasks are required so that users can access the database.

11. A. An index is designed for fast data retrieval.

12. A. A procedure is precompiled, stored code that is stored with the database and can be executed by name.

13. A. Instances open only a single database.

14. A. Starting an instance is what makes databases available for users to use.

15. D. The only time a control file gets created is when the database is initially created. After that, the control file is essential for the operation of the database.

16. C. A database has to have at least two redo log files.

17. B. A database has to have at least one database file.

18. B. The Listener process looks for clients that are attempting to connect to Oracle and hands them off to the appropriate process.

19. C. Net8 is the set of communication standards that Oracle clients and servers use to communicate. While option A (TCP/IP) may seem to be correct, TCP/IP by itself does not allow clients to communicate with Oracle servers.

20. C. Designing the database is usually done by the analysts and programmers, while operators usually work on managing existing databases.

Chapter

2

Installing and Configuring Oracle8i

✓ **How to Install Oracle Database Software**

- Identify the appropriate tool required to install Oracle database software

- Install the Oracle server, Oracle Enterprise Manager, Net8, and SQL*Plus products

✓ **Where to Find Important Oracle Files**

- Create a password file that is used to authenticate a user

- Identify the contents and location of the database trace files

✓ **Network Administration**

- Identify the location and purpose of the Net8 configuration files

- Create the Net8 configuration files using Net8 assistant

Exam objectives are subject to change at any time without prior notice and at Oracle's sole discretion. Please visit Oracle's Training and Certification Web site (http://education.oracle.com/certification/index.html) for the most current exam objectives listing.

This chapter covers Oracle8i installation on the server, client software installation for Oracle, as well as both server and client configuration.

This chapter will first take a look at the default directories of an Oracle installation and what each directory contains. It will then examine the major configuration files of an Oracle database including the password, parameter, and configuration files.

It'll then move on to tackle a Linux installation of Oracle, with details on configuring Linux to best support Oracle. Windows NT will be the next operating system installation covered. It'll then cover how to install Oracle on NetWare.

Starting and stopping an Oracle instance, as well as the various parameters for the STARTUP and SHUTDOWN commands will be covered.

Configuring the Listener and installing and configuring the Oracle client will finish the chapter.

Oracle8i Directory Structure

This section gives you a preview of the directory structure created during a basic Oracle server installation and the locations and functions of important configuration files.

When you install Oracle8i, you will select a destination for your Oracle files. The root of the Oracle directory tree is ORACLE_BASE. It typically follows the format D:\Oracle\ on Windows NT, although it can be named whatever you like, so long as its path does not contain any spaces.

Within ORACLE_BASE, the *Oracle Universal Installer* creates three directories: \ORACLE_HOME, \ADMIN, and \ORADATA.

The \ADMIN and \ORADATA directories both contain at least one \<DB_NAME> directory, where <DB_NAME> is the unique name for a specific database. Each \ADMIN\<DB_NAME> directory contains database administration files for that specific database. Each \ORADATA\DB_NAME directory contains the actual database files. If more than one database is installed on the server, you will see multiple directories in \ADMIN and \ORADATA.

In previous versions of Oracle, the database files were stored in the \ORACLE_HOME\DATABASE directory. In Oracle8i, the database files are stored in the \ADMIN and \ORADATA directories. The \ORACLE_HOME\DATABASE directory contains a copy of INIT<SID>.ORA, where SID is the unique name for an Oracle database instance. If you were to read its contents, you would see that this file contains only one line, which points to the actual working copy of INIT.ORA (for example: IFILE='D:\Oracle\admin\sales\pfile\init.ora').

The \ORACLE_HOME\ directory contains the Oracle products. Table 2.1 shows the directories likely to be explored by a database operator. Not all directories are listed, and if you install additional Oracle products, other directories will also be created in \ORACLE_HOME\.

TABLE 2.1   Oracle Directories and Contents

Directory	Contents
\BIN	Executables
\CLASSES	Oracle Enterprise Manager files
\DATABASE	Password file(s) and initialization file(s)
\DOC	HTML documentation library
\NETWORK	Net8 files
\PLSQL	SQL scripts, sample files, and message files for PL/SQL
\RDBMS	Oracle Server files
\SQLPLUS	SQL*Plus files
\SVRMGL	Server Manager files
\SYSMAN	Oracle Enterprise Manager files

Initialization Parameter Files (INIT.ORA)

Every database instance has a corresponding initialization file that contains parameters used to configure various aspects of database operation. For example, you can configure memory management and rollback segments, define the location of archive logs, control files, and trace files, and specify whether a password file is required for database operation. The INIT.ORA file is an ASCII text file and can be edited with any ASCII text editor. By default, the working copies of the initialization parameter files are located in ORACLE_BASE\admin\DB_NAME\pfile. There is also a sample initialization parameter file located in ORACLE_BASE\admin\sample\pfile that contains examples of many common settings. The initialization parameter file is only read when the database starts, so if you make any changes, you will have to shut down and restart the database instance.

The parameter file is also covered in Chapter 5, "Creating and Managing Databases," and Appendix B, "Performance and Tuning."

Password Files (PWD.ORA)

The PWD<SID>.ORA file contains username and password information for users who need System DBA or System DBO access to the database and the ability to start and shut down the database instance. Password files are located in the ORACLE_HOME\DATABASE directory. If you installed the starter database during the server installation, a password file is automatically created; it contains the users INTERNAL (password: oracle) and SYS (password: change_on_install).

Creating password files is covered in Chapter 5 ,"Creating and Managing Databases." System DBA and System DBO rights are covered in Chapter 6, "Oracle Users and Security."

Adding Users to the Password File

Once you have created the password file, you can add additional users with System DBA or System DBO privileges. Do not attempt to manually edit the password files. The SQL*Plus program should be used to add additional users. The steps to do so are as follows:

1. Start SQL*Plus.

2. Connect as user INTERNAL if it does not automatically prompt you to enter your username.

   ```
   SQL> CONNECT INTERNAL
   ```

3. Grant privileges to each user who will need to perform database administration.

   ```
   SQL> GRANT SYSDBA TO SCOTT;
   ```

4. You are then able to connect to the database as user SCOTT with System DBA privileges.

   ```
   SQL> CONNECT SCOTT/TIGER AS SYSDBA
   ```

Note that you can only add users to the password file if they already exist as an Oracle database account. SQL*Plus is covered in more detail in Chapter 3, "Oracle8i Enterprise Manager and Other Tools."

General Client Preferences (SQLNET.ORA)

*S*QLNET.ORA is used to store client preferences such as the location of trace and log files, routing options, and the preferred order for naming methods. Like the TNSNAMES.ORA file, SQLNET.ORA is commonly edited using the configuration tools *Net8 Configuration Assistant* and Net8 Assistant and is stored in the \ORACLE_HOME\NETWORK\ADMIN directory. A sample of a SQLNET.ORA file with examples and instructions for defining all of the client parameters is included in the \ORACLE_HOME\NETWORK\ADMIN\SAMPLE directory.

Installing Oracle8i on Linux

This section explains how to install and configure Oracle8i on Linux. It is assumed that you are already familiar with the Linux operating system and that this is the first installation of the Oracle8i software on the machine.

Because the DBO test was written to be operating system generic, detailed knowledge of how to install Oracle8i on a Linux server will probably not be tested.

This section covers the installation of Oracle8iR2 for Linux because release 2 of Oracle for Linux works much better than earlier versions.

The computer setup for this example installation is a dual PII 300Mhz with 392MB RAM and a 9GB SCSI hard drive running Red Hat 6.1, which was installed with a slightly modified default GNOME workstation option, and it is expected that this will be a dedicated Oracle server. The necessary modifications to the basic Red Hat Linux install are described in the following sections.

Oracle's Oracle8i for Linux documentation is available at http://technet .oracle.com or on the Oracle8i CD-ROM.

Hardware and Software Installation Requirements

These are the minimum hardware and software requirements as set forth by Oracle. If your system does not meet these requirements, the installation will not be successful.

Hardware

The hardware requirements are as follows:

- Physical memory of 128MB RAM (256MB is recommended)
- Swap space equal to twice the amount of RAM or at least 400MB
- CD-ROM (if installing from CD)
- About 750MB of free disk space

Software

The software requirements are as follows:

- Linux kernel version 2.2 or higher
- GLIBC package version 2.1
- Windows Manager that supports Motif version 1.2 (such as fvmw)

Linux Install

When installing the Linux operating system, the following will serve as a general guide for your disk partitioning:

/boot	16M
/usr	1600M
/opt	4200M
/	1024M
/var	1024M
/tmp	500M

This partitioning setup is optimized for a dedicated Oracle server. The /opt partition will contain the Oracle software and databases and should generally be as large as possible.

You should use two swap files, each 128MB. It is generally advisable to create two swap partitions for fault tolerance.

With some versions of Linux, it is sometimes necessary to modify some kernel parameters and recompile the kernel as specified in the guides available in the Documentation section at `technet.oracle.com`. This is not necessary with Red Hat 6.1.

Tasks to Be Performed as User Root

Make sure TCP/IP is up and running correctly. If you will be installing from a CD-ROM, make sure the CD-ROM is mounted.

If you don't have the Oracle8i CD, you can go to `technet.oracle.com` and download Oracle8i. You will need to set up an account for technet (which is free) in order to do this. Note that this file is almost 300MB in size. In this example, the file was downloaded into /tmp.

Once downloaded, expand the file in the /usr/local/src directory. This will create an Oracle8iR2 directory with all of the install files necessary in the /usr/local/src directory. You can use the sample commands to create the directory and untar the files.

```
cd /usr/local/src
tar -zxvf /tmp/oracle8161.tar.gz
```

Create the mount points for the Oracle installation. This example uses /opt/u01 and /opt/u02 for the mount points. You must have at least two mount points, one for the software and one for the database files. You can create the mount points using these sample commands:

```
mkdir /opt/u01

mkdir /opt/u02
```

Oracle recommends that installations follow the Optimal Flexible Architecture (OFA) standard, which contains guidelines for fast, reliable Oracle databases that require little maintenance. To follow the OFA standard, you must also add the /opt/u03 and /opt/u04 mount points, all four of which (u01–u04) should actually be on separate disks. Further discussion of OFA is beyond the scope of this book; however, for more information on OFA, see Appendix A of the *Oracle8i Administrator's Reference for Linux on Intel* available from `technet.oracle.com/docs`.

Create the Linux groups for database administration and software installation and maintenance. Group dba contains all of the administrators of the Oracle databases. Group oinstall contains users who own the Oracle Universal Installer's oraInventory directory and who can install and uninstall parts of the Oracle server. The oracle user account that runs the Oracle server installation must have the oinstall group as its primary group. You can add the groups using these sample commands:

```
groupadd dba
groupadd oinstall
```

Create the Linux user named oracle who will own the Oracle software, setting the primary group as oinstall and the secondary group as dba with the home directory set to be /home/oracle (which is merely the home directory of the oracle user and has nothing to do with the location of the Oracle software). Then set a password for that user account. You can add a new user with this sample command:

```
adduser -g oinstall -G dba -d /home/oracle oracle
```

NOTE

Use the oracle account only for installing and maintaining the Oracle software. Never use it for anything other than Oracle software setup. Never use the root account to install or administer the Oracle software.

Next, give the user account oracle and group oinstall ownership of the mount points into which you will be installing the Oracle software and databases. You can give ownership using these sample commands:

```
chown -R oracle:oinstall /opt/u01
chown -R oracle:oinstall /opt/u02
chown -R oracle:oinstall /opt/u03
chown -R oracle:oinstall /opt/u04
```

Tasks to Be Performed as User Oracle

It is a good idea to verify that the groups are configured correctly by logging in to the Linux box as oracle and typing the command **GROUPS**. The group oinstall should be listed first, followed by dba.

You should make sure that the user oracle's umask is 022. Do this by logging in as oracle and typing the command **UNMASK**. If umask returns anything other than 022, edit oracle's profile file (i.e., .bash_profile) and add umask 022 as a line.

You should also set up the environmental variables for the Oracle software install. To do so, edit user oracle's profile file (i.e., .bash_profile), and then add the environmental variables. For Bourne or Korn shells, the format is as follows:

```
VARIABLE=setting
export VARIABLE
```

Be sure to use the appropriate syntax for your shell program. The following example uses bash.

```
DISPLAY=workstation_name:0.0
export DISPLAY
ORACLE_BASE=opt/u01/app/oracle
export ORACLE_BASE
ORACLE_HOME=$ORACLE_BASE/product/8.1.6
export ORACLE_HOME
PATH=$PATH:$ORACLE_HOME/bin:/etc
export PATH
ORACLE_SID=SID
export ORACLE_SID
```

Since you may have multiple databases running on one machine, the SID, or Oracle System Identifier, is the unique identifier that Oracle uses to identify a specific database process. The SID is usually the first four letters of the database name.

Log out and log in again so that the settings will take effect. Type the command **ENV** to ensure that you have properly added all of the environmental variables, or type **echo $VARIABLE** to see a specific variable setting.

Installing Oracle 8.1.6 on Linux

To install Oracle on a Linux computer, follow the steps in Exercise 2.1.

EXERCISE 2.1

Installing Oracle on a Linux Server

1. Within your Windows Manager, start the Oracle Universal Installer (OUI) by issuing these commands:

```
startx

cd /usr/local/src/Oracle8iR2

./runInstaller
```

If you downloaded Oracle, you will have to untar or unzip the file into /usr/local/src for this exercise to work as written. If you have the CD, you will have to cd into the directory in which you mounted the CD. Once you have the files in the right place, you will need to open a command line interface window to issue the cd /usr/local/src/Oracle8iR2 and the ./runInstaller commands.

2. The first screen you see is a Welcome screen. Click Next to continue.

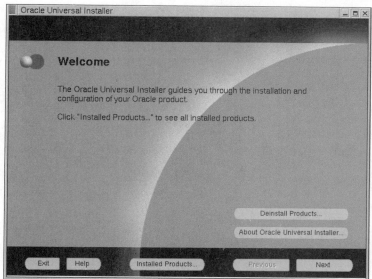

3. You will see the File Locations screen. The Source location is the location of the install files for the software you want to install. The Destination location is the $ORACLE_HOME directory that you configured in your profile file. Click Next to take the default path and to continue.

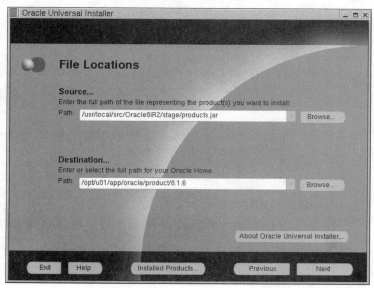

4. You will see the Inventory Location screen. Set the Inventory location to /opt/u01/app/oracle/oraInventory, and then click OK to continue.

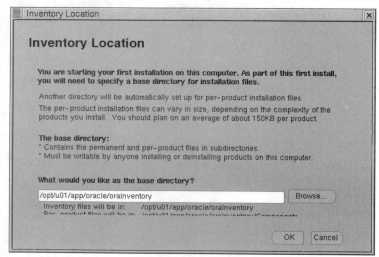

5. You will then see the Unix Group Name screen. This is the group that will be given to Oracle accounts that need Install rights to the Oracle software. Add oinstall, then click Next to continue.

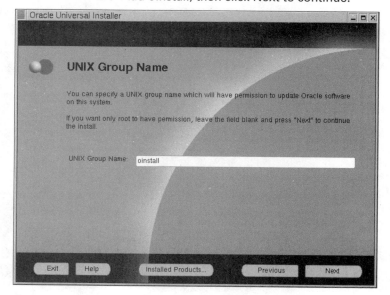

6. You will see the Root Tasks screen of the Oracle Universal Installer. Take note of the instructions in the Root Tasks screen, and follow them exactly. As you do so, you'll see the script run in a separate window.

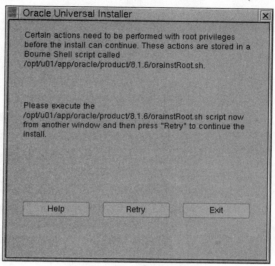

7. Once you have finished, return to the Root Tasks screen and click Retry. You will then see the Available Products screen.

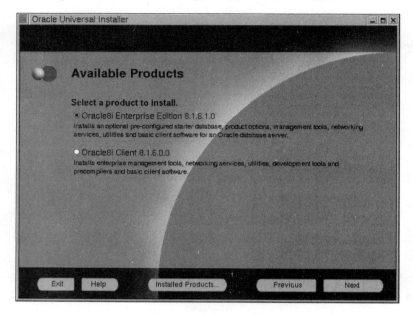

8. Select the server installation, and click Next. You will then see the Installation Types screen.

9. Select Typical, and click Next. You will then see the Database Identification screen.

10. Enter your server's Global Database Name, then select a SID. It is usually best to make things straightforward by keeping the SID you set in your profile file. Click Next.

11. You will then see the Database File Location screen. For performance reasons, the database software and the databases themselves should be on separate disks. However, it is entirely possible to run both software and databases from one disk, and a discussion of Optimal Flexible Architecture (OFA) is beyond the scope of this book. So, for the sake of this exercise, you should simply set the directory for your database files to /opt/u02, and click Next. You will then see the Summary screen.

EXERCISE 2.1 *(continued)*

12. Click Install to begin the installation. You might as well grab a snack at this point. The install process may take a long time, even on a fast machine. Eventually, you will see the Setup Privileges screen.

13. Make note of the instructions on the Setup Privileges screen, and follow them exactly. Click OK to continue.

14. You will then see the Configuration Tools screen, and Net8 Configuration Assistant and the Oracle Database Configuration Assistant will automatically install. As they are doing so, notice the Details section of the screen. It gives a brief description of the actions taking place.

15. Make note of the account names and passwords that appear on the final screen. Click OK to continue. You will see the Installation Complete screen, at which point you can click Exit to close the Oracle Universal Installer.

If your installation failed, you must run the Oracle Universal Installer again and uninstall all files. Then completely remove (rm –R) the $ORACLE_HOME you just created, and begin again.

This is only a basic configuration setup. For more sophisticated configurations, see the *Oracle8i Administrator's Reference for Linux on Intel* viewable at technet.oracle.com/docs.

Post-Installation Tasks

There are a couple of items you may wish to do once Oracle is installed in order to automate certain Oracle functions.

Automate Database Startup and Shutdown

It is important for you to know that you can use dbstart and dbshut to start and shut down your databases, respectively. However, you may also automatically start and stop the Oracle software on a Red Hat system. This section describes in detail the steps necessary to do so.

First edit the /etc/oratab file. Each ORACLE_SID that you wish to start automatically whenever dbstart is run must have a *Y* instead of an *N* at the very end of the line.

In some circumstances, the startup script $ORACLE_HOME/bin/dbstart does not correctly identify the Oracle software version as 8.1. Test to see if you have this problem by running dbshut to shut down any Oracle software that may already be running, then run the dbstart command. If you run ps -eafx and you see that no Oracle software is actually running, then you must edit the $ORACLE_HOME/bin/dbstart file, insert a new line at line 71 of this file, and add VERSION="8.1"; on a line by itself. This must come before the if statement on line 72 but after line 70.

As user root, create two files in the /etc/rc.d/init.d directory. The first one should be named dbora_start, and the second should be named dbora_stop.

Type the following code into the dbora_start file:

```sh
#!/bin/sh
# Set ORA_HOME to be equivalent to the ORACLE_HOME
# from which you wish to execute dbstart and
# dbshut
# set ORA_OWNER to the user id of the owner of the
# Oracle database in ORA_HOME
ORA_HOME=/opt/u01/app/oracle/product/8.1.6
ORA_OWNER=oracle

#Start the listener
if [ ! -f $ORA_HOME/bin/lsnrctl ]
then
echo "LISTENER startup: cannot start"
exit
else
su - $ORA_OWNER -c "/opt/u01/app/oracle/product/8.1.6/
    bin/lsnrctl start"
fi

# Starting the Database
if [ ! -f $ORA_HOME/bin/dbstart ]
then
echo "Oracle startup: cannot start"
exit
```

```
else
# Start the Oracle databases:
# The following command assumes that the
      oracle login will not prompt the
# the user for any values
su - $ORA_OWNER -c $ORA_HOME/bin/dbstart
fi
```

Type this into the dbora_stop file:

```
#!/bin/sh
# Set ORA_HOME to be equivalent to the ORACLE_HOME
# from which you wish to execute dbstart and
# dbshut
# set ORA_OWNER to the user id of the owner of the
# Oracle database in ORA_HOME
ORA_HOME=/opt/u01/app/oracle/product/8.1.6
ORA_OWNER=oracle

#Stop the listener
if [ ! -f $ORA_HOME/bin/lsnrctl ]
then
echo "LISTENER stopping: cannot stop"
exit
else
su - $ORA_OWNER -c "/opt/u01/app/oracle/product/8.1.6/
      bin/lsnrctl stop"
fi

if [ ! -f $ORA_HOME/bin/dbshut ]
then
echo "Oracle stopping: cannot stop"
exit
else
# Stop the Oracle databases:
# The following command assumes that the
      oracle login will not prompt
# the user for any values
su - $ORA_OWNER -c $ORA_HOME/bin/dbshut
```

```
fi
Next, change permissions for the new files ·
     to make them executable.
chmod 755 /etc/rc.d/init.d/dbora_start
chmod 755 /etc/rc.d/init.d/dbora_stop
Then make symbolic links for the dbora_start
     and dbora_stop files in the appropriate
     rc.d runlevel directories.
ln -s /etc/rc.d/init.d/dbora_start /etc/rc.d/rc3.d/
     S99dbora_start
ln -s /etc/rc.d/init.d/dbora_start /etc/rc.d/rc5.d/
     S99dbora_start
ln -s /etc/rc.d/init.d/dbora_stop /etc/rc.d/rc0.d/
     K10dbora_stop
ln -s /etc/rc.d/init.d/dbora_stop /etc/rc.d/rc6.d/
     K10dbora_stop
```

Edit the /etc/services file, and add the following line to reserve a port for the Oracle Listener. LISTENER is the default name for the Listener.

```
LISTENER 1521/tcp #Net8 Listener
```

You will need to update just a few more environmental variables. As user oracle, update Oracle's .bash_profile file, adding the lines that follow. Once you have done so, log out and log back in to ensure that the profile changes take effect.

```
LD_LIBRARY_PATH=$ORACLE_HOME/lib:$ORACLE_HOME/ctx/lib
export LD_LIBRARY_PATH
CLASSPATH=$ORACLE_HOME/JRE:$ORACLE_HOME/jlib:$ORACLE_HOME
     /rdbms/jlib:$ORACLE_HOME/network/jlib
export CLASSPATH
TNS_ADMIN=$ORACLE_HOME/network/admin
export TNS_ADMIN

ORAENV_ASK=NO
export ORAENV_ASK
. /usr/local/bin/oraenv
```

Finally, you can edit your $ORACLE_HOME/dbs/init.ora file to further customize the installation. This, however, is optional.

Installing Oracle8i on Windows NT

This section shows you how to install Oracle on Windows NT. Prior knowledge of Windows NT is assumed.

Because the DBO test was written to be operating system generic, detailed knowledge of how to install Oracle8i on a Windows NT server will probably not be tested. This section was written to help you get Oracle installed and running on a Windows NT system.

Installation Requirements

Following are the minimum requirements as set forth by Oracle. If your system does not meet these requirements, the installation will not be successful.

Hardware

- Physical memory of at least 96MB of RAM (256MB recommended)
- Virtual RAM space equal to twice the amount of RAM or at least 400MB
- CD-ROM (if installing from CD)
- At least 1.5GB of free space if using FAT partitions or 1GB of free space if using NTFS partitions 0

Software

- Windows NT 4 or higher

Tasks to Do Before Installing Oracle

Before you install Oracle on your server, you should confirm your network connectivity, the naming convention for the server, and the TCP/IP port you will use (if different from the default) and determine what directory and volume you will install Oracle on.

Because the Oracle installation program is all graphical, running the setup program is actually relatively easy.

Installing Oracle 8.1.6 on Windows NT

To install Oracle8i on a Windows NT server, do as shown in Exercise 2.2.

EXERCISE 2.2

Installing Oracle on a Windows NT Server

1. Run the SETUP.EXE program from the staging area, either the CD-ROM or the location in which you have stored your downloaded and uncompressed installation files. You will see the Welcome screen. Click Next to continue.

2. You will then see the File Locations screen. Note that the Installer automatically selects a location for the Oracle Home. If you choose to change the Oracle Home location, make sure that the path you select does not contain any spaces. Select Next to continue.

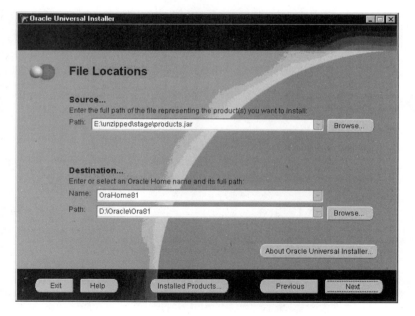

EXERCISE 2.2 *(continued)*

3. At the Available Products screen, select Oracle8i Enterprise Edition, then select Next to continue. The other two options, Oracle8i Client and Oracle8i Management Infrastructure are normally installed on workstations.

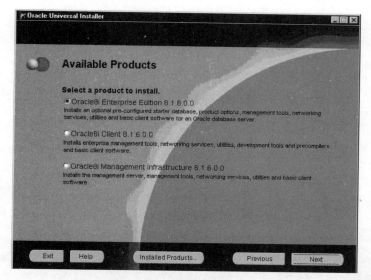

4. At the Installation Types screen, select Typical. Note that you could also select Minimal or Custom if you wish to select individual components to install. Select Next to continue.

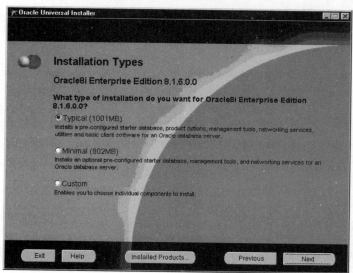

EXERCISE 2.2 *(continued)*

5. At the Database Identification screen, you will be prompted to enter the Global Database Name and the Oracle System Identifier (SID), which will identify the database instance running on the server. For the purposes of this exercise, the database sales will be created on the ackme.com domain. Select Next to continue.

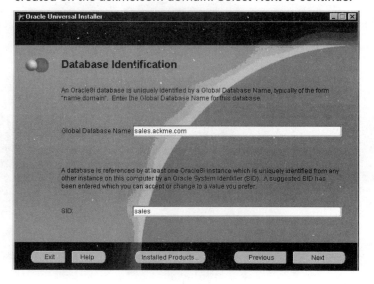

6. The Summary screen displays a list of the products to be installed. Select Install to begin the installation. Since a typical installation type was selected for this exercise, Net8 is automatically configured and a database is automatically created once installation of the server software is complete.

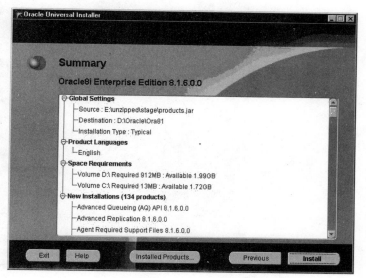

EXERCISE 2.2 *(continued)*

7. After database configuration, you will see an Alert box that contains the Global Database Name, system identifier, SYS account password (change_on_install), and SYSTEM account password (manager). Select OK to close the Alert box.

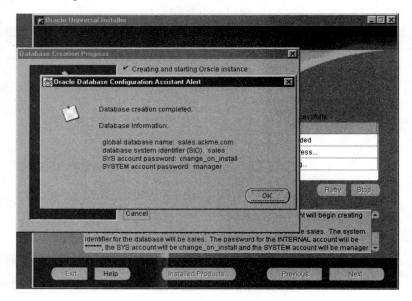

8. Once the configuration tools are finished, select Next to finish the install process.

After install is complete, open your NT services by selecting Start ➤ Settings ➤ Control Panel ➤ Services. You will see that several new Oracle services have been created and that the database services for sales (OracleServiceSALES) and the Listener (OracleOraHome81TNSListener) are already configured to start up automatically.

Installing Oracle8i on Novell NetWare

This section will show you how to install Oracle on NetWare. Prior knowledge of NetWare is assumed.

Because the DBO test was written to be operating system generic, detailed knowledge of how to install and configure Oracle8i on a NetWare server will probably not be tested. This section was written to help you get Oracle installed and running on a NetWare system.

Installation Requirements

As with other operating systems, the installation requirements for NetWare are basically the equivalent of a medium-powered server. You should also look to see if the existing server load is light enough so that installing Oracle won't have a major impact on applications that are currently running.

Hardware

- Physical memory of at least 96MB of RAM (256MB recommended)
- Virtual RAM space equal to twice the amount of RAM or at least 400MB
- CD-ROM (if installing from CD)
- At least 1GB of free space

Software

- NetWare 4.11 or higher

Tasks to Do Before Installing Oracle

Before you install Oracle on your server, you should make sure of your network connectivity, the naming convention for the server, and the TCP/IP port you will use (if different from the default) and determine what directory and volume you will install Oracle on.

Because the Oracle installation program is all graphical, running the setup program is actually relatively easy. Follow Exercise 2.3 to install Oracle on a NetWare server.

EXERCISE 2.3

Installing Oracle on NetWare

1. Shut down any Oracle applications that are running on the Net-Ware server by running the ORAUNLD command.

2. Insert the installation CD-ROM into the server, and mount the CD-ROM.

3. Load the NWCONFIG application.

4. Select Product Options, choose Install a Product Not Listed, then press F3 to specify the path to the Oracle software install directory.

5. Enter the location of PINSTALL.NLM, for example, O8INW:\install\netware (if the Oracle CD is mounted with the default name of O8INW).

6. The Oracle Universal Installer will load. It looks and behaves much the same as it does under Windows NT.

7. At the File Locations box, note that the default location for ORACLE_HOME is SYS:\OraHome1. It is generally advisable to install the Oracle software on its own volume; Oracle databases can quickly grow to enormous sizes. The volume on which Oracle software will be installed should not use compression or block suballocation.

8. During install, you will be prompted for a System DBA password. Avoid non-alphanumeric characters when selecting a password.

9. You will then be prompted to select the protocol(s) that Net8 will use. If you select TCP/IP, you will be prompted to supply your server's IP address.

Once the Oracle server software is installed, you can add the batch file ORALOAD.NCF to the end of your AUTOEXEC.NCF file to load the Oracle server NLMs automatically upon startup. The ORASTART.NCF batch file can be used to start the default database instance once all of the NLMs have been loaded.

Managing Oracle Trace Files

Oracle8i creates various trace files when an instance is running. The trace files can be found in the \ORACLE_HOME\ADMIN\ <SID> folder. The major trace file created is the <SID>ALRT.LOG, which is in the \BDUMP folder. Oracle also creates a <SID>ARC0.TRC file when ARCHIVELOG mode is enabled.

Oracle trace files are cumulative files and never get overwritten by default. In order to keep hard drives cleaned up, you should periodically look at the trace files, back them up, and delete them. You can delete trace files even when the instance is running—Oracle will just make a new file the next time it needs to write something in it.

Other trace files are kept in the \UDUMP folder, which contains user errors and problems, such as deadlocks.

Using Server Manager to Start Up and Shut Down Oracle Databases

Server Manager is a command line utility that can be used to start and stop database services, to control logging and recovery, and to execute SQL queries. You must be logged in to Oracle as a System DBA or System DBO privileged user to start up or shut down a database. This section describes how to use Server Manager to manually start and stop database services.

Instance Manager is a graphical utility that can be used to start and stop an instance. Instance Manager is covered in Chapter 3, "Oracle8i Enterprise Manager and Other Tools."

Starting Oracle

The syntax to start up an instance using Server Manager is as follows:

```
STARTUP <option> pfile=<path to the init.ora file>
```

There are four commonly used options to start up a database instance.

STARTUP OPEN

STARTUP OPEN is the default option for starting Oracle. It starts the instance, attaches the database, and opens the database. If you issue only the STARTUP command, it is as if you issued the STARTUP OPEN command. Figure 2.1 shows database startup in normal mode.

FIGURE 2.1 Starting a database in OPEN mode

STARTUP NOMOUNT

STARTUP NOMOUNT starts an instance without mounting the database. This is commonly used when creating a new database. Creating databases is covered in Chapter 5, "Creating and Managing Databases."

STARTUP MOUNT

STARTUP MOUNT will start the instance and open the control file, but it will not open the database files. This is commonly used when doing a database recovery. Database recovery and backups are covered in Chapter 10, "Backups and Restorations."

STARTUP RESTRICT

STARTUP RESTRICT will start the instance and open a database, but all users except those with the System DBA or the Restricted privilege will be unable to connect to the database.

Stopping Oracle

There are four common options used to shut down an Oracle instance. Again, you must be connected to the database as a user with System DBA privileges in order to shut down the database. The syntax to shut down is as follows:

SHUTDOWN <option>

There are four commonly used options to shut down a database instance.

SHUTDOWN NORMAL

SHUTDOWN NORMAL is the slowest, safest, and most commonly used shutdown option. Oracle will not allow any new connections and will wait for all users to log off. Once they have done so, Oracle closes and dismounts the database; then shuts down the instance. This is the default SHUTDOWN mode.

WARNING Because SHUTDOWN NORMAL waits for all connections to disconnect, any users or processes that don't disconnect will keep Oracle from shutting down. This could cause serious problems, especially if you have off-line backups scheduled to run (since they would end up not running because the database never shut down). SHUTDOWN TRANSACTIONAL may be a better choice, or even SHUTDOWN IMMEDIATE, if the database has to shut down immediately.

SHUTDOWN TRANSACTIONAL

SHUTDOWN TRANSACTIONAL is used when you need to shut down quickly, but you do not want active clients to lose any work. Oracle will not allow any new connections, and any connected clients will be disconnected as soon as they complete their current transactions. Once all transactions are finished, the database and instance are shut down.

SHUTDOWN IMMEDIATE

SHUTDOWN IMMEDIATE is used when you need to shut down the database right away, possibly because of an instability in the database or one of its applications. Currently processing transactions are not completed, the transactions are rolled back, all users are disconnected, and the database and instance shut down.

Figure 2.2 shows a database shutdown in SHUTDOWN IMMEDIATE mode.

FIGURE 2.2 Shutting the database down immediately

```
C:\WINNT\System32\command.com
Microsoft(R) Windows NT DOS
(C)Copyright Microsoft Corp 1990-1996.

C:\>svrmgrl

Oracle Server Manager Release 3.1.6.0.0 - Production

Copyright (c) 1997, 1999, Oracle Corporation. All Rights Reserved.

Oracle8i Enterprise Edition Release 8.1.6.0.0 - Production
With the Partitioning option
JServer Release 8.1.6.0.0 - Production

SVRMGR> connect internal@sales
Connected.
SVRMGR> shutdown immediate
Database closed.
Database dismounted.
ORACLE instance shut down.
SVRMGR>
```

SHUTDOWN ABORT

SHUTDOWN ABORT is only used when the database must be shut down immediately, or when no other SHUTDOWN mode will work. Current trans-actions are immediately terminated, users are disconnected, and uncommitted transactions are not rolled back. After a SHUTDOWN ABORT, the next time the database is started, it will automatically begin an instance recovery. You will not be able to open the database until the instance recovery is complete. Since instance recovery can take a very long time and you risk data loss, you should avoid using the abort option.

Be sure you know the common modes for database startup and shutdown and under what circumstances you would use them.

Listener Configuration (LISTENER.ORA)

LISTENER.ORA is used to set parameters for your network listener process on the server. The LISTENER.ORA file is also stored in the \ORACLE_HOME\network\admin directory and edited using the configu-ration tools Net8 Configuration Assistant and Net8 Assistant.

Unlike previous versions of Oracle, when you install Oracle8i server with the sample database, the Oracle Universal Installer prompts you for basic Net8 and Listener information and automatically configures both Net8 and the Listener during install.

There are two utilities that you can use to modify the Net8 and Listener configuration. Net8 Configuration Assistant allows you to configure basic network services after installation through a simple wizard-like interface. Net8 Assistant provides a more advanced environment for configuring and managing Net8. Both programs can be found by selecting Start ➤ Programs ➤ Oracle OraHome81 ➤ Network Administration on a Windows NT server. Running EASYCFG.NCF starts the Configuration Wizard on a NetWare server.

On the server, Net8 Assistant allows you to create and modify Listeners to receive client connections; these settings are stored in LISTENER.ORA. Net8 Assistant also allows you to configure various naming methods that will resolve the simple names that client connections will use when connecting to the database (like sales.ackme.com).

If you are using DNS to resolve names, the DNS server must be functioning, reachable by the client, and aware of the names you wish to use.

If you use the Local naming method, then these settings are stored in a file called TNSNAMES.ORA, and each client must also be configured (using the client's Net8 Assistant) to have its own TNSNAMES.ORA file. Using Net8 Assistant on the client to configure the Local naming method and to connect to the server is described in the section "Client Installation," found later in this chapter.

Starting and Stopping the Listener

On Windows NT, you can use the NET START <service> and NET STOP <service> commands to start (and stop) instances and Listeners, as shown in Figure 2.3.

FIGURE 2.3   Starting the Oracle instance and Listener

For greater control over the Listener process, use the Listener Control utility LSNRCTL. LSNRCTL is a command line program that can be run in either interactive or batch mode. To start LSNRCTL, run the command LSNRCTL at the command prompt of the Oracle server system. LSNRCTL behaves the same on Windows NT, NetWare, and Unix systems. If the Listener is named something other than the default (which is listener), then use the syntax lsnrctl <name>, where *name* is the name of the Listener you wish to administer. Figure 2.4 shows LSNRCTL started in interactive mode and its basic help function.

FIGURE 2.4   The LSNRCTL utility

All of these Listener configuration tasks can also be accomplished using the Instance Manager in the Oracle Enterprise Manager (OEM). Instance Manager and OEM are described in detail in Chapter 3, "Oracle8i Enterprise Manager and Other Tools."

Client Installation

Net8 and the client software must also be installed and configured on every workstation that will be accessing the Oracle server software. In Exercise 2.4, you install the Oracle client software.

EXERCISE 2.4

Installing the Oracle Client

1. To install Net8 and the Oracle client software, start the Oracle Universal Installer by running the same setup program you used to install the Oracle server software. After the Welcome screen, you will again see the File Locations screen that allows you to select the source and destination directories for the Oracle software. Once you proceed to the Available Products screen, select Oracle8i Client, then click Next.

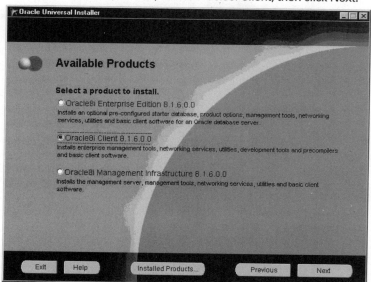

2. You will then be presented with the Installation Types screen. The Administrator, Programmer, and Application User installation types all include the basic client software that can be used to configure Net8 connectivity to the database; you should select the installation type appropriate for your uses. For the purpose of this exercise, however, Administrator should be selected, then click Next.

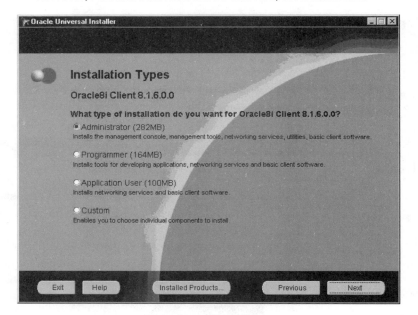

3. The Summary screen will show all of the products that will be installed. Select Next to install the software.

4. After the software is installed, the Net8 Configuration Assistant will automatically start. If a directory service is running on your server, you can select that option. Otherwise, use the Net8 Configuration Assistant to create a local file on your workstation (TNSNAMES.ORA) that will contain mappings from the simple service names to the network location and identification of the service.

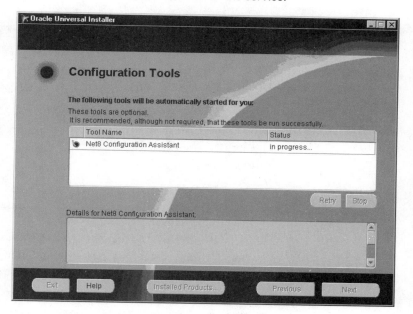

EXERCISE 2.4 *(continued)*

5. You will then select the version of the Oracle database or service you wish to access; Oracle8i should be your selection in this example. Select Next to continue.

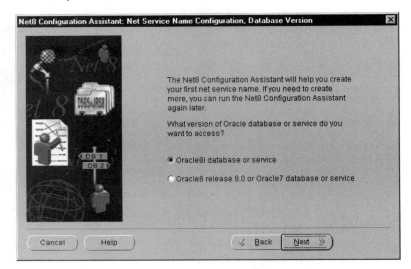

6. You will then see the first Net Service Name Configuration screen that prompts you for the service name that you wish to access. In this example, your service name is sales.ackme.com. Select Next to continue.

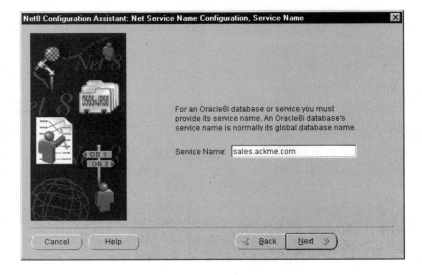

7. You are then prompted to select the protocol used to connect to the database. Select Next to continue.

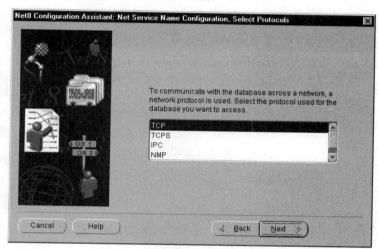

8. Depending on which protocol you select, the following screens will allow you to configure settings specific to that protocol. You would use IPC to connect to a database that is on the same physical machine as the client software, but in this example the client will be making a connection over a TCP/IP network, so fill in the server name, leave the port at the default of 1521, and choose Next to continue.

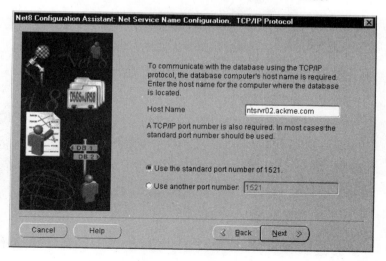

9. After you have configured Net8 for your protocol, you will have the opportunity to test the connectivity to the database. If the test fails, the resulting screen will provide diagnostic information. For example, the first screen shows that Net8 Configuration Assistant cannot locate a Listener. Once the Listener is started on the server, the test is successful, as shown in the next screen. Note that the username that Net8 Configuration Assistant uses to connect to the database is scott and the password is tiger. This user exists by default in all Oracle databases. If user scott has been removed, use any other login for that database.

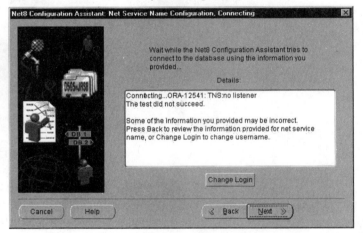

EXERCISE 2.4 *(continued)*

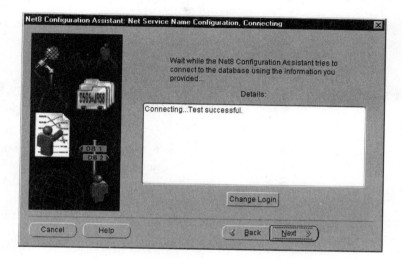

10. You will then be prompted to select a name for the service. After you click Next, you will be given the option to create another net service name or exit Net8 Configuration Assistant. Once Net8 Configuration Assistant is finished, you will return to the Oracle Universal Installer, which will inform you that the installation is finished.

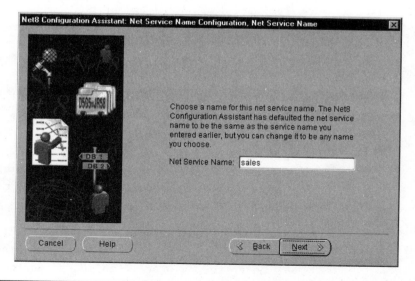

If OUI persistently crashes after Net8 Configuration Assistant runs, reinstall and make sure that you deselect the Test option.

Net8 Configuration (TNSNAMES.ORA)

*T*NSNAMES.ORA is an ASCII text file that contains the mapping between the short connect string that you would use when you log in to an instance and the full connection information. The mapping (called a service or alias) contains the actual connect descriptor that includes the Oracle service information such as the SID, the host machine's network address or name, and the port number on which the Listener listens for incoming client connection requests.

A copy of TNSNAMES.ORA is stored in the \ORACLE_HOME\network\admin folder on each machine (including the server) from which users will be logging in to the database. In the example that follows, SQL*Plus is used to connect as scott with connect string sales.

```
D:\Oracle> sqlplus scott@sales
SQL*Plus: Release 8.1.6.0.0 -
     Production on Sun Sep 17 14:55:23 2000
(c) Copyright 1999 Oracle Corporation.
     All rights reserved.
Enter password:
Connected to:
Oracle8i Enterprise Edition Release 8.1.6.0.0 -
     Production With the Partitioning option
JServer Release 8.1.6.0.0 - Production
SQL>
```

SQL*Plus connected to the database corresponding to the connect string as it is defined in the TNSNAMES.ORA file. In the following example, a simple TNSNAMES.ORA file was used:

```
# TNSNAMES.ORA Network Configuration File:
# D:\Oracle\Ora81\network\admin\tnsnames.ora
# Generated by Oracle configuration tools.
```

```
SALES =
  (DESCRIPTION =
    (ADDRESS_LIST =
      (ADDRESS = (PROTOCOL = TCP)
      (HOST = 192.168.3.5)(PORT = 1521)))
    (CONNECT_DATA =
      (SERVICE_NAME = sales.ackme.com)))
```

The connect string may be any short name that you define, and it does not need to match the database or server name. However, it is usually most straightforward to use the database name as your connect string.

Net8 is initially installed and configured during client software installation, but you can use Net8 Configuration Assistant and/or Net8 Assistant to modify the Net8 configuration for that workstation at any time. The programs look the same as the server version of the Net8 configuration tools, but since they are used to configure settings for the client machine on which they are installed, you will notice that the Listener Administration sections are left blank or disabled.

Summary

Oracle8i installs to what is called the ORACLE_HOME directory, which you enter during installation. Oracle8i must be installed on the server as well as any clients that you wish to have connected to the server.

Oracle8i supports Unix, Windows NT, and NetWare operating systems. The Oracle Universal Installer (OUI) program operates very similarly on all three platforms.

Server Manager is a command prompt utility that can be used to stop and start an instance. The syntax to start an instance is STARTUP <option> pfile=<path to init.ora>.

The Listener is an application that listens for incoming requests from clients and passes the requests to Oracle8i. The Listener is automatically installed and configured during a normal Oracle server install. The Listener configurations are stored in a file called LISTENER.ORA.

Additional configurations for both the server and client are held in SQLNET.ORA.

Clients are also installed using the OUI. Part of the client installation is to create the TNSNAMES.ORA file, which stores a database alias that contains all of the information needed to connect to a particular Oracle instance.

The Easy Configuration utility and the Net8 Configuration Assistant can both be used to create an alias (which modifies the TNSNAMES.ORA file). The Net8 Configuration Assistant can also be used to modify Listener settings.

A database consists of a parameter file (INIT.ORA), a password file (PWD.ORA), at least one control file (CTL.ORA), at least one database file (USER.USR), and at least two redo log files (REDO1.LOG, REDO2.LOG).

Key Terms

Before you take the exam, make sure you're familiar with the following terms:

Instance Manager

LISTENER.ORA

Net8 Configuration Assistant

Oracle Universal Installer (OUI)

Server Manager

SHUTDOWN ABORT

SHUTDOWN IMMEDIATE

SHUTDOWN NORMAL

SHUTDOWN TRANSACTIONAL

SQLNET.ORA

STARTUP MOUNT

STARTUP NOMOUNT

STARTUP OPEN

STARTUP RESTRICT

TNSNAMES.ORA

Review Questions

1. You need to back up all of the database files. You have several lazy users who never log out of their application. Which of these would you not want to use?

   A. SHUTDOWN ABORT

   B. SHUTDOWN NORMAL

   C. SHUTDOWN TRANSACTIONAL

   D. SHUTDOWN IMMEDIATE

2. You need to back up all of the database files. You have several users who run complex transactions that are hard to duplicate. Which of these would you use?

   A. SHUTDOWN ABORT

   B. SHUTDOWN NORMAL

   C. SHUTDOWN TRANSACTIONAL

   D. SHUTDOWN IMMEDIATE

3. Which file contains the connection configurations for a client?

   A. LISTENER.ORA

   B. SQLNET.ORA

   C. INIT.ORA

   D. TNSNAMES.ORA

4. Which file contains the configurations for the Listener services?

   A. LISTENER.ORA

   B. SQLNET.ORA

   C. INIT.ORA

   D. TNSNAMES.ORA

5. What directory holds the Oracle executables?

   A. \BIN

   B. \NETWORK

   C. \RDBMS

   D. \SVRMGL

6. What directory holds the Server Manager files?

   A. \BIN

   B. \NETWORK

   C. \RDBMS

   D. \SVRMGL

7. Where does the SQLNET.ORA file reside?

   A. \BIN

   B. \NETWORK

   C. \NETWORK\CONFIGS

   D. \NETWORK\ADMIN

8. What is the name of the program used to install Oracle on a server?

   A. Oracle Setup

   B. Oracle Universal Installer

   C. Oracle Configuration Wizard

   D. Oracle Manager

9. Which of the files is not an ASCII file?

   A. PWD.ORA

   B. INIT.ORA

   C. SQLNET.ORA

   D. TNSNAMES.ORA

10. Which command prompt utility is used to start and stop the instance?

    A. Instance Manager

    B. Oracle Universal Installer

    C. Server Manager

    D. Enterprise Manager

11. You need to create a new database using SQL syntax. Which mode should you start in?

    A. OPEN

    B. NOMOUNT

    C. MOUNT

    D. RESTRICT

12. You need to keep users out of the database while you create some new tables. Which mode should you start in?

    A. OPEN

    B. NOMOUNT

    C. MOUNT

    D. RESTRICT

13. What utility edits the TNSNAMES.ORA file on the client?

    A. Connection Wizard

    B. Net8 Configuration Assistant

    C. Oracle Universal Installer

    D. Client Setup

14. What is the default port when using TCP/IP?

    A. 1500

    B. 1520

    C. 1521

    D. 1550

15. If you configure an IPC connection, which Oracle servers can you connect to? (Select all that apply.)

    A. The server running on that particular computer

    B. Any server in your subnet

    C. Any server you can see across a router

    D. Any server

16. If you configure a TCP/IP connection, which Oracle servers can you connect to? (Select all that apply.)

    A. The server running on that particular computer

    B. Any server in your subnet

    C. Any server you can normally see across a router

    D. Any server in your company

17. Which graphical utility is used to start and stop an instance?

    A. Instance Manager

    B. Oracle Universal Installer

    C. Server Manager

    D. Oracle Setup

18. The following code would be found in which file?

```
SALES =
  (DESCRIPTION =
    (ADDRESS_LIST =
      (ADDRESS = (PROTOCOL = TCP)
      (HOST = 192.168.3.5)(PORT = 1521)))
    (CONNECT_DATA =
      (SERVICE_NAME = sales.ackme.com)))
```

    A. LISTENER.ORA

    B. TNSNAMES.ORA

    C. SQLNET.ORA

    D. PWD.ORA

19. What is the password for the default user scott?

    A. scott

    B. winner

    C. tiger

    D. smith

20. Which of the options would start an instance?

    A. STARTUP FILE=c:\database\init.ora

    B. STARTUP PFILE=c:\database\init.ora

    C. STARTUP PARAMETER=c:\database\init.ora

    D. STARTUP OPEN=c:\database\init.ora

Answers to Review Questions

1. B. SHUTDOWN NORMAL waits for all users to disconnect (which they may never do if their application is left open).

2. C. Because you have transactions running (which you wish to preserve), you don't want to issue SHUTDOWN ABORT or SHUTDOWN IMMEDIATE, and if you issue SHUTDOWN NORMAL, shutdown may never take place.

3. D. The TNSNAMES.ORA file contains connection configurations.

4. A. The LISTENER.ORA file contains the configurations for the Listener service.

5. A. The \BIN folder contains the Oracle executables.

6. D. The \SVRMGL folder holds the Server Manager files.

7. D. The SQLNET.ORA file resides in the NETWORK\ADMIN folder.

8. B. Oracle is installed on the server using Oracle Universal Installer.

9. A. The password file is not ASCII—the rest are.

10. C. Server Manager is used to stop and start the instance.

11. B. You need to start the instance in NOMOUNT mode to create a new database.

12. D. The RESTRICT option keeps all users out, unless they are a System DBA or have the Restrict privilege.

13. B. The Net8 Configuration Assistant edits the TNSNAMES.ORA file on the client.

14. C. Port 1521 is the default port for Oracle.

15. A. IPC connections are only good for communicating with servers that are installed on that particular box.

16. A, B, C. If you use the TCP/IP protocol, you should be able to connect to any server you can normally see across the router. There may be some servers in your company that you cannot get to via TCP/IP. In that case, the Oracle client can't get to those servers either.

17. A. Instance Manager is a graphical tool used to start and stop instances.

18. B. TNSNAMES.ORA contains aliases (Sales in this case) with all of the connection information necessary to find the Oracle instance.

19. C. The default password is tiger for the default user scott.

20. B. The PFILE option points to the parameter file in the STARTUP command.

Oracle8i Enterprise Manager and Other Tools

ORACLE8i DBO EXAM OBJECTIVES OFFERED IN THIS CHAPTER:

✓ **How to Install Oracle Database Software**

- Identify the appropriate tool required to install Oracle database software
- Install the Oracle server, Oracle Enterprise Manager, Net8, and SQL*Plus products

✓ **Tools Are Used to Access an Oracle Database**

- Define the SQL and PL/SQL languages
- Define the appropriate tool used to achieve tasks within the database: Designers, Developers, End-Users, DBAs, and DBOs
- Set up a repository and a management server for Oracle Enterprise Manager
- Start and stop the intelligent agent
- Manage your services from the Console

✓ **How to Stop and Start an Oracle Database**

- Use OEM Instance Manager to shut down the database
- Shut down the database in different modes
- Use Instance Manager to start up the database in different modes
- Configure the init.ora parameters by using Instance Manager

Exam objectives are subject to change at any time without prior notice and at Oracle's sole discretion. Please visit Oracle's Training and Certification Web site (http://education.oracle.com/certification/index.html) for the most current exam objectives listing.

racle8i Enterprise Edition comes with a variety of graphical tools and utilities that not only make administration of databases easier, some tools can even perform sophisticated analyses on your data and usage. Because there is such a wide variety of tools, one of the challenges is knowing which tool to use for a given purpose.

This chapter will cover how to install the various tools and utilities, as well as how to use them for database operations. The tools that will be covered are as follows:

Enterprise Manager The overall management tool

Instance Manager Allows you to start and stop an Oracle instance

Storage Manager Used to manage database files and tablespaces

Schema Manager Used to manage database objects

Security Manager Used to configure users, roles, and security

SQL Worksheet Allows you to send SQL code to Oracle

Diagnostics Pack Used to find common problems

Tuning Pack Used to better Oracle performance

In previous versions of Oracle8 and Oracle8i, the Diagnostics, Change Management, and Tuning Packs had to be purchased and installed separately from the core utilities. Starting with Enterprise Manager 2.1 (available with Oracle8i), those three packs are now a standard feature.

Because the Diagnostics Pack, Change Management, and Tuning Pack all require Enterprise Manager, when you run the Setup program provided with those utilities, Enterprise Manager will be installed if it isn't already. You can also choose to install just Enterprise Manager without any of the additional packs.

Installing Enterprise Manager

Starting with Oracle8i, Enterprise Manager and the various other utilities are independent of the Oracle8i server and thus need to be installed separately. You will first need to install the Oracle8i server (see Chapter 2, "Installing and Configuring Oracle8i") before you can install Enterprise Manager.

Oracle8i uses a management server to hold the repository for administration, which is basically a set of configurations and preferences used when managing servers. Unlike Oracle8, many different users can use the same repository in Oracle8i.

To install Enterprise Manager, run the Setup program from the Enterprise Manager CD-ROM or downloaded directory. In Exercise 3.1, you install Enterprise Manager as part of the Diagnostics Pack.

EXERCISE 3.1

Installing Enterprise Manager and the Diagnostics and Tuning Packs

1. Run the Setup program from the Diagnostics Pack CD-ROM. Click the Begin Installation button.

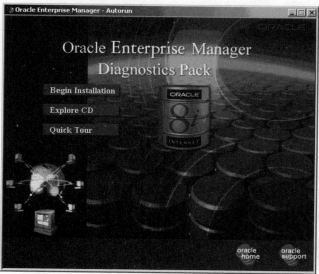

2. At the Welcome page, note that you can choose to view installed programs and de-install, as well as install, products. To continue, choose the Next button.

EXERCISE 3.1 *(continued)*

3. At the File Locations screen, enter a unique path and name for your Oracle8i installation if you are installing Enterprise Manager on the same box as Oracle. Otherwise, accept the default name and location. Choose Next to continue.

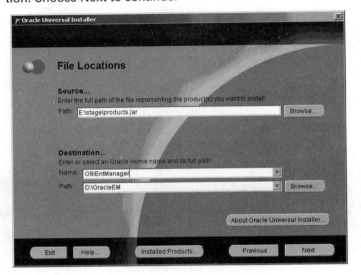

4. Note that the Installer program will scan the products to install and then go to the Available Products page. From here, select Diagnostics Pack, Management Server, and Enterprise Manager Client if it is the first Oracle utility installed. If you already have Enterprise Manager installed and are just adding the Diagnostics Pack, leave it at the default setting. Choose Next to continue.

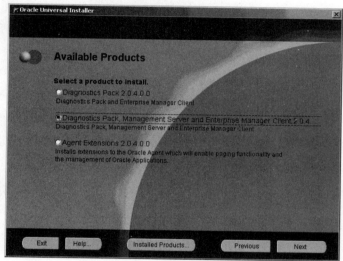

5. From the Installation Types screen, leave the default setting of Typical, unless you know there are certain modules you want to add or subtract. Select Next to continue.

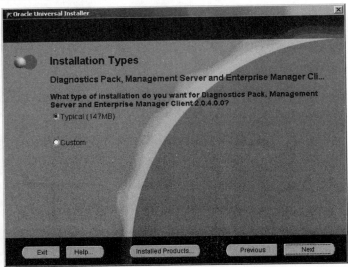

6. On the Summary page, you can see exactly what will be installed and where it will go. Choose Install to start the installation.

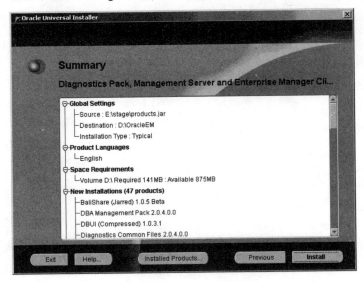

7. Once the install has completed, the Configuration Assistant will start. Page 1 of the Assistant has you log in to a database where the repository will be created. Enter the appropriate information, and choose Next.

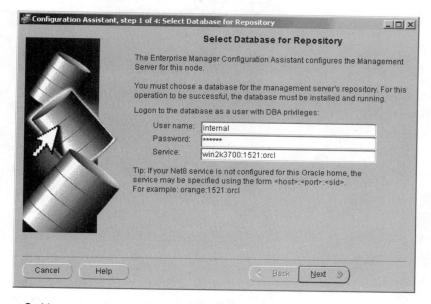

8. You may get a warning about processes set too low. If you do, go ahead and create the repository anyway.

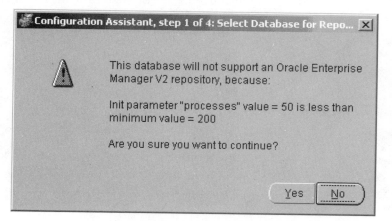

EXERCISE 3.1 *(continued)*

9. The Repository Login Information screen allows you to create the user who will own the repository. Enter the user name and their password, and choose Next to continue.

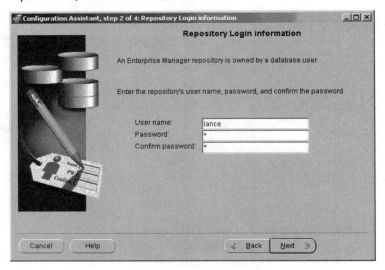

10. You will be asked where to put the repository. Use the default location, unless you have a good reason not to (like a full hard drive). If you are reinstalling Enterprise Manager or creating a new repository, you may get a warning about overwriting an old repository. If you are sure you want to create a new one, choose No.

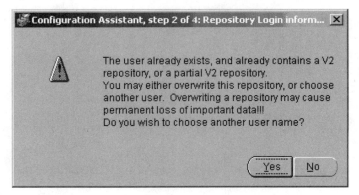

11. The Create Repository Summary screen should appear. It will allow you to back up and make changes if you need to. To create the repository, choose Finish.

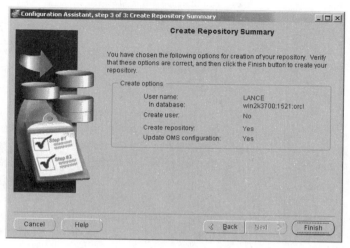

12. The Configuration Action Progress screen will show the progress of the repository installation. When it is done, a Close button will appear. Choose Close to close the screen.

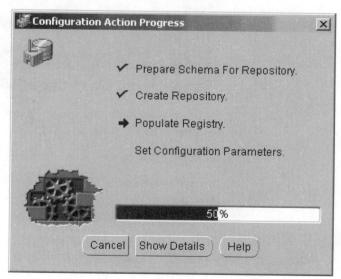

EXERCISE 3.1 *(continued)*

13. To install the Tuning Pack, insert the CD-ROM or run Setup from the Tuning Pack directory.

14. Choose Begin Installation.

15. Select Next at the Welcome screen.

16. Select the name and the path that you used in step 3 so that the Tuning Pack is installed in the same location as Enterprise Manager. Choose Next.

17. At the Available Products screen, select just the Tuning Pack if you have already installed Enterprise Manager. Select Next to continue.

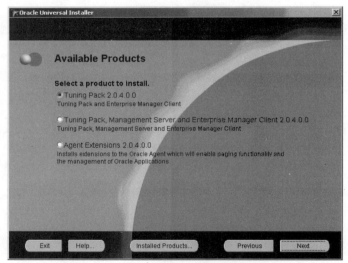

18. At the Installation Types screen, choose to do a Typical installation and then choose Next.

19. Choose Install at the Summary screen to install the Tuning Pack.

20. Once the installation is complete, choose Exit to quit the Setup program.

Once Enterprise Manger is installed, the Oracle Enterprise Manager Management Service must be started. On Windows NT, go to Control Panel ➤ Services; on Windows 2000, go to Computer Management ➤ Services and Applications ➤ Services, as shown in Figure 3.1.

FIGURE 3.1   The Enterprise Manager Management Service

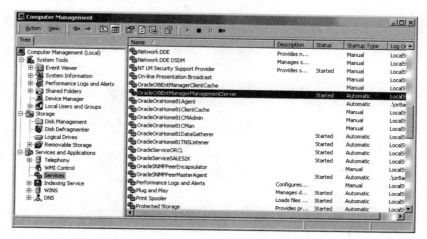

If you don't have the service started, you will get an error stating such when you attempt to log in.

Oracle Enterprise Manager

Oracle *Enterprise Manager* (OEM) is the main management and configuration tool that comes with Oracle. Once Enterprise Manager is installed (see Exercise 3.1), you will need to log in to the repository with a user that has sufficient rights. To start Enterprise Manager (on Windows) go to Start ≻ Programs ≻ (Installed Name) ≻ Oracle Enterprise Management ≻ Enterprise Manager Console.

If this is your first time, you may want to look at the Quick Tour, which shows you basic features of Enterprise Manager.

You will get a Connection box (see Figure 3.2) prompt when you start Enterprise Manager. Enter the name and password of the user account (the default is sysman with a password of oem_temp), and select the management server you wish to attach to. If there is no management server listed, click the browser button next to the server name, which will allow you to add the management server, as shown in Figure 3.3.

FIGURE 3.2 Connecting to the management server

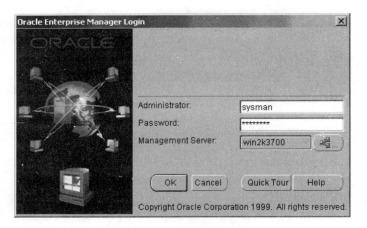

FIGURE 3.3 Entering a management server

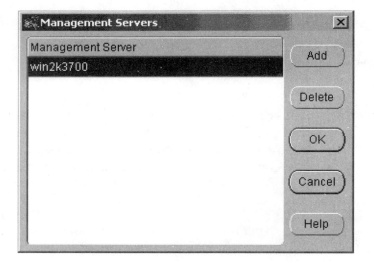

 The default user is sysman with a password of oem_temp when connecting to the management server for the first time. You will be prompted to change your password at the first login. Make sure you don't lose the password (before you make additional administrators), or you will have to delete and re-create the repository.

Once you are in Enterprise Manger, you will see four panes, as shown in Figure 3.4. The upper-left pane shows databases, Listeners, and nodes (servers). The upper-right pane shows groups of databases, the lower-left pane shows active and past jobs, and the lower-right pane shows alerts, registered events, and historic events.

FIGURE 3.4 Enterprise Manager

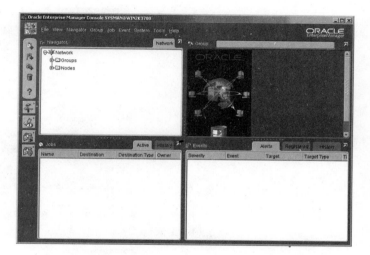

Discovering Databases

In order to manage a database, you must first discover the database. If you add additional databases, you can simply go to Navigator ➢ Discover Nodes and refresh Enterprise Manager. Your new databases should show up. In Exercise 3.2, you discover databases running on a node (server).

EXERCISE 3.2

Discovering Databases

1. Start Enterprise Manager, and log in.

2. Make sure the SNMP agent is running on the node you wish to discover. For NetWare servers, run LOAD DBSNMP; on Windows NT servers, make sure the Oracle Agent service is running, and on Unix, run the SNMP service.

3. Make sure you have a service name configured for each database instance. See Chapter 2, "Installing and Configuring Oracle8i," for more details.

4. From Enterprise Manager, choose Navigator ➤ Discover Nodes.

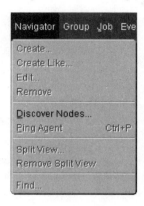

5. Enter the name of the node (server) you wish to discover databases on, and choose OK.

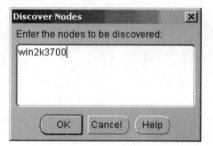

6. You should get back a status report that the node was processed and that its status is Added. Choose Close.

7. The Network pane (upper left) should now have Databases and Listeners folders, in addition to the Groups and Nodes folders. Open the Databases, Listeners, and Nodes folders in order to see what was discovered.

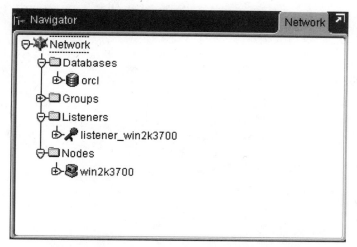

Configuring Preferences

In order for you to connect to various databases and nodes, you must either supply security credentials every time you wish to connect or set your preferences beforehand. You can set default preferences for all databases, nodes, and Listeners and can also set credentials for specific databases, etc. that would override your default settings.

Credentials for individual databases, Listeners, and nodes override default settings, if default settings are present.

In Exercise 3.3, you set the preferences for the sysman account.

Configuring Preferences

1. Start Enterprise Manager, and log in.

2. Go to the System ➤ Preferences menu.

3. Note that you can change passwords from this screen. Go to the Preferred Credentials screen.

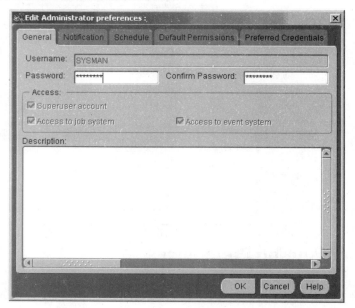

4. From the Preferred Credentials screen, note that you can set default credentials for all databases, Listeners, or nodes, as well as specific ones. Set the credential for the default database as internal, with a password of oracle (or whatever your current one is), and set the account for SYSDBA rights. Choose OK to save your changes.

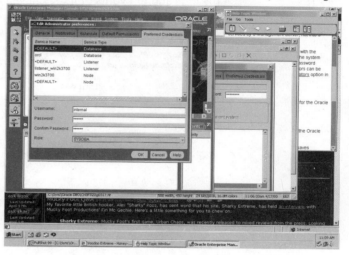

5. To test your credentials, highlight a database and go to Tools ➢ Database Applications ➢ Security Manager. You should go right in without any prompts.

Adding Administrators to the Management Server

More than likely you will want additional people to be able to use Enterprise Manager. Such people are called administrators, and they can easily be added to the list. In Exercise 3.4, you add additional administrators to the Oracle Management Server.

Adding Enterprise Manager Administrators

1. Start Enterprise Manager, and log in.

2. Go to System ➢ Manage Administrators.

EXERCISE 3.4 *(continued)*

3. Note that you see the current list of administrators. Choose Add, and enter the name and password of the account (adding lance is shown below).

4. You can also choose whether the new administrator has access to the jobs and/or events or if they have access to all Enterprise Manager functions. Make this user a superuser in Enterprise Manager. Choose OK to save the account.

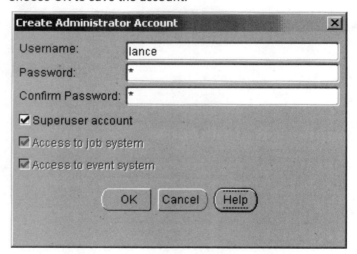

5. From the main screen, you should now see the new account. Note that if you choose to edit an account, you go directly to the Preferences window, as shown in Exercise 3.3. Choose Close to close the account. You can now log in to Enterprise Manager with the new account.

Creating Groups

Groups of related databases, Listeners, and nodes can be created for both ease of management and status checking. Another great feature of groups is that they can be overlayed on a map, which allows you to quickly check their status by location. Groups are displayed by default in the upper-right pane of Enterprise Manager.

To create a new group simply go to the Group ≻ Create Group menu. From here, give it a name (such as US) and a path to a bitmap (in the format of ...\images\usa.gif), as shown in Figure 3.5.

FIGURE 3.5 Creating a Group

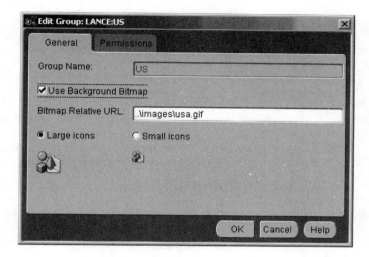

Once a group is created, you can manage the group as if it were a single entity. For example, you can target a group for a job just as you would an individual database.

Creating Jobs and Events

Enterprise Manager allows you to proactively manage your servers by automating common tasks. To automate common tasks, you create jobs and watch for certain circumstances by registering events.

Jobs are commonly used to back up the database on a regular basis, as well as import or export data on a schedule. Jobs can also be set to run when a particular circumstance occurs. Jobs can send SQL commands, as well as operating system commands. Jobs are shown by default in the lower-left pane of Enterprise Manager.

Events are commonly used to watch for certain things such as the database or Listener going up and down and volumes and tablespaces getting full. Oracle comes with many prebuilt events and also gives you the ability to easily create your own. Events are shown by default in the lower-right pane of Enterprise Manager.

Jobs and events are covered in detail in Chapter 9, "Proactive Management of an Oracle Server."

Using the Enterprise Manager Configuration Assistant

There may be times when you need to fix a damaged repository, create a new repository, or delete an old one. The Enterprise Manager Configuration Assistant does all three functions.

> When you first install Enterprise Manager, the Assistant is run as part of the installation in order to create the initial repository.

To run the Assistant, simply log in to the Assistant utility with a user account and password, and choose the appropriate action. You will then be prompted to specify which action you wish to do. See Figure 3.6.

FIGURE 3.6   The Enterprise Manager Configuration Assistant

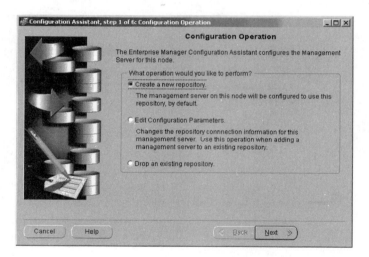

Managing Instances with Instance Manager

There are two ways to start an instance. They are as follows:

- At command prompt, using Server Manager and issuing the STARTUP command

- Graphically (with Instance Manager as the main utility used)

The advantage to using the STARTUP command is that it is quick and can be automated. The main disadvantage is that you need to know the exact syntax to use.

The advantage to using graphical tools such as *Instance Manager* is that you can easily start and stop the instance without knowing a single SQL command. Some disadvantages are that it is slower starting Instance Manager than Server Manager and that you may choose the wrong menu item from within Instance Manager.

Instance Manager is best used on databases other than the database your repository is stored in. For example, we stored our repository in the ORCL database, which means Instance Manager should be used to stop and start databases other than ORCL. Instance Manager can still be used to manage connections to and transactions in the repository database.

You can run Instance Manager separately from Enterprise Manager, or you can start Instance Manager from within Enterprise Manager.

Instance Manager can also save the settings located in the INIT<SID>.ORA file to a local file so that you can use your local copy of the parameters when you start an instance.

If you update the original INIT<SID>.ORA file, make sure you update your local copy of the settings. Otherwise, you may find yourself using old (and quite possibly wrong) settings when you start the instance.

In Exercise 3.5, you use Instance Manager to stop and start an instance.

In order to make Exercise 3.5 work, you have to create an additional database called SALES2K, which is detailed in Chapter 5, "Creating and Managing Databases."

EXERCISE 3.5

Using Instance Manager to Start and Stop an Instance

1. Start Instance Manager from within Enterprise Manager or by going to Start ➤ Programs ➤ <Oracle Home> ➤ DBA Management Pack ➤ Instance Manager.

2. Log in to the management server or connect directly to the database with the appropriate credentials. Note that you may be prompted for additional connection information if you don't have preferred credentials set up for your user account in the management server (see Exercise 3.3).

3. Click the + key for the SALES2K database, and highlight the Database icon. You should get a red, yellow, and green traffic light in the right pane.

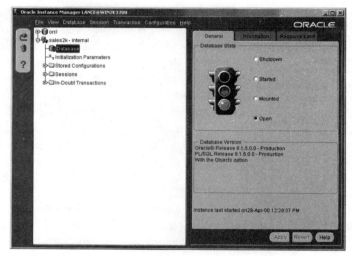

4. Go to the Information tab to see the current log mode, archive destination, and SGA information.

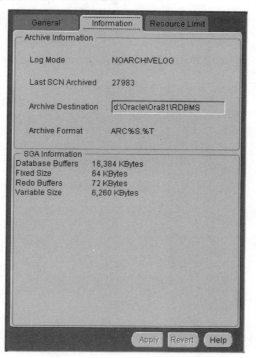

5. Go to the Resource Limit tab to see information about the current and maximum parameters such as processes, sessions, and locks.

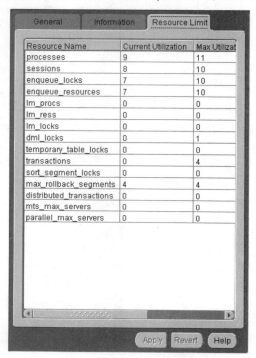

Resource Name	Current Utilization	Max Utilizat
processes	9	11
sessions	8	10
enqueue_locks	7	10
enqueue_resources	7	10
lm_procs	0	0
lm_ress	0	0
lm_locks	0	0
dml_locks	0	1
temporary_table_locks	0	0
transactions	0	4
sort_segment_locks	0	0
max_rollback_segments	4	4
distributed_transactions	0	0
mts_max_servers	0	0
parallel_max_servers	0	0

6. Go back to the General tab.

7. Click Initialization Parameters to see the settings for the INIT file. Notice there are Basic Tuning, Instance Specific, Advanced Tuning, and Derived tabs.

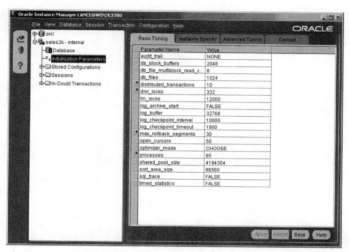

8. Save a local copy of the INIT parameters by choosing the Save button at the lower-right of the screen. Call the settings Default Settings with a description of Initial Settings for Database SALES2K. Choose OK to save your settings.

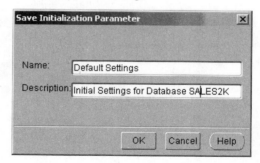

9. Click the Sessions folder to see what connections are in the database. Note that you can right-click a particular connection and either disconnect it immediately or after the current transaction.

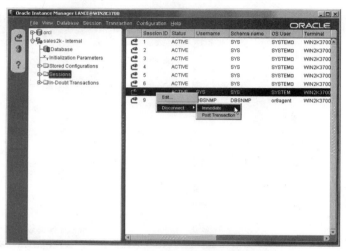

10. Go to the In-Doubt Transactions folder. Normally, you will not have any transactions here.

11. Change the instance to allow only users with the Restrict Session right by choosing Session ➤ Restrict.

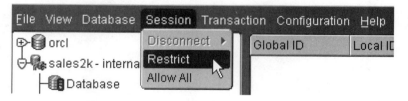

12. Change the instance to allow everyone to connect by choosing Session ➤ Allow All.

13. Click the Database icon again.

14. Stop the instance by choosing Shutdown and then the Apply button. Set it to a Transactional shutdown with a timeout of 30 seconds.

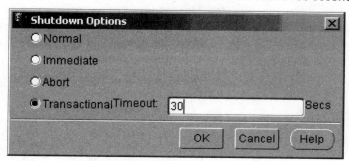

15. You should see a Shutdown in Progress activity bar. When the database has shut down, choose OK.

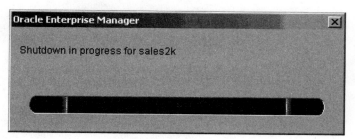

16. To restart the instance, select the Open button, and then the Apply button. You will be prompted for the location of the INIT parameter file. Use the browser to find the appropriate INIT file for the database. You can also use the local configuration settings you saved in step 8 (called Default Configuration). Choose the local settings and OK to start the instance.

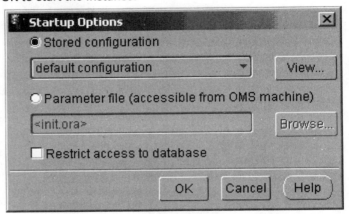

17. After the Startup Progress bar finishes, you should get a box saying the instance was opened. Choose OK to dismiss the box.

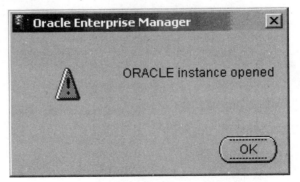

SQL Commands and SQLPlus Worksheet

SQLPlus Worksheet is used to make a direct connection to the Oracle instance. SQLPlus Worksheet runs on the client. In order to use SQLPlus Worksheet you must have the following:

- Valid username and password

- Connection and object rights

- Configured database service (alias)

- Running database instance

Users, passwords, and rights are covered in Chapters 6, "Oracle Users and Security," and 7, "Installing and Managing Applications." Configuring the database service is covered in Chapter 2, "Installing and Configuring Oracle8i," as is starting the database instance. SQLPlus Worksheet is graphical and consists of two panes: one for the commands and one for the output.

To run a command, click the Run icon or use the F5 key.

SQLPlus Worksheet is used extensively in Chapter 4, "Introduction to SQL and PL/SQL." In Exercise 3.6, you connect via SQLPlus Worksheet and issue a simple command.

EXERCISE 3.6

Using SQLPlus Worksheet to Run SQL Commands

1. Start SQLPlus Worksheet from within Enterprise Manager using the Tools ➤ Database Applications ➤ Oracle SQL*Plus Worksheet menu or by going to Start ➤ Programs ➤ <Oracle Home> ➤ DBA Management Pack ➤ SQLPlus Worksheet.

2. If you started SQLPlus Worksheet from within Enterprise Manager, you should not see any prompts (providing you have set up preferred credentials). If you start the program directly, enter the user Scott with a password of Tiger to the ORCL service.

> **EXERCISE 3.6**
>
> 3. Enter the command Select * from   emp;
>   Hit **F5** or click the lightning bolt icon to run the query. Your result should look something like this.
>
>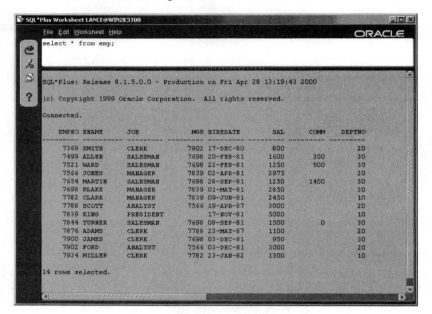
>
> 4. Close SQLPlus Worksheet.

SQL Commands and SQL*Plus

Another client tool used to send SQL commands to the Oracle instance is SQL*Plus. *SQL*Plus* is a single-paned graphical tool, which operates on the client very much like Server Manager does on the server.

SQL*Plus comes with the Oracle engine and is installed under the Oracle Home ➢ Application Development program group.

In Exercise 3.7, you connect to the database using SQL*Plus and issue a simple command.

EXERCISE 3.7

Using SQL*Plus to Run SQL Commands

1. Start SQL*Plus by going to Start ➤ Programs ➤ Application Development ➤ SQL*Plus.

2. Connect to the ORCL instance with the username Scott and the password Tiger.

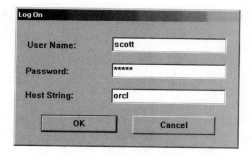

3. Enter the command Select * from emp; and hit Return. You should get results similar to this.

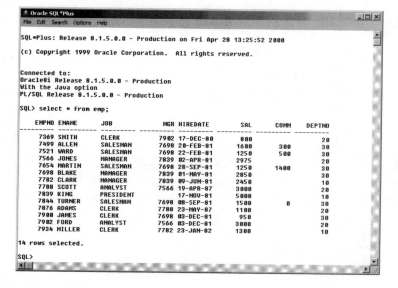

4. Close SQL*Plus.

Server Manager

Server Manager is much like SQL*Plus, except it runs on the server. Server Manager is a command prompt utility and is started differently, depending on which operating system (and even which version of Oracle) you are on.

Server Manager is installed as part of the Oracle installation, which means that you should always be able to run Server Manager, even if you don't have SQLPlus Worksheet or SQL*Plus.

You can use SQL*Plus and SQLPlus Worksheet to stop an instance, but you can't use them to start an instance because they require a connection. You can, however, use Server Manager to both stop and start instances.

Server Manager was used extensively in Chapter 2, "Installing and Configuring Oracle8i," to start and stop the database. Remember that if you are running Server Manager on a Windows NT (or Windows 2000) server, use the SVRMGRL command. For NetWare, start Server Manager by issuing the SVRMGR31 command. For UNIX, issue the SVRMGRL command.

Storage Manager

Storage Manager is primarily concerned with the physical files and tablespaces that make up the database. Storage Manager can be used to modify existing datafiles, add new datafiles, or delete old ones.

Storage Manager is also used to create, modify, and delete tablespaces, which are a logical grouping of one or more physical files. When a logical object (such as a table or index) is created, the object is created on a tablespace. By using Storage Manager, the database operator can decide exactly what files make up the tablespace and can dynamically modify tablespaces by adding additional files or increasing the ones present.

Tablespaces and datafiles are covered in more detail in Chapter 7, "Installing and Managing Applications."

Schema Manager

*S*chema Manager is used to manage existing schemas or sets of objects. A schema is a group of objects owned by the same user. For example, the Sales schema may contain tables, indexes, and views owned by the user called Sales.

Schema Manager can show objects grouped by owner or by type of object. Existing objects can be easily modified using Schema Manager, and new objects can be created as well.

Creating objects is covered in more detail in Chapter 7, "Installing and Managing Applications."

Security Manager

*S*ecurity Manager is used to manage the rights of users and roles (groups) to the Oracle system and to individual objects. Just as in most operating systems, rights granted to roles are automatically given to any members of the role. For example, if the Librarians role has Select rights to the Checkout table, and Sue is a member of the Librarians role, she would have the Select right to the Checkout table.

Security Manager can also be used to assign disk quotas to users and profiles for advanced features such as complex password checking, limits on CPU usage, etc.

Security is covered in more detail in Chapter 6, "Oracle Users and Security."

Backup Manager

*O*racle8i ships with a full service backup and restore utility, which is accessed through Backup Manager. Backup Manager is used to back up and restore the database.

There are several methods for performing backups, including backing up the entire database and backing up just the data that has changed. Whatever the method used, performing and testing backups are a critical step in maintaining the database.

Backup Manager, backups, and restorations are covered in more detail in Chapter 10, "Backups and Restorations."

Diagnostics Pack

The *Diagnostics Pack* includes programs such as Capacity Planner, Performance Manager, Top Sessions, Trace Manager, and Trace Data Viewer. The various Diagnostics Pack utilities are used to see what is going on in the Oracle instance for troubleshooting as well as baselining the system.

The various Diagnostics Pack utilities are covered in detail in Appendix B, "Performance and Tuning."

Tuning Pack

The *Tuning Pack* utilities are designed to help you optimize your Oracle database and instance. The Tuning Pack utilities consist of the Oracle Expert, SQL Analyze, and Tablespace Manager.

The Tuning Pack utilities are covered in more detail in Appendix B, "Performance and Tuning."

Summary

Oracle Enterprise Manager (OEM) and its related tools are graphical utilities that allow you to easily manage your database.

When installing Enterprise Manager for the first time, you will need to choose a Management Server, as well as a user to own the repository. The repository is the set of tables and objects that Enterprise Manager (and the other related utilities) use to track jobs, events, etc.

If you need to check, create, or delete a particular repository, you can use the Enterprise Manager Configuration Assistant. The reasons you may wish to delete a repository include: cleaning up after users who leave the company or combining various management servers into one.

You should set the preferred credentials for the management accounts, so that when you manage a resource you are not prompted for connection information.

You can start the other management utilities from within Enterprise Manager, or you can start them by themselves.

Instance Manager is used to stop and start an Oracle instance. Storage Manager is used to manage physical data files and tablespaces. Schema Manager is used to manage objects. Security Manager is used to manage users and roles and their rights to objects. Backup Manager is used to back up and restore the database. The Diagnostic Pack utilities are used to troubleshoot problems and baseline the system for future growth, and the Tuning Pack utilities are used to optimize existing databases.

SQLPlus Worksheet and SQL*Plus are used on the client to enter SQL commands, while Server Manager is used on the server to do the same thing.

Key Terms

Before you take the exam, make sure you're familiar with the following terms:

Diagnostics Pack

Enterprise Manager

Instance Manager

Schema Manager

Security Manager

SQL*Plus

SQLPlus Worksheet

Storage Manager

Tuning Pack

Review Questions

1. What utility would you use to start the instance?

   A. Schema Manager

   B. Security Manager

   C. Storage Manager

   D. Instance Manager

2. What utility would you use to create tablespaces?

   A. Schema Manager

   B. Security Manager

   C. Storage Manager

   D. Instance Manager

3. What utility would you use to create users and roles?

   A. Schema Manager

   B. Security Manager

   C. Storage Manager

   D. Instance Manager

4. What utility would you use to create tables?

   A. Schema Manager

   B. Security Manager

   C. Storage Manager

   D. Instance Manager

5. What utility would you use to restore the database?

   A. Backup Manager

   B. Security Manager

   C. Storage Manager

   D. Instance Manager

6. What utility would you use to create a new datafile?

   A. Schema Manager

   B. Security Manager

   C. Storage Manager

   D. Instance Manager

7. What utility would you use to create automated jobs?

   A. Schema Manager

   B. Security Manager

   C. Storage Manager

   D. Enterprise Manager

8. What utilities would you use to optimize the database?

   A. Schema Manager

   B. Diagnostics Pack

   C. Tuning Pack

   D. Enterprise Manager

9. What utilities would you use to find out who is running the largest queries?

   A. Schema Manager

   B. Diagnostics Pack

   C. Tuning Pack

   D. Enterprise Manager

10. What utility would you use to give rights to users?

   A. Schema Manager

   B. Security Manager

   C. Storage Manager

   D. Instance Manager

11. Where are related tables that are used for Enterprise Manager stored?

    A. Vault

    B. Repository

    C. Schema

    D. Index

12. What is the default user for Enterprise Manager?

    A. Sys

    B. Internal

    C. Sysman

    D. Manager

13. What does saving a local configuration do in Instance Manager?

    A. It saves the layout of the windows and toolbars.

    B. It saves the user login settings.

    C. It saves the INIT parameters to a local file.

    D. It saves the user session to an output file.

14. What does setting a preferred credential do in Enterprise Manager?

    A. It sets your current rights.

    B. It sets your rights to databases, Listeners, and nodes when you connect to them.

    C. It sets your rights to the repository.

    D. It sets your object rights to data in the database.

15. If you had a default database credential of Sue with a password of red, and a credential for the Sales database of Katie with a password of blue, what would happen if you tried to connect to the Sales database?

    A. You would be prompted, since you have conflicting credentials.

    B. The credentials with the most rights would be used.

    C. The credential of Sue would be used.

    D. The credential of Katie would be used.

16. By default, what is shown in the lower-left pane of Enterprise Manager?

   A. Jobs

   B. Events

   C. Groups

   D. Databases, Listeners, and Nodes

17. By default, what is shown in the lower-right pane of Enterprise Manager?

   A. Jobs

   B. Events

   C. Groups

   D. Databases, Listeners, and Nodes

18. What program can you use to change database parameters?

   A. The Console

   B. Server Manager

   C. Instance Manager

   D. Database Manager

19. When do changed database parameters take effect?

   A. Immediately

   B. After the RESET command is issued

   C. After the SHUTDOWN command is issued

   D. When the instance is restarted

20. What computer does Server Manager run on?

   A. The management server

   B. The client

   C. The Oracle server

   D. Both the Oracle server and management server

Answers to Review Questions

1. D. Instance Manager is used to start and stop instances.

2. C. Storage Manager is used to create tablespaces.

3. B. Security Manager is used to create users and roles.

4. A. Schema Manager is used to create tables and other objects.

5. A. Backup Manager is used to back up and restore the database.

6. C. Storage Manager is used to create and modify datafiles.

7. D. Enterprise Manager is used to create and manage jobs.

8. C. Tuning Pack is used to optimize the database.

9. B. Diagnostics Pack is used to find out who is running the largest queries.

10. B. Security Manager is used to give rights to objects.

11. B. The repository is where related tables used by Enterprise Manager and other utilities are stored.

12. C. Sysman is the default user for Enterprise Manager.

13. C. A local configuration is a copy of the INIT parameters that Instance Manager can use at startup.

14. B. Preferred credentials set up how you will connect to a particular database, Listener, or node.

15. D. Default credentials are used only if there are no specific credentials. If there are specific credentials, those are the ones that will be used.

16. A. Jobs are shown in the lower-left pane of Enterprise Manager.

17. B. Events are shown in the lower-right pane of Enterprise Manager.

18. C. Instance Manager can be used to change database parameters.

19. D. Parameters are read when the instance starts.

20. C. Server Manager runs on the Oracle server.

Chapter 4

Introduction to SQL and PL/SQL

ORACLE8i DBO EXAM OBJECTIVES OFFERED IN THIS CHAPTER:

- ✓ Oracle SQL: Basic SELECT Statements
- ✓ Oracle SQL: Data Retrieval Techniques

The "objectives" for this chapter are not official Oracle8i DBO exam objectives like those covered in the rest of the chapters, but it is assumed that these topics are known and understood before you take the Oracle Internet Database Operator exam, and it is, therefore, vital that you know this information well.

Exam objectives are subject to change at any time without prior notice and at Oracle's sole discretion. Please visit Oracle's Training and Certification Web site (http://education. oracle.com/certification/index.html) for the most current exam objectives listing.

Some of the basic job skills of a database operator are the abilities to enter data into the database, modify the data, and get data back out from the database. Although graphical tools and applications may be used, a strong foundation in the SQL language can only help an operator.

The original design of a SQL database allowed for interaction between the client and server via a language designed to be easy to understand and use, Structured English Query Language (SEQueL or *SQL* for short). Most major software vendors support the most common SQL syntax, although they sometimes add various enhancements. See Figure 4.1.

FIGURE 4.1 SQL support among various vendors

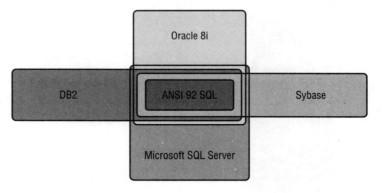

Thus, there are two basic methods that enable the client to communicate with the server:

- PL/SQL code
- Applications

Oracle uses a version of SQL called PL/SQL (which stands for Procedural SQL). PL/SQL code is basically SQL with enhancements designed specifically for Oracle databases, such as variable support and conditional processing. Most users, however, access Oracle databases via some sort of application, so they may never see the PL/SQL code. Typical applications that are used to access the Oracle database are either prepackaged, such as SAP, PeopleSoft, and other LOB (line of business) applications, or custom built. Applications may be custom written using Visual Basic, Delphi, Oracle Application Development tools, or other such programs.

This chapter mainly covers the use of PL/SQL for queries and simple updates. Later chapters will show you how to create objects and manage security using PL/SQL.

As a database operator, you will need to know some PL/SQL programming, as you may be called on to create custom reports that an application may not be able to do, as well as to modify the data directly.

Default Security

Although security issues are covered in detail in Chapter 6, "Oracle Users and Security," you will need to know about the default security that Oracle uses so that you can connect to the database to run the commands in this chapter. Oracle has several default users including those that follow:

Internal   This default user has a default password of oracle and is created for backwards compatibility, but it can be useful for connecting to the server to perform initial configurations.

Sys   This default user has a default password of change_on_install and is used for overall system tasks.

System   This default user has a default password of manager and is used for overall system tasks.

Scott   This default user has a password of tiger and can be used to connect to the sample database.

Demo This default user has a password of demo and can be used to connect to the sample database.

The tables in the default database are contained in the tablespaces under the users Demo and Scott and appear as follows.

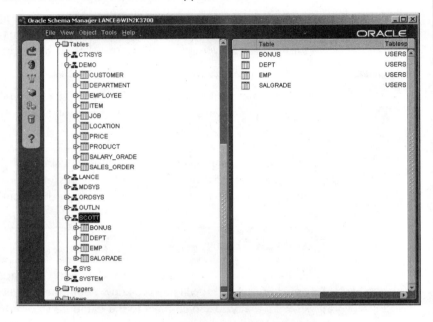

PL/SQL Tools

There are three major tools you can use to submit PL/SQL commands to the Oracle database engine.

- SQL*Plus
- SQLPlus Worksheet
- Server Manager (command line mode)

*SQL*Plus* is a simple shell that allows you to write commands and have them immediately execute in the same screen. Server Manager is similar.

SQLPlus Worksheet is a more complex tool that allows you to create commands in one screen and have the reports appear in another.

In this book, SQLPlus Worksheet is used, unless stated otherwise.

Server Manager is a command line program used to submit PL/SQL commands to the Oracle engine primarily from the server itself. Server Manager is started by running SVRMGR31 on NetWare servers, and SVRMGRL on Windows NT and Unix servers.

Starting SQLPlus Worksheet

To start SQLPlus Worksheet, go to Start ➢ Programs ➢ <ORACLE_HOME> ➢ DBA Management Pack ➢ SQLPlus Worksheet. You will be prompted for the username and password to connect, as shown in Figure 4.2.

FIGURE 4.2   Logging in to Oracle to start SQLPlus Worksheet

You will need to connect as an existing user. For our example, you would connect as Scott with a password of tiger. Leave the Service field blank to connect to the default instance or enter **orc1** for the instance if the default instance is not set. To test the connection, you would then enter the command SELECT * FROM emp; and hit F5 or the Run icon. You should get results similar to that shown in Figure 4.3.

FIGURE 4.3 Running a simple query in SQLPlus Worksheet

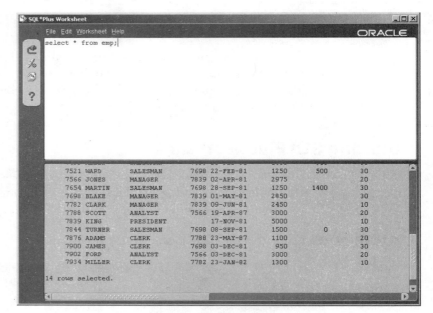

Starting Server Manager

Server Manager allows you to connect to the Oracle instance from the Oracle server in case you don't have the regular Oracle client installed. To start the Server Manager at the NetWare console, enter the command SVRMGR31. On a Windows NT computer, the command is SVRMGRL; on Unix, either SVRMGRL or SVRMGRLO. To connect to the database, enter the command CONNECT Scott/Tiger; You should get a message that says you are connected. See Figure 4.4. Once you are connected, you can issue any command that you normally could from SQL*Plus or SQLPlus Worksheet. To exit, use the command EXIT.

FIGURE 4.4 Connecting to Oracle via Server Manager

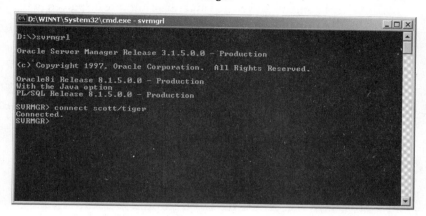

If you have more than one instance running, you should also enter the command DISCONNECT, followed by the command SET INSTANCE <service name> to make sure you are in the right instance.

Starting SQL*Plus

SQL*Plus is a graphical, one-pane utility that allows you to send SQL commands to the Oracle database and see the results. To start SQL*Plus on the client, go to Start ➢ Programs ➢ <ORACLE_HOME> ➢ SQL*Plus. Enter the appropriate connection information in the Log On box, as shown in Figure 4.5.

FIGURE 4.5 Connecting to Oracle via SQL*Plus

Enter the command SELECT * FROM emp; When you hit Enter, the command is executed and the results are displayed in the same screen as the command. See Figure 4.6.

FIGURE 4.6 Running a simple query in SQL*Plus

```
± Oracle SQL*Plus                                                        _ □ X
File Edit Search Options Help

SQL*Plus: Release 8.1.5.0.0 - Production on Tue Apr 18 20:13:02 2000

(c) Copyright 1999 Oracle Corporation.  All rights reserved.


Connected to:
Oracle8i Release 8.1.5.0.0 - Production
With the Java option
PL/SQL Release 8.1.5.0.0 - Production

SQL> select * from emp;

    EMPNO ENAME      JOB            MGR HIREDATE       SAL      COMM     DEPTNO
--------- ---------- --------- -------- --------- --------- --------- ---------
     7369 SMITH      CLERK         7902 17-DEC-80       800                  20
     7499 ALLEN      SALESMAN      7698 20-FEB-81      1600       300        30
     7521 WARD       SALESMAN      7698 22-FEB-81      1250       500        30
     7566 JONES      MANAGER       7839 02-APR-81      2975                  20
     7654 MARTIN     SALESMAN      7698 28-SEP-81      1250      1400        30
     7698 BLAKE      MANAGER       7839 01-MAY-81      2850                  30
     7782 CLARK      MANAGER       7839 09-JUN-81      2450                  10
     7788 SCOTT      ANALYST       7566 19-APR-87      3000                  20
     7839 KING       PRESIDENT          17-NOV-81      5000                  10
     7844 TURNER     SALESMAN      7698 08-SEP-81      1500         0        30
     7876 ADAMS      CLERK         7788 23-MAY-87      1100                  20
     7900 JAMES      CLERK         7698 03-DEC-81       950                  30
     7902 FORD       ANALYST       7566 03-DEC-81      3000                  20
     7934 MILLER     CLERK         7782 23-JAN-82      1300                  10

14 rows selected.

SQL> |
```

The SELECT Statement

Now that you know how to use the PL/SQL tools, let's take a look at the SELECT statement. The SELECT statement is an important feature; you should make sure you're able to read and understand what simple SELECT statements are doing.

All SQL and PL/SQL commands must end with a semi-colon ";".

The *SELECT statement* can be used to retrieve specific rows and columns of information from one or more tables in one or more databases. There are three basic components to every SELECT statement: SELECT, FROM, and WHERE.

The syntax for a simple SELECT statement is as follows:

```
SELECT <column_list>
FROM <table(s)>
WHERE <search_criteria> ;
```

One of the simplest SELECT statements is to select all columns from a single table. You use the "*" operator to do this. For example, the following statement will select all columns and all rows from the emp table.

```
SELECT * FROM emp;
```

The results would look like that shown in Figure 4.6.

You can specify individual columns in the column list parameter. This is sometimes called vertical partitioning because you are only selecting certain columns. For example, if you wanted to get only the employee's number, name, job title, and date of hire, you could run the following query:

```
SELECT empno, ename, job, hiredate
FROM emp;
```

The result set would look like this:

EMPNO	ENAME	JOB	HIREDATE
7369	SMITH	CLERK	17-DEC-80
7499	ALLEN	SALESMAN	20-FEB-81
7521	WARD	SALESMAN	22-FEB-81
7566	JONES	MANAGER	02-APR-81
7654	MARTIN	SALESMAN	28-SEP-81
7698	BLAKE	MANAGER	01-MAY-81
7782	CLARK	MANAGER	09-JUN-81
7788	SCOTT	ANALYST	19-APR-87
7839	KING	PRESIDENT	17-NOV-81
7844	TURNER	SALESMAN	08-SEP-81

```
7876 ADAMS      CLERK     23-MAY-87
7900 JAMES      CLERK     03-DEC-81
7902 FORD       ANALYST   03-DEC-81
7934 MILLER     CLERK     23-JAN-82
```

Let's take a look at specifying search criteria by using the WHERE clause. The WHERE clause is used to discriminate between rows of information. This is also known as horizontal partitioning because you are only selecting certain rows of information. For example, if you wanted to get information on all employees that have a last name that begins with the letter "M" you could run this query:

```
SELECT empno, ename, job, mgr
FROM emp
WHERE ENAME LIKE 'M%';
```

```
EMPNO      ENAME      JOB        MGR
---------- ---------- ---------- ----------
      7654 MARTIN     SALESMAN        7698
      7934 MILLER     CLERK           7782
2 rows selected.
```

You can also order your result sets in either ascending (default) or descending order. For example, if you wanted to list employee information in descending order (Z–A) by last name, you could run this query:

```
SELECT ename, job
FROM emp
ORDER BY ename DESC;
```

Your results would look like the following:

```
ENAME      JOB
---------- ---------
WARD       SALESMAN
TURNER     SALESMAN
SMITH      CLERK
SCOTT      ANALYST
```

```
MILLER      CLERK
MARTIN      SALESMAN
KING        PRESIDENT
JONES       MANAGER
JAMES       CLERK
FORD        ANALYST
CLARK       MANAGER
BLAKE       MANAGER
ALLEN       SALESMAN
ADAMS       CLERK
14 rows selected.
```

You can also order numeric columns by ascending order (smallest to largest) or by descending order (largest to smallest). You can also specify a second sort column if there is a tie in the first column. For example, to rank employees by salary (from largest to smallest) and list employees by last name if there is a tie on salary, use this command:

```
SELECT ename, job, sal
FROM emp
ORDER BY sal desc, ename;
```

```
ENAME       JOB         SAL
----------  ----------  ----------
KING        PRESIDENT   5000
FORD        ANALYST     3000
SCOTT       ANALYST     3000
JONES       MANAGER     2975
BLAKE       MANAGER     2850
CLARK       MANAGER     2450
ALLEN       SALESMAN    1600
TURNER      SALESMAN    1500
MILLER      CLERK       1300
MARTIN      SALESMAN    1250
WARD        SALESMAN    1250
ADAMS       CLERK       1100
JAMES       CLERK        950
SMITH       CLERK        800
14 rows selected.
```

Renaming Columns

You don't have to accept the default names of columns in your result set. To rename columns, simply use the keywords = or *as*. For example, if you want *sal* (stored in the column sal) to show as *salary*, use the "sal as 'salary'" query.

```
SELECT ename as "Last Name", job as "Job", sal as "Salary"
FROM emp
ORDER BY sal desc, ename;


Last Name   Job         Salary
----------  ---------   ----------
KING        PRESIDENT      5000
FORD        ANALYST        3000
SCOTT       ANALYST        3000
JONES       MANAGER        2975
BLAKE       MANAGER        2850
CLARK       MANAGER        2450
ALLEN       SALESMAN       1600
TURNER      SALESMAN       1500
MILLER      CLERK          1300
MARTIN      SALESMAN       1250
WARD        SALESMAN       1250
ADAMS       CLERK          1100
JAMES       CLERK           950
SMITH       CLERK           800
14 rows selected.
```

Selecting Tables from Other Schemas

A *schema* is defined as a collection of tables and other database objects that are owned by the same user. If a person is using his own tables, only the table name is necessary. For example, when Scott wants to use the EMP table, SELECT * FROM emp; works correctly. But, if Scott wants to use the tables owned by DEMO, the owner of the table must be appended to the name of the table. For example, to see all of the columns and rows from the JOB tables in the DEMO tablespace, use this command:

```
SELECT * FROM demo.job;
JOB_ID     FUNCTION
---------- ------------------------------
       667 CLERK
       668 STAFF
       669 ANALYST
       670 SALESPERSON
       671 MANAGER
       672 PRESIDENT
6 rows selected.
```

This example only works on systems where the Demo user and sample tables are installed. Oracle on Unix does not install the Demo user.

Arithmetic Functions

Oracle and the SQL language support a variety of mathematical functions on numeric columns, including ^, /, *, +, -, which are explained in Table 4.1.

TABLE 4.1   Oracle Mathematical Symbols

Symbol	Description
^	to the power of
/	divided by
*	multiplied by
+	added to
−	subtracted from
=	equal to
<>	not equal to

TABLE 4.1 Oracle Mathematical Symbols *(continued)*

Symbol	Description
>	greater than
<	less than
>=	greater than or equal to
<=	less than or equal to

The order of precedence is as listed, but it can always be overridden using parentheses "()".

COUNT (*) and COUNT (condition) are used to find the number of rows that match a condition.

You can test for equality using =, <> or !=, >=, and <=. You can also use IN when comparing a list of numeric values. For example, to compute a yearly total for employees, run this command:

```
Select ename, sal, comm, sal*12+comm as
      "Total $" from emp;
ENAME          SAL          COMM        Total $
----------  ----------  ----------  ----------
SMITH                     800
ALLEN                    1600          300       19500
WARD                     1250          500       15500
JONES                    2975
MARTIN                   1250         1400       16400
BLAKE                    2850
CLARK                    2450
SCOTT                    3000
KING                     5000
TURNER                   1500            0       18000
ADAMS                    1100
JAMES                     950
FORD                     3000
MILLER                   1300
14 rows selected.
```

Character Functions

As stated earlier, you can use the LIKE function to search for certain character strings. You can also use the percent character (%) as a multiple character wildcard and the underscore character (_) for a single character wildcard.

To concatenate columns together, you can use two consecutive straight bar characters (||). For example, to combine the first name and last name of each employee in the EMPLOYEE table of the DEMO database, use this command:

```
Select first_name ||last_name as "Name"
FROM demo.employee;
Name
--------------------------------
JOHNSMITH
KEVINALLEN
JEANDOYLE
...
BARBARAMILLER
ALICEJENSEN
JAMESMURRAY
32 rows selected.
```

To add characters to a SELECT statement, use the CONCAT operator. For example, to list a person and their job, use this query:

```
select concat (concat (ename, ' is a '), job)
     as "Job Title"
FROM emp
ORDER BY job;
Job Title
-------------------------
SCOTT is a ANALYST
FORD is a ANALYST
SMITH is a CLERK
ADAMS is a CLERK
MILLER is a CLERK
JAMES is a CLERK
JONES is a MANAGER
CLARK is a MANAGER
BLAKE is a MANAGER
KING is a PRESIDENT
```

```
ALLEN is a SALESMAN
MARTIN is a SALESMAN
TURNER is a SALESMAN
WARD is a SALESMAN
14 rows selected.
```

NULL Values

NULL *values* represent data that could exist but doesn't for that particular person or thing. In the EMP table, for example, there are columns for salary and commission. Several of the employees listed in the EMP table earn a salary but not a commission. Their commission data could be stored as a 0, but that could imply a very lazy employee who could earn a commission but has not rather than one to whom commissions just do not apply. By storing NULL in the commission column, it is easy to recognize that commissions just don't apply to that person. Another example is a table for data about people. Your company policy may be that every person requires a phone number (NOT NULL) while a person's e-mail address is optional (NULL).

When you compute the minimum, maximum, and average salaries, any columns that have NULL will be excluded from the computation. To include all rows in a computation, use the COUNT (*) function. It returns all rows, not just those with values. You can specifically search for NULL values by using the IS NULL comparison. You can also search for rows that do not have NULL by using the IS NOT NULL comparison. For example, to find all employees that do not get a commission, use the following command:

```
Select ename, sal, comm from emp where comm is null;
ENAME       SAL         COMM
---------- ----------  ----------
SMITH                  800
JONES                  2975
BLAKE                  2850
CLARK                  2450
SCOTT                  3000
KING                   5000
ADAMS                  1100
JAMES                  950
FORD                   3000
MILLER                 1300
10 rows selected.
```

Logical Operators

The logical operators AND, OR, and NOT can be used in a query in a WHERE clause to create complex conditions. In so doing, you may need to use parentheses to ensure processing is done as intended. For example, to find employees that have a salary of at least 2000 or a salary of 1500 plus 100 or more in commission, use the following query:

```
select ename, sal, comm
     from emp
     where (sal > 2000) or (sal> 1500 and comm > 100);
ENAME        SAL          COMM
----------   ----------   ----------
ALLEN            1600         300
JONES            2975
BLAKE            2850
CLARK            2450
SCOTT            3000
KING             5000
FORD             3000
7 rows selected.
```

Summarizing Data

In many circumstances, you may wish to see summary values instead of all of the detail rows. The following functions compute and show summary values:

Min   Shows the minimum value

Max   Shows the maximum value

Avg   Shows the average value

Sum   Shows the aggregate value

You can find the minimum, maximum, and average salary of the employees in the EMP table with the following command:

```
Select min (sal), max(sal), avg (sal)
from emp;


MIN(SAL)   MAX(SAL)   AVG(SAL)
800        5000       2073.21429
1 row selected.
```

Using the Group By Command

Sometimes you may wish to see data organized by category, such as the average salary by department. Use the GROUP BY command to get subtotals. Try the following command:

```
SELECT deptno, avg(sal), avg(comm)
FROM emp
GROUP BY deptno;

    DEPTNO  AVG(SAL) AVG(COMM)
--------- --------- ---------
       10 2916.6667
       20      2175
       30 1566.6667       550
```

Using the Having Clause

Just as the WHERE clause limits detail rows, the HAVING clause limits summary rows. For example, if you want to see only those departments that have an average salary greater than $2,000, you would use the HAVING clause in a command like the following:

```
SELECT deptno, avg(sal), avg(comm)
FROM emp
GROUP BY deptno
HAVING AVG(sal)> 2000;

    DEPTNO  AVG(SAL) AVG(COMM)
--------- --------- ---------
       10 2916.6667
       20      2175
```

UNION Operator

You can combine the results of two or more queries into a single result set by using the *UNION operator*. The UNION operator combines result sets and eliminates redundant results, while the UNION ALL operator shows all resulting rows.

Other useful operators are the INTERSECT and MINUS operators. The INTERSECT operator only returns rows if both result sets have the row. The

MINUS operator returns rows that are in the first result set and not in the second result set.

Note that each of the result sets should be similar. To find employees and their salaries from both the EMP (from the Scott schema) and EMPLOYEE (from the Demo schema) tables run this query:

```
select ename, sal from emp
union
select last_name, salary from demo.employee;
ENAME            SAL
---------------  ----------
ADAMS                  1100
ALBERTS                3000
ALLEN                  1600
BAKER                  2200
BLAKE                  2850
CLARK                  2450
DENNIS                 2750
DOUGLAS                 800
DOYLE                  2850
DUNCAN                 1250
FISHER                 3000
FORD                   3000
JAMES                   950
JENSEN                  750
JONES                  2975
KING                   5000
LANGE                  1250
LEWIS                  1800
MARTIN                 1250
MILLER                 1300
MURRAY                  750
PETERS                 1250
PORTER                 1250
ROBERTS                2875
ROSS                   1300
SCOTT                  3000
```

SHAW	1250
SMITH	800
SOMMERS	1850
TURNER	1500
WARD	1250
WEST	1500

32 rows selected.

Joining Tables

Relational databases function by splitting related data into separate tables. To retrieve data from relational databases, you will usually need to recombine the data from two or more tables before you can retrieve the data you're interested in. Joining tables is the way this is done. There are several ways to join tables, including the following:

- Inner Joins or Equijoins
- Outer Joins
- Cross Joins or a Cartesian Product

If the type of join is not specified, an inner join will be performed. Another term for inner joins is equijoins, which are performed the majority of time. The technical definition of an equijoin is when two or more tables are joined using values they have in common (equal), while a non-equijoin is when tables are joined using non-equal values.

Note that if the same table is used, a self join is created. Inner and self joins can consist of multiple tables, while outer and cross joins only join two tables.

Inner Joins (Equijoins)

Inner joins only show results where rows from both tables have matching data. A graphical representation of an inner join is shown in Figure 4.7.

FIGURE 4.7   Inner joins (equijoins) between tables

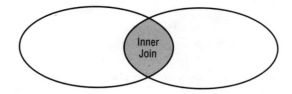

For more complex queries, you can join information from three or more tables at the same time. An inner join lets you pick and choose individual columns from the tables you are joining. To find out which employees belong to which departments in the Scott schema, you would need to join the EMP table and the DEPT table and then display results based on a deptno match between the EMP and DEPT tables. For example, see the following query:

```
SELECT ename, job, mgr, dname
FROM emp, dept
WHERE emp.deptno= dept.deptno
ORDER BY dname;
```

Your results would look as follows:

ENAME	JOB	MGR	DNAME
CLARK	MANAGER	7839	ACCOUNTING
KING	PRESIDENT		ACCOUNTING
MILLER	CLERK	7782	ACCOUNTING
SMITH	CLERK	7902	RESEARCH
ADAMS	CLERK	7788	RESEARCH
FORD	ANALYST	7566	RESEARCH
SCOTT	ANALYST	7566	RESEARCH
JONES	MANAGER	7839	RESEARCH
ALLEN	SALESMAN	7698	SALES
BLAKE	MANAGER	7839	SALES
MARTIN	SALESMAN	7698	SALES
JAMES	CLERK	7698	SALES
TURNER	SALESMAN	7698	SALES
WARD	SALESMAN	7698	SALES

14 rows selected.

Outer Joins

Outer joins are useful for showing all of the rows from one table, with any matching rows of a second table. A graphical representation of an outer join is shown in Figure 4.8.

FIGURE 4.8 Outer joins between tables

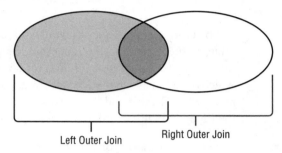

Left Outer Join   Right Outer Join

For example, you may have a customers table and a sales_order table. An inner join would show you all the customers that placed orders. An outer join would show you all customers, regardless of the fact if they placed orders or not. Any orders placed would be shown for that particular customer, and customers without orders would have NULL generated for the order columns. An example of an outer join that would show all employees regardless of whether or not they had a department assigned to them would be as follows:

```
SELECT ename, job, mgr, dname
FROM emp, dept
WHERE emp.deptno (+) = dept.deptno
ORDER BY dname;
```

There are two types of outer joins: left outer joins and right outer joins. A left outer join simply means that the left-most table in the statement has the + sign and will go through every row. A right outer join means that the second table or right table has the + sign and will go through all of its rows, whether or not there is a match from the left table. If you reverse the order of the tables in the statement, a left outer join would become a right outer join, and vice versa.

Cross Joins (Cartesian Products)

In a *cross join*, every row of one table is listed against every row of another table. A cross join is sometimes referred to as a Cartesian product, as every possible result is computed. A graphical representation of a cross join is shown in Figure 4.9.

FIGURE 4.9   Cross or Cartesian join

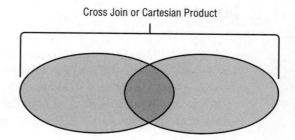

Cross Join or Cartesian Product

For example, if there are 50 customers and 100 orders, a cross join would produce a result set of 5,000 rows, which would be meaningless. Cross joins are used to create lots of dummy data for testing performance, but are not useful for any business situation.

Cross joins are performed when the WHERE clause is left off of a JOIN statement. If you are attempting to run a join, but it is taking an extraordinary amount of time, you may have triggered a cross join, such as in this code:

```
SELECT ename, job, mgr, dname
FROM emp, dept;
```

Adding Comments to SQL Code

You can add comments to your PL/SQL code by one of the following methods:

- Start the comment with /*. Enter the body of the comment, which can span multiple lines. End the comment with */.

- Start the comment with -- (two hyphens).

- Use the REMARK keyword.

The following example utilizes each method.

```
/*This is a comment*/
--This is also a comment
REMARK This is also a comment
```

You might want to comment your code to make it easier to debug, to show where changes have been made to the original code, or to show who wrote which pieces. Documenting your code makes it much easier if you ever need to go back and add or fix something.

Updating Rows

The *UPDATE command* is used to edit or update existing rows in the database. To use the UPDATE command, simply specify the UPDATE command with the table name, then use the SET command with the new data followed by the WHERE clause to limit the update. For example, to update Allen's commission from 300 to 500, use this command:

```
UPDATE emp
SET comm = 500
WHERE ename = 'ALLEN';

1 row processed.
```

WARNING Make sure you always specify a WHERE clause when you do an UPDATE, or you will make the same change to every row!

Inserting Rows

To insert a row, simply use the INSERT INTO <table name> VALUES (col1, col2, col3...) command. For example, to insert a new employee into the EMP table, use this command:

```
INSERT into emp values
    (7985,'LEWIS','Clerk', 7902,sysdate,900,NULL,20);
1 row processed.
```

Procedures

Procedures (also called stored procedures) are precompiled PL/SQL statements that are stored on the Oracle server itself.

Because procedures are precompiled, they run much more quickly and efficiently than regular queries do. The compiler doesn't have to think about what it needs to do in order to run a stored procedure. The work order or blueprint is saved with the stored procedure. All the Oracle server has to do is load the information and run it. Another advantage of procedures is that they run the same way every time, no matter what application calls them.

Creating procedures is done with the CREATE PROCEDURE command. For example, to create a procedure that adds a commission amount to an employee, run the following statement:

```
create procedure add_comm(emp_id number, new_comm number)
as
begin
update emp set comm=comm+new_comm where empno = emp_id;
end;
end add_comm;
/
Statement processed.
```

Let's just make sure that the old commission for Allen is 500.

```
SQLWKS>select ename, sal, comm from emp where empno=7499;
ENAME       SAL        COMM
---------- ---------- ----------
ALLEN             1600        500
1 row selected.
```

Then, to execute the procedure for Allen (whose ID is 7499), enter this command (assuming you have created the add_comm procedure):

```
execute add_comm (7499, 500);
Statement processed.
```

If the procedure works, it should look like this:

```
SQLWKS>select ename, sal, comm from emp where empno=7499;
ENAME         SAL          COMM
----------    ----------   ----------
ALLEN               1600         1000
1 row selected.
```

You can run stored procedures from any of the SQL utilities. To run the procedure created earlier, you would enter **execute** and then the name of the procedure.

Summary

As a database operator you will need know how to communicate directly with the Oracle database engine using PL/SQL, which was designed to be relatively easy to use.

In this chapter, default security was covered, including how to log in as System, Sys, Internal, Scott, and Demo. You need to have enough rights in the database in order to select data. Chapter 6, "Oracle Users and Security," covers rights in more detail, as well as how to create users beyond just the default ones.

We learned how to submit PL/SQL commands to the Oracle database engine using the various PL/SQL tools, including SQLPlus Worksheet, SQL*Plus, and Server Manager.

We also learned a bit about the SELECT statement. As a DBO, it's important to know how to vertically and horizontally partition tables and then sort your result set in either an ascending or descending fashion, as well as to know how to do a simple query with multiple tables involved.

Various functions were covered, from concatenating character columns to dealing with NULL data to aggregating numeric columns.

Updating existing rows was covered, as well as inserting new rows into tables.

Finally, a discussion on creating and using procedures wrapped up the chapter. Procedures are simply stored PL/SQL code that have been given a name and stored in the database. Procedures can be executed by name, and variables can be supplied.

Key Terms

Before you take the exam, make sure you're familiar with the following terms:

cross join

inner join

INSERT command

NULL values

outer join

Schema

SELECT statement

Server Manager

SQL

SQL*Plus

SQLPlus Worksheet

UNION operator

UPDATE command

Review Questions

1. What does the following PL/SQL script do?

```
SELECT Employee.FirstName, Employee.LastName,
WorkInfo.YearsExp
FROM Employees, WorkInfo
WHERE Employee.EmpID = WorkInfo.EmpID.
```

   A. It displays all information in an employee record along with all of the employee's associated work information.

   B. It displays the first name and last name listed in an employee record, and if the employee has work experience, it will display that, too.

   C. It displays all employees' first names, last names, and work experience for those employees with records in the Employee table that have a matching employee ID in the WorkInfo table.

   D. It displays all employees first names, last names, and work experience for those employees with records in the Employee table whether or not they have a matching employee ID in the WorkInfo table.

2. What are the benefits of procedures? (Select all that apply.)

   A. They are precompiled and therefore run more efficiently than normal queries.

   B. They can be run from any application.

   C. They run more efficiently than normal queries because they are not precompiled, and the optimizer can therefore look at the current conditions and make the necessary optimizations real-time.

   D. They can only be run from the application that created them.

3. Which of the following commands would show just those departments with an average salary greater than $2,000?

A. SELECT deptno, avg(sal), avg(comm)
   FROM emp
   GROUP BY deptno
   WHERE AVG(sal)> 2000;

B. SELECT deptno, avg(sal), avg(comm)
   FROM emp
   GROUP BY deptno
   WHERE AVG(sal)< 2000;

C. SELECT deptno, avg(sal), avg(comm)
   FROM emp
   GROUP BY deptno
   HAVING AVG(sal)< 2000;

D. SELECT deptno, avg(sal), avg(comm)
   FROM emp
   GROUP BY deptno
   HAVING AVG(sal)> 2000;

4. You have two tables—one for customers and one for orders. The Customers table contains the names of the customers, while the Orders
table contains dates and details about the orders. Which type of join
would you use to find the names of just those customers who have
ordered from you in the last month?

A. Inner join (equijoin)

B. Outer join

C. Self join

D. Cross join

5. You have two tables, one for employees (including department ID) and one for department details (including the names of the departments). Which type of join would you use to list all employees and their respective department names, even including employees who don't have a department?

   A. Inner join (equijoin)

   B. Outer join

   C. Self join

   D. Cross join

6. Which type of join would you use to generate test data?

   A. Inner join (equijoin)

   B. Outer join

   C. Self join

   D. Cross join

7. Which operator can be used to show all of the parts that are in both this year's and last year's parts catalog?

   A. UNION

   B. UNION ALL

   C. INTERSECT

   D. MINUS

8. Which operator can be used to show, employees from two different tables, including duplicates?

   A. UNION

   B. UNION ALL

   C. INTERSECT

   D. MINUS

9. Which operator can be used to show all of the managers who manage employees in the company when the data is stored in three different Employee tables? You only need to list a manager once.

   A. UNION

   B. UNION ALL

   C. INTERSECT

   D. MINUS

10. Which operator can be used to show all of the managers who have employees in the Sales, Accounting, and Marketing Employee tables?

    A. UNION

    B. UNION ALL

    C. INTERSECT

    D. MINUS

11. What is the default password for System?

    A. oracle

    B. change_on_install

    C. manager

    D. tiger

12. What is the default password for Sys?

    A. oracle

    B. change_on_install

    C. manager

    D. tiger

13. For a column that holds e-mail addresses for customers who come in off the street, how should you set the column?

    A. Primary Key

    B. NOT NULL

    C. NULL

    D. Foreign Key

14. For a column that holds e-mail addresses for customers who come from the Internet, how should you set the column?

    A. Either NULL or NOT NULL—doesn't matter

    B. NOT NULL

    C. NULL

    D. Restricted

15. Which program comes installed with your Oracle server that you can run and send SQL commands to your database with?

    A. Server Manager

    B. Server Admin

    C. Oracle Manager

    D. Oracle Admin

16. Which of these will not designate a remark in SQL?

    A. –

    B. Remark

    C. /* */

    D. **

17. You have 1,000 customers in your database and 1,000 rows in your Order Details table. Of your customers, 100 brought 1 product last year, 200 bought 2 products, and 100 bought 3. If you do an equijoin to list all of your customers and their orders for last year, how many rows would you have?

    A. 600

    B. 700

    C. 800

    D. 1,000

18. You have 1,000 customers in your database. Of those customers, only 200 have ordered something this year. You do a left outer join, with the Customers table on the left and the Current Year Orders table on the right. How many rows will be in the result set?

  A. 200

  B. 1,000

  C. 1,200

  D. 1,300

19. You have 1,000 customers in your database and 1,000 rows in your Order Details table. Of your customers, 100 brought 1 product last year, 200 bought 2 products, and 100 bought 3. If you do a cross join between the Customers table and the Order Details table, how many rows will be in the result set?

  A. 1,000

  B. 2,000

  C. 1,000,000

  D. 2,000,000

20. Which keyword comes before the name of the table in a SELECT statement?

  A. DataFrom

  B. From

  C. Database

  D. Get

Answers to Review Questions

1. C. The WHERE clause indicates that there must be a matching record in the Employee and WorkInfo tables.

2. A, B. Stored procedures are precompiled and thus run much faster and can be run from any application.

3. D. The HAVING clause eliminates summary data after the summarization.

4. A. An inner join (equijoin) comparing the Customers and Orders tables would work as long as you used the WHERE clause to limit orders to the last month.

5. B. An outer join will show you all employees, regardless of what department they are in (and even if they are not in a department).

6. D. A cross join or Cartesian product can be used to generate test data quickly.

7. C. The INTERSECT function only shows rows that are in both result sets.

8. B. The UNION ALL function will show all of the rows from two or more result sets and will not eliminate duplicates.

9. A. The UNION function will combine all of the results from the two queries and delete any duplicates.

10. C. The INTERSECT function will only show rows that appear in all three result sets, which is what you want.

11. C. The default password for the System account is manager.

12. B. The default password for the Sys account is change_on_install.

13. C. Because many customers who come in off the street may not have e-mail addresses, you should set the column to allow NULL values.

14. B. Because your customers come from the Internet, you can assume that they will have an e-mail address (which you want) and can set the column to NOT NULL, thus making it a required field.

15. A. Server Manager is the program you can run on the Oracle server to connect to the Oracle database.

16. D. Remarks are designated with Remark, --, or /* */, but not **.

17. C. You will get one row for each match of customer and order details, so you will get 100+400+300 or 800 rows.

18. B. Outer joins list all of the rows from one table, whether or not there is a corresponing row in the other table.

19. C. A cross join produces x * y for the number of rows in the result set, so in this case 1,000 × 1,000 or 1,000,000.

20. B. The From keyword is used to designate the table data is coming from.

Creating and Managing Databases

ORACLE8i DBO EXAM OBJECTIVES OFFERED IN THIS CHAPTER:

✓ **How to Create an Oracle Database and Services**

- Create a database by using the Database Assistant tool
- Identify the files required to create and open a database
- Identify the directory in which the Oracle database files are stored
- Display the database services using the NT control panel services utility

Exam objectives are subject to change at any time without prior notice and at Oracle's sole discretion. Please visit Oracle's Training and Certification Web site (http://education.oracle.com/certification/index.html) for the most current exam objectives listing.

As an Oracle database operator, your chief job will probably consist of maintaining one or more databases. This chapter will cover not only how to maintain existing databases, but also how to create new databases using syntax, as well as the graphical tools. Oracle Storage Manager, which is used to manage existing databases and their database files, will also be covered.

Performance and Placement of Database Files

Placing your database files in the appropriate location is very dependent on the hardware and software that you have available to you. There are very few fast and hard rules when it comes to databases. In fact, the only definite rule is that you should spend more time designing your solution than implementing it. The more you plan and design your system, the less work it will be later.

There are several issues to keep in mind when you are attempting to decide where to place your database files. They include planning for fault tolerance and reliability, planning for speed, and planning for growth.

You should rank these three categories in order of importance for your particular database. For instance, if your database can easily be reproduced (from monthly mainframe tapes, for example), speed may be more important than fault tolerance. A database that supports a critical application that generates a lot of data may have growth as its most important issue, with fault tolerance a close second.

Let's look at fault tolerance and reliability first.

Planning for Fault Tolerance and Reliability

Fault tolerance simply involves eliminating a single point of failure in your operation. For example, if you have UPS power systems, or even a spare power generator, you have a fault tolerant power system.

There are several different things you can do to ensure the reliability and consistency of your database. In servers, you can set up your hard drives and volumes to become fault tolerant or capable of withstanding a single item failing. There are several different methods of ensuring fault tolerant hard drives, including different levels of RAID (Redundant Array of Inexpensive Drives). Each method has certain features and drawbacks. Take a look at the different RAID levels and what they entail.

You should also use name brand servers with good support policies. Also, make sure your routers, hubs, and workstations have a UPS installed if you want network connectivity in case of power failure.

RAID 0

RAID 0 uses *disk striping*. What this does is it writes data across multiple hard disk partitions in what is called a stripe set (see Figure 5.1). This can greatly improve speed as multiple hard disks are working at the same time. RAID 0 can be implemented through the use of Windows NT, NetWare, Linux, and other operating system software or on third-party hardware. While RAID 0 gives you the best speed, it does not give you any fault tolerance. If one of the hard disks in the stripe set is damaged, you lose all of your data.

FIGURE 5.1 RAID 0 or disk striping

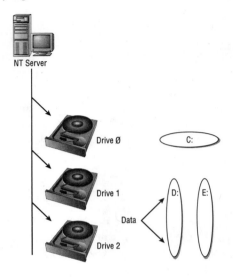

 RAID 0 is the fastest way to set up your drives, but remember that if any of the drives in the array fail, the entire array is ruined.

RAID 1

RAID 1 uses disk mirroring. *Disk mirroring* actually writes your information to disk twice: once to the primary file and once to the mirror file (see Figure 5.2). This gives you excellent fault tolerance, but it is somewhat slow as you must write to disk twice. Reads from two drives are somewhat faster than reads from a single drive.

The main disadvantage of disk mirroring is that you lose half of your drive space to fault tolerance. For example, if you have two 18GB drives in a RAID 1 configuration, you have only 18GB of usable space. NetWare, Windows NT, and Linux include the ability to mirror your hard disks. RAID 1 only requires a single hard disk controller.

FIGURE 5.2 RAID 1 or disk mirroring

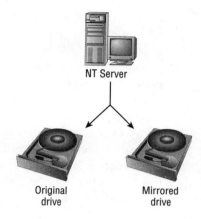

Disk Duplexing

Disk duplexing is similar to RAID 1 in that it does involve mirroring, but it uses two separate hard disk controllers instead of one (see Figure 5.3). This is more efficient and more fault tolerant than RAID 1, but it still requires twice the amount of hard disk space as RAID 0.

Although hard drives fail a lot more often than disk controllers, a disk controller failure will corrupt both mirrored drives, so disk duplexing is highly recommended over disk mirroring.

FIGURE 5.3 Disk duplexing

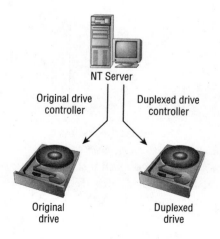

RAID 5

RAID 5 is called striping with parity. What this does is write data to the hard disk in stripe sets with the addition of a fault tolerant parity check bit. One of the disks in your stripe set (you must have at least three) will not store data, but will store parity checksums for the other disks (see Figure 5.4). This gives you excellent fault tolerance, as well as good read speeds with a reasonable amount of overhead. You will lose $1/n$ of your drive space where n is the number of drives in the array. For example, if you had three 18GB hard drives in a RAID 5 array, your total usable space would be 36GB (you would lose 1/3 of your drive space). As you add more drives, the array becomes more efficient. For example, if you have five 18GB drives in your array, your usable drive space is 72GB, as you would still lose just a single drive (18GB) or 1/5 of the total drive space.

FIGURE 5.4 RAID 5 or the Striped with Parity drive

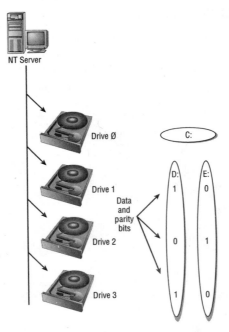

The parity checksums can be used to re-create information lost if a single disk in the stripe set fails (see Figure 5.5). If more than one disk in the stripe set fails, you will lose all of your data. Windows NT and Linux support RAID 5 in a software implementation. If you can afford a hardware implementation of RAID 5, I highly suggest that you use it. It will be faster and more reliable than using an operating system's software implementation of RAID 5.

FIGURE 5.5 Dynamically reconstructing a lost RAID 5 drive in RAM

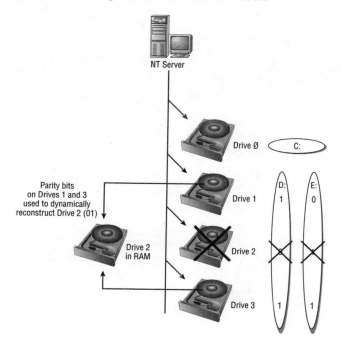

 The major disadvantage of RAID 5 is slow writes because every write to the drive has to have a parity bit computed and then written to the array. A general rule of thumb is that if the database is over 10 percent writes, RAID 5 should be avoided.

RAID 10

RAID 10 is the big daddy. This level of RAID should be used in mission critical systems that require 24/7 uptime and the fastest possible access. RAID 10 implements striping with parity as in RAID 5 and then mirrors your stripe sets. You still have excellent speed and excellent fault tolerance, but you also have the added expense of using more than twice the disk space as RAID 0. Then again, I am talking about an instance of Oracle that can afford *NO* downtime.

The other issue that you need to keep in mind when working with a database is communication. Oracle can only have database files on what it deems a local hard disk. Your local hard disks can be on your local machine or a hardware device that is connected directly to the Oracle machine (like a hardware RAID array). Although you have this limitation with your active database files, this rule does not apply to your backups. Backups can be placed anywhere in your enterprise, including a named pipe, local hard disks, networked hard disks, or a tape.

For efficiency's sake, you may wish to place the redo log files on RAID 10 (since the files are very write intensive) and the database files on RAID 5 (to save money).

Planning for Speed

One of the first things to look for when planning for speed is bottlenecks. There is no sense in spending thousands of dollars on a new server if the old server was not running even close to capacity.

For example, many companies are still on 10Mbps Ethernet, which limits the network to only a fraction of the maximum output of a server. Shared hubs instead of switches may also cause contention on the network.

When planning for maximum speed for a given server, there are several other items to look at beside bottlenecks. They include the following:

- CPUs
- RAM
- Network Bandwidth
- Disk Controllers
- Disk Drives
- Disk Configurations

Relational databases are very CPU and RAM intensive. I once had a student who ordered a four-CPU server with only 128MB of RAM. In his case, the additional CPUs did him no good without additional RAM. For today's fast CPUs, I would suggest at least 128MB of RAM per CPU.

There's an old joke. Question: "What is the fastest hard drive read you can make?" Answer: "One that never happens." In other words, RAM used for caching is much faster than reading the data off of the drive.

Poor network performance will choke even the fastest server. For example, if your clients are going through routers that take two seconds to get through and back, your queries will be slow because of the additional network overhead, even if your server is instantaneous.

You should always buy name brand servers and disk controllers. Disk drives tend to be the bottleneck of a server because they are really the only physical part of a computer. That is why extra RAM for caching can have a tremendous impact on a database server.

See Appendix B, "Performance and Tuning," for more details on performance and tuning.

Planning for Growth

There are two ways to grow database files:

- You can add additional files to the database.
- You can make existing files larger.

There are advantages to both methods. When adding additional files to a database you can put the files on a different volume than the original datafiles for either performance or space reasons. You can also adjust all of the extents and other parameters separately for each individual file, which could be useful. For example, you may want smaller extents for datafiles associated with tables with lots of little data rows, while you would probably want larger extent sizing for datafiles associated with tables with large rows.

An advantage to extending existing datafiles is that it is simpler to have as few datafiles as possible. You can manually extend the file when it looks like it is close to getting full or enable the Autoextend function (or both). Autoextend allows datafiles to automatically grow as needed, which saves you from getting a call at 2:00 A.M. because someone added a large amount of data.

Adding additional datafiles, as well as modifying existing ones is covered in greater detail below.

Where to Put the Database

Once you've looked at fault tolerance, speed, and reliability issues and have determined a plan for growth, you can more easily determine where to place the database.

All other things being equal, placing your database files on a RAID 0 or striped drive will provide the best performance. Placing your files on a RAID 10 drive will give you the best performance and fault tolerance. RAID 5 drives have the worst write performance of any configuration, but in very expensive drive arrays ($100,000+) drive performance is no longer an issue, as the bottleneck moves to another part of the server or to the network.

You may want to consider putting the files for tables, indexes, and redo logs on separate drives, especially if you are not striping your drives. If you are striping your drives, the tables, indexes, and redo logs are already on the same physical drives, although putting them on different volumes will tend to spread them out over the different drive heads and platters.

Wherever you place your datafiles, you should document where they are in case of any sort of failure. Knowing what you have and where it was placed are key components of a successful backup and restore strategy.

Understanding Database Files and SIDs

Now that you know where to place your database files, let's talk about exactly what database files will be created when you create an Oracle database.

An Oracle database is composed of several database files, including parameter, password, control, data, and redo logs, which are all discussed below. You can store several databases in the same directory because each database should use a distinct naming convention, although Oracle8i separates them into different directories.

Let's look at some database naming conventions, as well as the database files that are created in an Oracle database.

System IDs (SIDs)

A database name is considered by default it's *System ID (SID)*. The SID is used as the default naming convention for all of the support files associated with a particular database. The SID is used after the prefix of a file to show which database the file is associated with. PWDORCL.ORA, for instance, is the password file for the ORCL database, and PWDSALES2K.ORA is the password file for the SALES2K database. Almost all files use ORA DBF, or LOG for the default extensions, so consistent use of prefixes and SIDs is essential for tracking which files belong to which databases.

A SID can only be 8 alpha-numerical characters or less (on Oracle8i). In previous versions of Oracle, it could only be 4 alpha-numerical characters or less. The SID will be designated by <SID> in examples in this book.

Although you don't have to use the SID of the database in its file name, it is highly recommended, especially if you have more than one database on your server.

Physical Components of a Database

An Oracle database is composed of many files. As a database administrator, you may be responsible for creating various database files either directly or indirectly. The various database files of the sample database ORCL, who creates them, and what purpose they serve are covered in Table 5.1.

TABLE 5.1 Database Files

File Type	Default Name	Contents	Created by
Parameter	INIT<SID>.ORA	Initial parameters	Admin
Password	PWD<SID>.ORA	Admin passwords	Admin
Control	CTL<SID>.ORA	Database parameters	Oracle
User data	USR<SID>.DBF	User data	Oracle
System data	SYS<SID>.DBF	System data	Oracle
Index data	IDX<SID>.DBF	Index data	Oracle
Rollback	RBS<SID>.DBF	Rollback data	Oracle
Redo (logs)	LOG<SID>.DBF	Redo log data	Oracle
Temporary	TMP<SID>.DBF	Temporary data	Oracle

Parameter File

The *parameter file* must exist to start a database instance and open a database. The parameter file points to the control file(s) and datafile(s) that should be used when the database is opened. If the control and database files do not already exist, they will be created. The parameter file is an ASCII file and can be edited by any text editor. Make sure you don't change the extension (ORA) when you edit it.

The parameter file is only read during the initialization of the database; thus, any changes you make to the file will not take effect until the next time you start the instance.

Oracle provides a sample parameter file called INITSEED.ORA. Note that the file not only contains parameters for the database, but because it is the initialization file for the instance, it contains various settings that control the way the instance will start. Parameter files and settings pertaining to the instance are covered in more detail in Chapter 2, "Installing and Configuring Oracle8i."

The INITSEED.ORA file contains good default parameters for most databases. If you create a database using syntax, simply copy the INITSEED.ORA file to INIT<SID>.ORA, edit the appropriate lines, and use the new file as your parameter file.

Password Files

A *password file* can be created to grant Sysdba access to those users who need it. To create a password file, use the appropriate tool for the operating system you are running on. Table 5.2 shows which tool to use for which operating system.

TABLE 5.2 Password File Tools and Their Operating Systems

Password File Tool	Operating System
ORAPWD	UNIX
ORAPWD	Windows NT
NWDBM80	NetWare

When you create the password file, you can enter the password for the Sysdba, as well as the maximum number of anticipated Sysdbas.

Make sure you enter a sufficient number of Sysdbas as this cannot be changed after the fact without deleting and re-creating the password file (and re-adding all the Sysdbas back into it).

Here is the syntax of the command:

```
orapwd file=<name> password=<password> entries=<users>
```

Enter the name of the file where <name> is, the password where <password> is, and the maximum number of administrators where <users> is. Save the file in the Database folder with PWD<SID>.ORA for the filename.

Control Files

A database needs to have one or more *control files* associated with it. In fact, if your database files are OK, but your control files are damaged, you will not be able to access your data. Control files are used by Oracle to keep track of various system information for the database. Control files are in binary format and are not editable.

For fault tolerance, you should always specify at least two control files on two separate hard drives. To specify two control files, simply add a semicolon ";" between the filenames and paths. For example, to specify two control files (CTL1DB1.ORA on the D: drive and CTL2DB1.ORA on the E: drive) use this command in the parameter (INIT<SID>) file:

```
control_files = D:\orant\DATABASE\CTL1DB1.ORA;
E:\orant\DATABASE\CTL2DB1.ORA
```

Datafiles

The database can be created after the instance is started in NOMOUNT mode.

Starting an instance in various modes is covered in Chapter 2, "Installing and Configuring Oracle8i."

When the database is created, various types of *datafiles* will be created, including user datafiles, system datafiles, and redo log files.

User Data

User data should always be stored on *user tablespaces*. When a user tablespace is created, you will create one or more datafiles to store the data. User tablespaces (and thus datafiles) are covered in Chapter 7, "Installing and Managing Applications."

System Data

Oracle uses the *system tablespaces* to store the data dictionary for the database. The system tablespaces are created on the *system datafiles*. To help preserve data integrity, you should create user tablespaces and assign users to use those tablespaces.

Redo Log Files

Oracle tracks changes in the *redo log files*. In case of a system failure, changes can be rolled forward from the redo log files. Oracle databases need at least two redo log files, as changes are written first to one file and then to the other. Redo log files and how to back them up are covered in Chapter 10, "Backups and Restorations."

Rollback Segments

Rollback segments are used to temporarily store transactions until they are finished. Creating and managing rollback segments are covered in Appendix B, "Performance and Tuning."

Creating Databases

Before you get started on creating a database, there are a couple of things you should do to make the creation go smoother, including checking prerequisites, creating the password file, and creating a parameter file. Once you have done your homework, there are basically two ways to create a database: using PL/SQL or the Database Configuration Assistant. Let's start with the more difficult way of creating a database, using PL/SQL. After that, we will use the Database Configuration Assistant to create a new database.

Checking Prerequisites

There are several items you need to check to ensure the successful creation and running of the database. You should make sure the hardware is sufficient to run the database. Speed and number of CPUs, memory, and hard drive space are all essential to check. Also be sure to check network traffic to make sure your network can support the database. General optimizing hints were covered earlier in the chapter, and tuning and optimizing the database are covered in Appendix B, "Performance and Tuning."

Creating the Password File

Create a password file using the appropriate program, as shown in Table 5.2. You should safeguard the password and change the default password of Oracle databases to ensure sufficient administrators can access the database. Changing passwords is done by using Security Manager and is covered in Chapter 6, "Oracle Users and Security."

Creating the Parameter File

You will need to create a parameter file if you're using PL/SQL to create the database. Simply copy either the INITSEED.ORA file or another parameter file that closely matches what you want, edit the file to change at least the name and paths to the control files, and save the new file using the name of the new database.

Starting and Restarting the Instance

Normally, starting an instance initializes the system memory structures and opens the database. To create a database, you have to start the instance in NOMOUNT mode, as there is no database to mount. Following is an example command to start the instance in NOMOUNT mode:

```
STARUP NOMOUNT pfile=D:\ORANT\DATABASE\initdb1.ora
```

Once the database is created, you will have to stop the instance and start it normally. Note that for best recoverability you should back up the database when you initially stop the instance.

Creating the Database Using PL/SQL

When you create a database, you should specify the logical name of the database, the physical filename where the database file will reside, and the size of the database file. Optional parameters include the maximum size that the database is allowed to grow to, as well as the growth characteristics. You also need to specify the number and filenames of the redo log files, as well as their size. Here is an example of the CREATE DATABASE statement:

```
create database db1
    controlfile reuse
    logfile group 1 ('C:\RANT\DATABASE\log1db1.dbf',
    'C:\ORANT\DATABASE\log2db1.dbf') size 200K reuse,
    group 2 ('C:\ORANT\DATABASE\log3db1.dbf',
```

```
'C:\ORANT\DATABASE\log4db1.dbf') size 200K reuse
datafile 'C:\ORANT\DATABASE\sys1db1.dbf'
size 10M reuse autoextend on  next 20M maxsize 200M
character set WE8PC850;
create rollback segment rb_temp storage(initial 50K next 50K);
```

Here are details on what the different parameters do:

CREATE DATABASE   Names the database, which, in this case, would be db1.

CONTROLFILE REUSE   States that the control files specified in the INIT<SID>.ORA file will be overwritten and rebuilt from scratch if they already exist.

LOGFILE GROUP1   Designates the first of at least two redo log file groups. Every database must have at least two redo log file groups. Each group must consist of one or more members. In this case, we have made two members of each group for redundancy purposes.

LOGFILE GROUP2   Designates the second of at least two redo log file groups. Note the size of the files and that if the file already exists it will be overwritten (reused).

DATAFILE   Designates the initial size of the database file expressed in megabytes. Keep in mind that this will pre-allocate hard disk space. In this case, it starts as a 10MB file, will overwrite any existing file, and will automatically grow 20MB to a maximum of 200MB. This is the system tablespace, which is used for system tables and data. Creating and using user tablespaces is covered in Chapter 7, "Installing and Managing Applications."

CHARACTER SET   Specifies the character set that the database supports.

CREATE ROLLBACK SEGMENT   Gives the name and size of the rollback segment. This rollback segment starts at 50KB and will grow by 50KB as needed. Rollback segments are covered in more detail in Appendix B, "Performance and Tuning."

Creating the Database Using Database Configuration Assistant

Oracle has supplied a Wizard, called the *Database Configuration Assistant*, to let you create databases using a GUI tool. The Database Configuration Assistant makes creating databases easy and allows you to set the most common parameters for both the database and the instance.

The Database Configuration Assistant is a program that is installed with the server, not the client software (not even with Oracle Enterprise Manager).

To start the Database Configuration Assistant in Windows NT, go to Start ➢ Programs ➢ Oracle Home ➢ Database Administration ➢ Database Configuration Assistant. In Exercise 5.1, you use the Database Configuration Assistant to create a new database.

EXERCISE 5.1

Creating Databases Using the Database Configuration Assistant

1. Start the Database Configuration Assistant by going to Start ➢ Programs ➢ Oracle Home ➢ Database Administration ➢ Database Configuration Assistant.

2. Choose Create a Database. Select Next to continue.

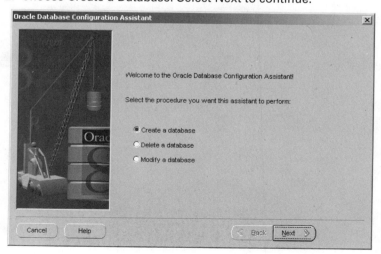

EXERCISE 5.1 *(continued)*

3. When you select Create a Database, you are prompted to use the typical or custom settings. Choose Custom, and select Next to continue.

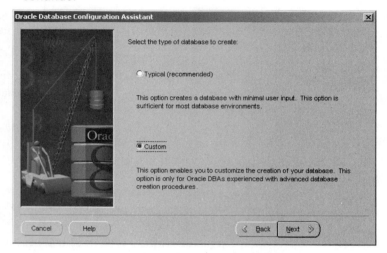

4. At the Environment page, you can select the type of applications that will be running with your database: Online Transaction Processing, Decision Support System, or a Hybrid. Unless your database is going to use primarily one type or another, you should choose Hybrid and then select Next to continue.

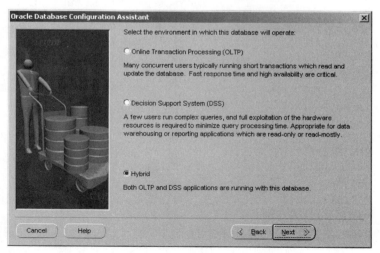

5. You should next enter the number of concurrent users the database will support. Note that I have changed it to 50. Select Next to continue.

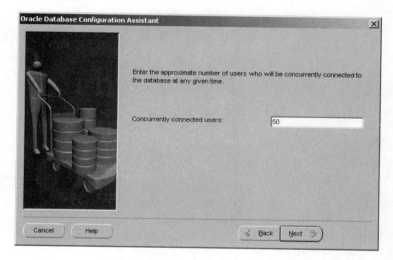

6. You can now select the mode the database will operate in. Dedicated Server Mode is better for OLAP-type applications, where OLTP applications will probably benefit from the Shared Server Mode. If you are unsure, leave the default settings and choose Next to continue.

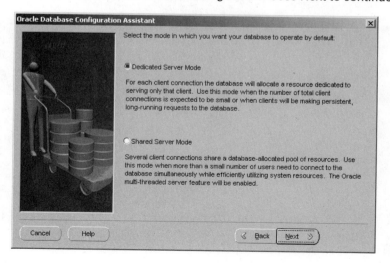

7. If you chose a custom installation, you next have a choice of optional data management cartridges to support, as well as advanced replication. For the purpose of the exercise, clear all the boxes, and choose Next to continue.

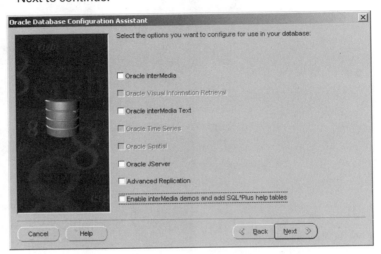

8. You can enter the name of the database in the next screen. Enter **sales2k** if you can't think of a better name. Select Next to continue.

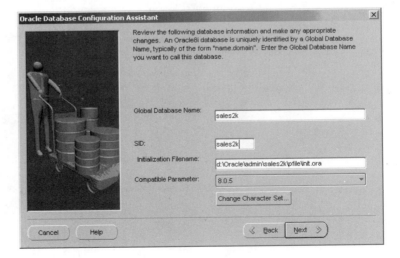

9. Enter the password for the INTERNAL account in this screen. Choose Next to continue.

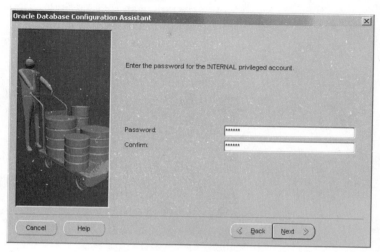

10. In the next screen, you can change the default names and paths of the control files, as well as data and log file parameters. Leave the default settings, and choose Next to continue.

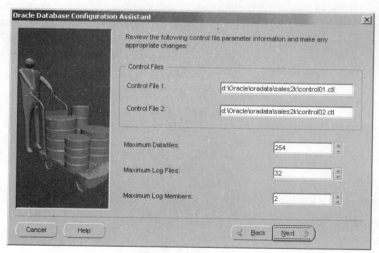

11. This screen is quite important, as it allows you to change the paths, names, autoextend parameters, and sizes of the default datafiles for the system, user, rollback, index, and temporary tablespaces. Note that the default extension for the datafiles is DBF. Adjust the datafiles as your design calls for, or, for this example, just take the defaults and choose Next to continue.

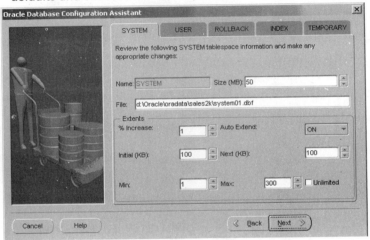

12. The next screen allows you to make changes to the default settings for the redo log files. Note that the default extension for redo log files is LOG, which you may want to change to match your database design. Leave the default settings for this example database, and choose Next to continue.

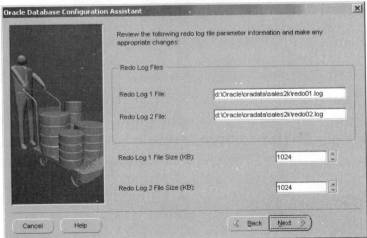

EXERCISE 5.1 *(continued)*

13. You can change the default checkpoint intervals, as well as set archive logging in the next screen. Take the default settings, and choose Next to continue.

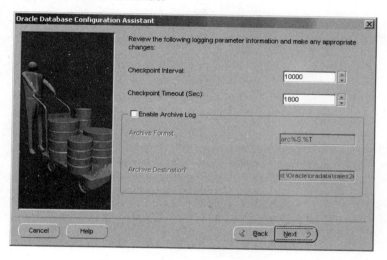

14. The SGA and other instance parameters can be changed from the next screen. Take the default settings, and choose Next to continue.

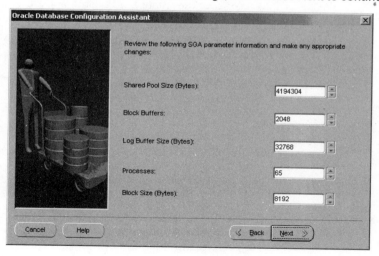

EXERCISE 5.1 *(continued)*

15. You can set the path for the trace files in the next screen. Take the defaults, and choose Next to continue.

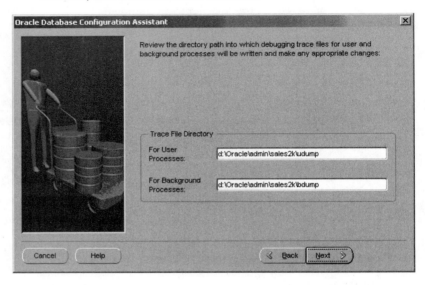

16. In the next screen, you can choose to create the database immediately or save the creation SQL commands to a script for later running. Choose to create the database now, and select Finish to continue.

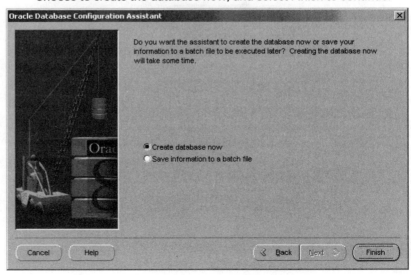

17. Answer yes at the prompt to start the database creation.

18. Once the database creation is in progress, you should see a Database Creation Progress screen such as this.

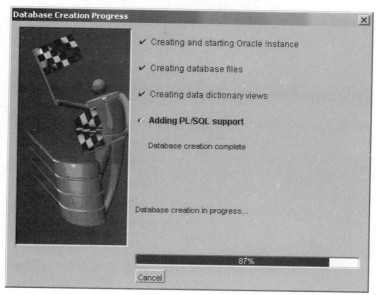

19. When the database is done, carefully note the database name, SID, and INTERNAL, SYSTEM, and SYS passwords. Choose OK to close the screen.

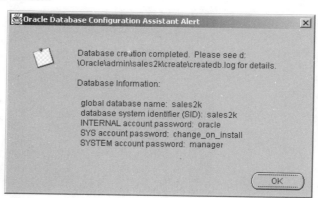

You will have to create a service name to connect to the database. See Chapter 2, "Installing and Configuring Oracle8i," for more information on creating database service.

Managing Database Files

Once the database is created, you will almost certainly want to manage the various database files. You can use the ALTER DATABASE command to manage most parameters of the database or the GUI interface called Storage Manager. Storage Manager was introduced in Chapter 3, "Oracle8i Enterprise Manager and Other Tools."

Storage Manager

Storage Manager is used to manage the various physical files and their associated database object. For instance, user tablespaces can be created or existing ones expanded onto additional datafiles.

To start Storage Manager, go to Start ➤ Programs ➤ Oracle Enterprise Manager Home ➤ DBA Management Pack ➤ Storage Manager. You can also start Storage Manager from within Enterprise Manager. You will have to connect to an existing database with at least DBA rights. Once you are in Storage Manager, you will see Tablespaces, Datafiles, and Rollback Segments folders. Click the + icon to expand the Tablespaces and Datafiles folders, as shown in Figure 5.6.

FIGURE 5.6 Storage Manager

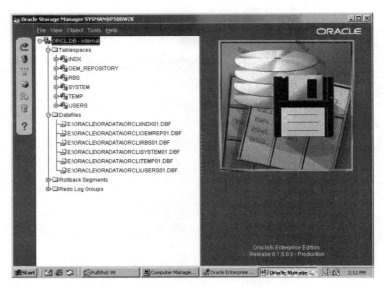

To add additional datafiles to a tablespace, simply choose Object ➤ Create, and highlight Datafile. You will need to enter the entire path of the datafile, as well as the tablespace it will be a part of and its starting size. See Figure 5.7.

FIGURE 5.7   Creating a new datafile

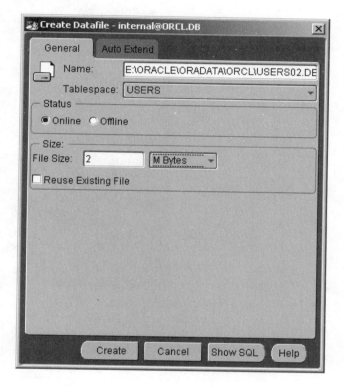

You may also want to enable autoextend by going to the Auto Extend tab and filling in the details, as shown in Figure 5.8.

FIGURE 5.8 The Autoextend properties of a datafile

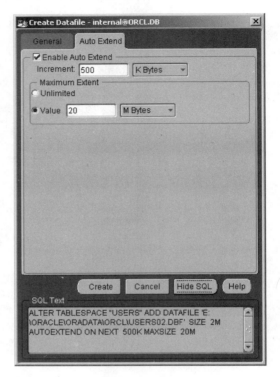

You can also edit the properties of existing datafiles by highlighting the file, right-clicking, and choosing Edit. By editing existing files, you can make them larger and/or enable autoextend for automatic growth.

Figure 5.8 also shows the SQL text that Storage Manager will generate—the Show SQL Text button was selected.

To create additional tablespaces, simply highlight the Tablespace folder, and select the + icon, or go to the Tablespace ➢ Create menu option. Give the tablespace a name, add one or more datafiles by using the Add button and filling in the details, and choose the Create button. Tablespaces and when to create new ones are covered in more detail in Chapter 7, "Installing and Managing Applications."

Rollback segments are covered in Appendix B, "Performance and Tuning," while redo log file groups are covered in Chapter 10, "Backups and Restorations."

Logical Components of a Database

After the database is created, it is ready to hold the logical objects. Remember from Chapter 1, "Introduction to Oracle and Relational Databases," that a database is composed of various logical objects such as tables, indexes, views, procedures, and triggers. Databases also contain users, each of whom will have rights to the various objects of the database. Creating and managing users is covered in Chapter 6, "Oracle Users and Security," while creating and managing logical objects will be covered in Chapter 7, "Installing and Managing Applications."

Summary

There is much more to data storage in Oracle than meets the eye. Oracle data storage structure is about more than just a file or a collection of files. It is an entire internal architecture designed for one purpose alone, to extract and modify your data as quickly and efficiently as possible.

This chapter covered what a database is. This included a discussion on datafiles and their placement as it relates to fault tolerance. You looked at the different levels of RAID and their advantages and disadvantages. Remember that for most installations, RAID 5 is the most inexpensive choice for maximizing fault-tolerance, with a small price to pay in additional storage. RAID 5 is, however, relatively slow for writes, which makes RAID 10 the best performing fault tolerant solution.

You then looked over the CREATE DATABASE statement and looked at all of the different options that are available to you. This included the ability to have your database automatically grow as needed. Remember that you should set the MAXSIZE parameter so that your data or redo log files don't fill an entire disk partition.

You also learned how to create databases using the Database Configuration Assistant, a Wizard from Oracle that lets you create databases easily from the GUI.

Storage Manager was the last topic of the chapter. Storage Manager is used to manage datafiles of existing databases. You can not only increase the size of datafiles, you can also edit their properties, including how they autogrow. You can also add additional datafiles to a database using Storage Manager.

Key Terms

Before you take the exam, make sure you're familiar with the following terms:

control files

Database Configuration Assistant

datafiles

disk duplexing

disk mirroring

disk striping

fault tolerance

parameter file

password file

RAID 0

RAID 1

RAID 5

RAID 10

redo log files

rollback segments

Storage Manager

system datafiles

System ID (SID)

system tablespaces

user data

user tablespaces

Review Questions

1. You want to choose a fault tolerant solution that will impact performance as little as possible. Which would you choose?

   A. RAID 0

   B. RAID 1

   C. RAID 5

   D. RAID 10

2. You are on a very limited budget but still have to have a fault-tolerant solution. Which would you choose?

   A. RAID 0

   B. RAID 1

   C. RAID 5

   D. RAID 10

3. The default extension for system datafiles when using the Database Configuration Assistant is which?

   A. USR

   B. DBF

   C. IDX

   D. DAT

4. The default extension for redo log files when using the Database Configuration Assistant is which?

   A. USR

   B. RED

   C. LOG

   D. REL

5. When will a change to a database parameter (initialization) file take place? Choose the best answer.

   A. Immediately

   B. When the database instance is restarted

   C. Never (as the change would only affect new databases)

   D. When the server is rebooted

6. What is the name of the password file creation tool in Windows NT?

   A. ORAPWDNT

   B. ORAPWD

   C. NWDBM80

   D. PWDADMIN

7. What is the name of the password file creation tool in UNIX?

   A. ORAPWD

   B. ORAPWD80

   C. NWDBM80

   D. PWDADMIN

8. Why would you want to specify two control files?

   A. You wouldn't for normal databases

   B. For performance reasons

   C. For fault tolerance reasons

   D. For user access reasons

9. What does the REUSE command do in the CREATE DATABASE command?

   A. REUSE is not a valid switch.

   B. REUSE makes the log files autowrap as needed.

   C. REUSE causes control files to reclaim fragmented memory space for the instance.

   D. REUSE causes existing files to be overwritten.

10. What is the name of the utility that can be used to easily create new databases?

    A. Enterprise Manager

    B. Instance Manager

    C. Storage Manager

    D. Database Configuration Assistant

11. What is the name of the utility that can be used to modify existing tablespaces or database files?

    A. Enterprise Manager

    B. Instance Manager

    C. Storage Manager

    D. Database Assistant

12. Which mode should you start an instance in to create a new database?

    A. OPEN

    B. NOMOUNT

    C. MOUNT

    D. CLOSED

13. Who creates the database control file?

    A. The administrator

    B. Oracle during database creation

    C. Each user upon connection

    D. The backup process

14. How can you have the database grow automatically?

    A. Enable autoextend

    B. Disable autoextend

    C. Enable autodatafile adds

    D. Disable autodatafile adds

15. What units can you specify datafiles in? (Choose all that apply.)

   A. KB

   B. MB

   C. GB

   D. Bytes

16. If you specify 10 administrators when you initially create the password file, what happens when you need to have 11 administrators?

   A. You can only add 10 administrators.

   B. The 10-administrator limit applies to concurrent admins, so they just can't all be in at the same time.

   C. The password file will grow automatically.

   D. You have to manually grow the password file.

17. Tablespaces have to have at least how many datafiles?

   A. Zero

   B. One

   C. Two

   D. Four

18. How can you minimize the immediate impact on your production server when running the Database Configuration Assistant?

   A. Walk slowly through the menus.

   B. Make the initial database small.

   C. Save the database creation script for later use.

   D. Hit Cancel at the end of the Wizard.

19. Which of these drive arrays can continue with a single hard disk failure? (Select all that apply.)

   A. RAID 0

   B. RAID 1

   C. RAID 5

   D. RAID 10

20. What is the name of the sample default database on most operating systems?

    A. ORACLE

    B. ORCL

    C. ENTMAN

    D. REPOSITORY

Answers to Review Questions

1. D. The fastest performing fault tolerant solution is RAID 10.

2. C. The most efficient (and thus cheapest) fault tolerant solution is RAID 5.

3. B. DBF is the default extension for system datafiles.

4. C. LOG is the default extension for redo log files.

5. B. The database (and instance) parameter file is read when the instance is started. Rebooting the operating system (D) may not cause the instance to automatically start, so B is still the best answer.

6. B. ORAPWD is the program used to create password files on a Windows NT computer.

7. A. ORAPWD is the program used to create password files on a UNIX computer.

8. C. If the control file becomes unreadable, the entire database is unreadable; thus, two or more copies of the control file should be used for fault tolerance.

9. D. The REUSE command overwrites existing files.

10. D. The Database Configuration Assistant can be used to create, delete, or modify databases.

11. C. Storage Manager can be used to manage existing databases and database files.

12. B. The instance must be started in NOMOUNT mode in order to create a new database.

13. B. Oracle creates the database control file, as specified in the parameter file, during database creation.

14. A. Enabling autoextend allows datafiles to grow automatically.

15. A, B. You can specify sizes for datafiles in KB or in MB.

16. A. Once you set a limit on the number of Sysdbas or Sysops in the password file, you have to delete and re-create the file to add users beyond your initial limit.

17. B. A tablespace has to have at least one datafile.

18. C. You can save the database creation script for later use when using the Database Configuration Assistant.

19. B, C, D. Of these, only RAID 0 is not fault tolerant concerning disk drives.

20. B. The sample database is called ORCL.

Chapter

6

Oracle Users and Security

This chapter focuses on security within the database. Just like you wouldn't want users to log in to a server with full rights, you don't want users to connect to a database with full rights to the data.

There are various ways you can secure access to the database. You can use object rights, disk quotas, and default tablespaces or grant or deny users the ability to give their rights to others.

This chapter will also go over the default rights of the system accounts and what rights are needed to perform various operations.

Understanding Object Security and Ownership

User accounts are created in an Oracle database so that individual people can have different security settings. Using separate accounts also allows you to audit database activity, thus allowing you to quickly see who is doing what in the database.

Oracle databases are composed of various objects. Chapter 7, "Installing and Managing Applications," goes into more detail on the various objects and how to create, modify, and delete them.

Users will normally log in to the operating system or network and then connect to the database instance. Once users are connected to the instance, they can use whatever rights have been granted to them on any particular object. See Figure 6.1.

FIGURE 6.1 Users and objects

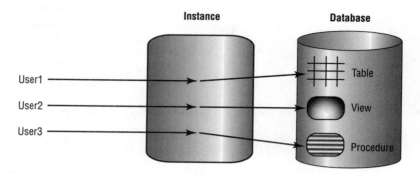

There are several basic rules that you should keep in mind to make it easier to administer security.

- The owner of an object has all rights on an object.

- If you are not the owner of an object, all rights have to be granted from the owner.

- Once rights are granted to a user, the user can grant those rights to another user only if they have been given the right to do so.

Default Users

When a database is first created, Oracle8i creates some default user accounts (shown in Table 6.1) to support additional components and so that you can connect as a user with enough rights to create additional users.

TABLE 6.1 The Default Users

Name	Default Password	Description
INTERNAL	ORACLE	An alias to the SYS account (used for backwards compatibility)
SYS	CHANGE_ON_INSTALL	The main system account
SYSTEM	MANAGER	The account that owns system tables

TABLE 6.1 The Default Users *(continued)*

Name	Default Password	Description
SCOTT	TIGER	A sample database user
DEMO	DEMO	A sample database user
DBSNMP	DBSNMP	User with an SNMPAgent role
OUTLN	OUTLN	User with a DBA role
MYSSYS	MSSSYS	A user account for MS Transaction Server
CTXSYS	CTXSYS	A user account for interMedia Text
MDSYS	MDSYS	A user account for Spacial and inter-Media
ORDSYS	ORDSYS	A user account for Time Series, VI Retrieval
ORD-PLUGIN	ORDPLUGIN	A user account for non-native plug-ins
COMDEMO	COMDEMO	A user account for COM automation

Creating New Users

In order for anyone to connect to Oracle8i, they must first have a user account created for them. Of course, the Oracle administrator must connect with one of the default system accounts to create the initial users in the database.

Users can be created by SQL code or by using *Security Manager* (first introduced in Chapter 3, "Oracle8i Enterprise Manager and Other Tools").

Figure 6.2 shows a new user being created in Security Manager. In Exercise 6.1, you create a new user yourself.

FIGURE 6.2 Creating a new user with Security Manager

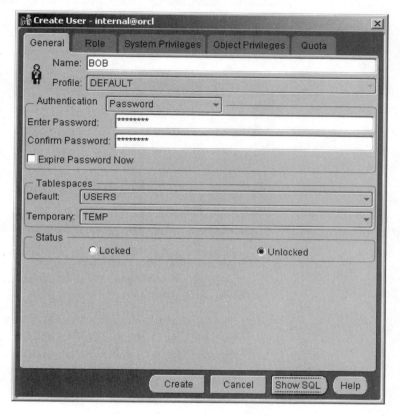

 For instructions on how to install and configure Oracle Enterprise Manager and Security Manager, see Chapter 3, "Oracle8i Enterprise Manager and Other Tools."

EXERCISE 6.1

Creating New Users

1. Start Security Manager from Tools ➢ Database Applications ➢ Oracle Security Manager in Oracle Enterprise Manager.

2. Connect to the ORCL database (or any other test database) using a user account that has System DBA rights (such as the Internal or Sys user accounts).

EXERCISE 6.1 *(continued)*

3. Click the + symbol to open the database.

4. Click the + symbol to open the Users folder.

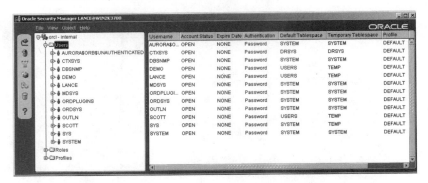

5. Right-click the Users folder, and choose Create; click the Create button (green) on the left pane; or choose Object ➤ Create from the menu, and choose User.

6. Enter Bob for the name and Password for the password, and then select the Users tablespace for his default tablespace and the Temp tablespace for his temporary one (see Figure 6.2).

7. Choose Create to make the new user. The new user should appear in the Users folder.

Many of the administration tools allow you to see the actual SQL code that will be sent to Oracle8i when you choose an action button (e.g., OK, Apply, Create, etc.). To see the code, select the Show SQL button, after which you will see the SQL language that is associated with the action you selected (see Figure 6.3).

FIGURE 6.3   The SQL language associated with creating a new user

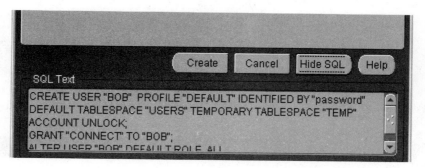

 Examining the SQL code before you apply it can not only help you learn SQL, but can also serve to double-check exactly what will take place when you click the Create button.

Assigning Tablespaces to Users

Every user needs both a default tablespace and a temporary tablespace assigned to them. If you don't specify a default or temporary tablespace, the System tablespace will be designated.

 Allowing the System tablespace to be used by normal users is usually a bad idea, as the System tablespace should be reserved for just System tables and objects. You certainly don't want to run out of space in the System tablespace because someone created a large temporary table!

When a user creates a database object, it will be created in the default tablespace, unless specified otherwise. You may wish to create unique tablespaces for various applications that are a part of a particular database. Tablespaces are discussed in more detail in Chapter 7, "Installing and Managing Applications."

Default and temporary tablespaces can be either assigned when a user is initially created or changed afterwards. To change the default tablespace of a user, open Security Manager, and then go to the General tab of a user (see Figure 6.4). Select the new default tablespace for the user, and choose Apply.

FIGURE 6.4 Changing default tablespaces

In Exercise 6.2, you change the tablespace of a user.

EXERCISE 6.2

Changing Tablespace Assignments of a User

1. Start Security Manager if it is not already started.

2. Open the Database folder by clicking the + key.

3. Open the Users folder by clicking the + key.

4. Click the folder for the user Bob (created in Exercise 6.1).

5. Go down to the Tablespaces section, and click the old tablespace assignment (in the Default section) to get a list of all potential tablespaces (see Figure 6.4).

6. Assign the Users tablespace as the default tablespace.

7. Go to the Temporary section, and select the Temp tablespace.

8. Select Apply to save your changes.

The SQL syntax to change Bob's default tablespace to App1 and his temporary tablespaces to Temp1 is as follows:

```
Alter User "Bob" Default Tablespace "App1"
        Temporary Tablespace "Temp1";
```

Default tablespaces are for convenience, not for security. Objects can be created in any tablespace the user has enough rights to, not just the assigned tablespace. Tablespaces other than the default can be easily designated when creating objects.

If a user has created objects in the wrong tablespace, simply copy the objects to the correct tablespace and delete them from the wrong tablespace. Objects and how to create and move them are covered in Chapter 7, "Installing and Managing Applications."

Managing Quotas for Users

Quotas allow you to specify who can create how much new material in a particular tablespace. If you want users to be able to create objects or add data to the database, they must have a quota other than "none" (which is the default).
Quotas can be set to the following designations:

None   No space can be used on that tablespace.

Unlimited   No restriction exists on that tablespace.

Value   A quota limit in kilobytes or megabytes exists.

To set quotas, go to the Quotas tab of the Users account in Security Manager, as shown in Figure 6.5.

FIGURE 6.5   Setting quotas for tablespace usage

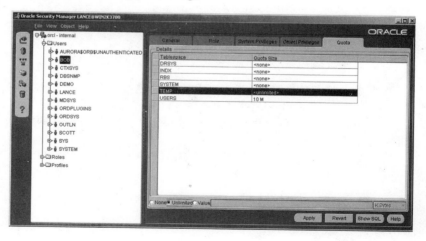

Note that you can specify quotas in kilobytes (K Bytes) or in megabytes (M Bytes). In Exercise 6.3, you set the quota for a user.

EXERCISE 6.3

Setting Quotas on Users

1. Start Security Manager if it is not already started.

2. Open the Database folder by clicking the + key.

3. Open the Users folder by clicking the + key.

4. Click the folder for the user Bob (created in Exercise 6.1).

5. Go to the Quota tab (see Figure 6.5).

6. Click the Users tablespace.

7. Go to the bottom left corner of the Quota screen, and change None to Value.

8. Enter 10 for the value, and change K Bytes to M Bytes.

9. Go to the Temp tablespace, and change None to Unlimited. Your screen should now look similar to Figure 6.5.

10. Click Apply to save your changes.

If a user has been granted the system privilege of Unlimited Tablespace, you cannot create quotas for that user. To create quotas for such a user, you must first remove the Unlimited Tablespace privilege.

The SQL syntax for setting a 10MB limit on Bob for the Users tablespace is as follows:

```
Alter User "Bob" quota 10 M on Users.
```

Database Roles

Managing security for a large number of users can easily be a full-time job if you don't use roles. A database *role* operates very similarly to an operating system group. Any rights assigned to the role automatically apply to all members of the role.

For example, if you have 10 salespeople who all need Select rights to five tables and you give individual rights to the tables, you would have to grant 50 individual rights (10 × 5). Doing this many grants causes problems not only in the initial grants (mistakes are easy to commit), but long-term maintenance is also a burden. Adding another salesperson requires five grants.

The long-term solution is to create and use a role. You should create a role (let's call it Sales_Group), grant rights to the five tables to the role, and then assign the salespeople who need those rights to that role.

Creating Roles

Roles can be created using Security Manager or SQL syntax. When you open Security Manager, you will see a folder called Roles with various system roles in it (see Figure 6.6).

FIGURE 6.6 Oracle database roles

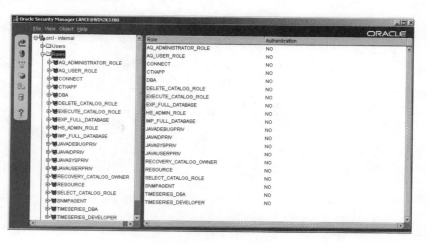

In Exercise 6.4, you create a role called Sales_Group.

EXERCISE 6.4

Creating Oracle Database Roles

1. Start Security Manager if it is not already started.

2. Open the Database folder by clicking the + key.

3. Open the Roles folder by clicking the + key.

4. Right-click the Roles folder, and choose Create; click the Create button (green) on the left pane; or choose Object ➤ Create from the menu, and then choose Role.

5. Enter the name of the new role (Sales_Group).

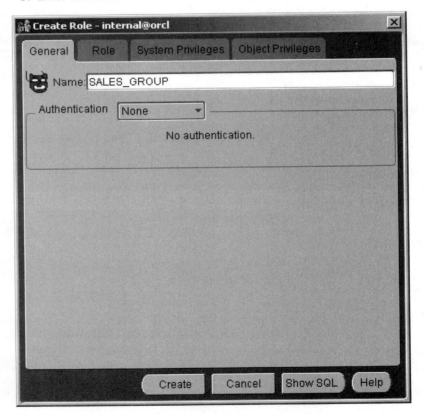

6. Click Create to create the role.

Roles can also be created using SQL syntax. To create a role called Sales_ Managers with SQL syntax, use the following command:

```
Create Role "Sales_Managers" not identified;
```

Granting Privileges and Role Membership to Roles

Once roles are created, they can be assigned system and object privileges just as with a user. You can even assign roles to roles (i.e., nest roles within roles) as long as you don't have circular assignments.

You can assign rights using Security Manager or SQL syntax. If you assign rights with the Admin option, then members of the pertinent role can also assign those right to others (just as with users). In Exercise 6.5, you grant rights to the Sales_Group role.

EXERCISE 6.5

Granting Privileges and Roles to Roles

1. Start Security Manager if it is not already started.

2. Open the Database folder by clicking the + key.

3. Open the Roles folder by clicking the + key.

4. Go down and select the Sales_Group role (created in Exercise 6.4).

5. Go over to the Role tab.

6. Make the Sales_Group role a member of the Connect role (just in case individual Sales users don't have Connect privileges), highlight the Connect role, and click the down arrow.

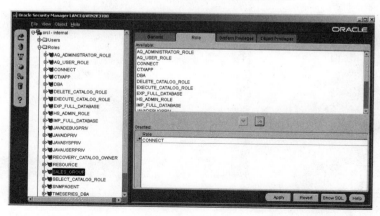

7. Go to the System Privileges tab.

EXERCISE 6.5 *(continued)*

8. Highlight the Create Any View privilege, and click the down arrow to grant that privilege.

9. Allow the Sales_Group to grant the Create Any View privilege to others by clicking the Admin Option setting until it shows a blue checkmark.

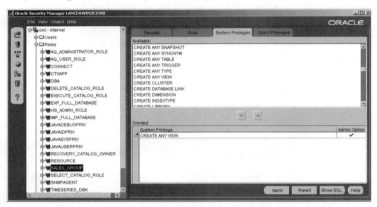

10. Go to the Object Privileges tab.

11. Open the Sys schema on the left of the screen.

12. Open the Views folder.

13. Highlight the All_All_Tables view.

14. Highlight the Select privilege, and click the down arrow.

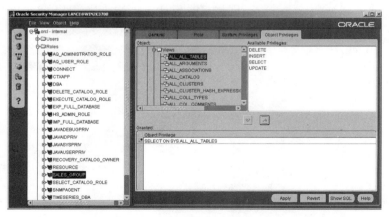

15. Select Apply to save your changes.

Roles can be granted rights using SQL syntax as well. Simply use the name of the role where you would normally use the name of a user in a normal GRANT statement.

Assigning Roles to Users

Once you have created database roles, you can assign users to that role. If the role is created before the user, you can make the assignment when you create the user. You can also easily edit existing users and assign them to roles.

In Exercise 6.6, you assign a user to a role.

EXERCISE 6.6

Assigning Users to Roles

1. Start Security Manager if it is not already started.

2. Open the Database folder by clicking the + key.

3. Open the Users folder by clicking the + key.

4. Click the folder for the user Bob (created in Exercise 6.1).

5. Go to the Role tab.

6. Highlight the Sales_Group role, and click the down arrow.

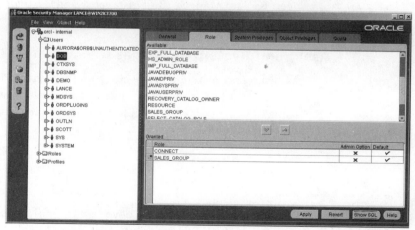

7. Click the Apply button to save your changes.

To assign Bob to the Sales_Group role using SQL, use the following command:

```
Grant "Sales_Group" to "Bob";
```

The two system roles we are most concerned about are the Connect role and the DBA role. The Connect role allows a user to connect to the instance and is required before the user can log in to Oracle. When you create a user using Security Manager, the Connect role is automatically assigned to the user. If you create users using SQL scripts, you must be sure to also assign the Connect role to them. The DBA role grants a user all rights in the database tables and should only be assigned to users who are actually in charge of the database.

System Privileges

System privileges allow you to fine-tune your security of the database so that users can do only what they need to do. Most of the system privileges are beyond the scope of this book; however, the two system privileges we are most concerned about are the following:

- System DBA
- System DBO

The System DBA role allows a user full rights in the instance. The user can use all of the administration tools, such as Security Manager, Storage Manager, Backup Manager, and Instance Manager, to do such things as stop and start an instance and back up and restore databases.

Assigning System Privileges

You can assign system privileges from the System Privilege tab of the Properties dialog box for users or roles. You can also grant system privileges by using SQL syntax. For example, to grant Sysdba privileges to Bob, run the following command:

```
Grant SYSDBA to "Bob";
```

The INIT<SID>.ORA file must have remote_login_passwordfile = exclusive (instead of shared) in order for you to grant Sysdba privileges to users other than the Sys user.

When Not to Assign System Privileges

Because anyone with Sysop or Sysdba privileges can affect the entire instance and not just a particular set of tables, you should grant these high-level system privileges sparingly. For example, you may have a database that supports a salesperson contact application, which is managed by Sue. The database may also support a human resources application, which is managed by Katie. If you grant both Sue and Katie Sysdba privileges, they would be able to affect data-files, tablespaces, and other items in each other's application, which may not be what you want.

If, for some reason or another, Katie needs Sysdba rights as part of the application maintenance, you may want to move Sue's application to another database and instance.

Object Permissions

Object permissions generally allow users to manipulate data that a database object controls. For example, to view the information in a table, you must first have *SELECT permission* on that table. If you want to run a stored procedure, you must first have *EXECUTE permission* on that stored procedure. Table 6.2 lists the object permissions and what objects they affect.

TABLE 6.2 Object Permissions

Permission	Performs	Objects Affected
DELETE	Deletes data from an object	Table, View
EXECUTE	Runs a stored procedure	Stored Procedure
INSERT	Adds new data to an object	Table, View
SELECT	Views data in an object	Table, View, Column
UPDATE	Modifies data in an object	Table, View, Column

Although you can grant permissions on columns, it is frowned upon, as any SQL statement that touches that table must check permissions on each column. You should create a view on the required columns and then assign permissions to that view. This way, permissions are checked only once on the entire view rather than on each column.

When a database user creates an object, she becomes an object owner and is automatically granted all object permissions (see Table 6.2) on that object. All other users (including Sysdba) are denied any permissions on that object unless the owner grants permissions to them.

In order for users to be able to give their rights to another user, they must have been given their rights with the With Grant option if using SQL syntax or the With Admin option if using Security Manager.

Profiles

Profiles allow you to set many items for more that one user at a time. A user will use the default profile if you don't specify one. Profiles hold settings such as limits on CPU time, connect time, concurrent sessions, and the size of a session. Passwords can also be controlled by defining advanced characteristics using profiles. Password expirations, history, complexity, and lockouts can also be set using profiles.

Creating and Editing Profiles

You can edit the existing profile (called Default) or you can create new profiles. New profiles can be created with Security Manager or SQL syntax. In Exercise 6.7, you create a new profile and edit some of its properties.

EXERCISE 6.7

Creating and Editing Profiles

1. Start Security Manager.

2. Open the Profiles folder.

3. Create a new profile by right-clicking and choosing Create; clicking the Create button (green) on the left pane; or choosing Object ≻ Create from the menu, and then choosing Profile.

4. Enter the profile name (Sales, in our case).

5. Leave the General tab settings at their default settings, and go to the Password tab.

6. Check the box next to Expire Password, then change the password's term of expiration to 30 days and the number of days after which the password will be locked to 3 days after expiration.

7. Check the box next to Keep Password History, then specify that an unlimited number of passwords are to be kept for 30 days.

8. Check the Enforce Password Complexity box, and leave the Complexity Function at its default.

9. Check Lock Account on Failed Logon, and set it so that after 10 bad attempts the account will be locked for one day.

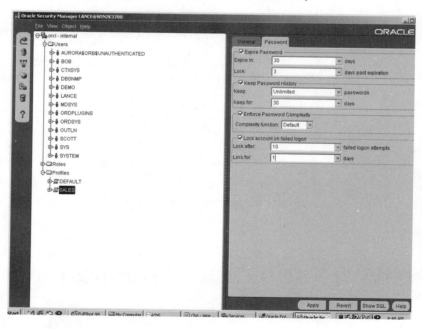

10. Choose Apply to save the profile.

Assigning Profiles

Assigning profiles to users is fairly simple. In Security Manager, simply go to the General tab of a user and select the new profile.

In Exercise 6.8, you assign the Sales profile to Bob.

EXERCISE 6.8

Assigning Profiles to Users

1. Start Security Manager.

2. Open the Users folder.

3. Click the folder for the user Bob.

4. On the General tab, pick Sales as the profile for Bob.

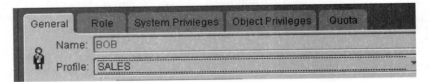

5. Select Apply to save your changes.

You can also use SQL to change a user's profile. The command to set Bob to use the Sales profile is as follows:

```
Alter User "Bob" Profile "Sales"
```

Don't forget that data (i.e. Bob and Sales) are case sensitive. If you put in BOB, this SQL statement would not work.

NetWare and Oracle Integration

NetWare users and groups can be linked to Oracle users and groups. Linking users or groups allows you to connect to Oracle without a password and to manage your Oracle accounts and rights from NetWare's NDS Administrator.

In order to integrate the two systems, there are several steps you must take. You must ensure that the following steps are taken:

- SQLNET.ORA must contain `sqlnet.authentication_services =` `(NDS)` on both the client and the server.

- Users or roles in Oracle must be set to External.

- An NDS Oracle Instance object must be created.

- Properties of the Oracle Instance object must be configured.

After you edit the SQLNET.ORA files on the client and server, you may need to restart the computers to have it take effect. Note that on NetWare clients the parameter may already be set.

Oracle also creates a default group in NDS called Oracle DBA.

Once you create the Oracle Instance object (see Figure 6.7), you can connect to the instance and manage your users by going to the User Configuration button (see Figure 6.8). You can also manage the security of the users by choosing to modify the user's profile and role membership. To log in with an NDS credential, simply use a forward slash (/) for the user name and leave the password blank, although you will still have to specify a service.

FIGURE 6.7   Creating an Oracle Instance NDS object

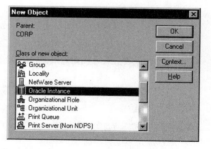

FIGURE 6.8   Properties of an Oracle Instance object

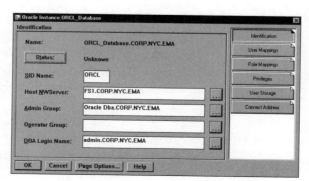

NT and Oracle Integration

Just as with NetWare servers, Windows NT users and groups can be linked to Oracle user accounts. To set up Windows and NT integration, you must set the server and the client to SQLNET.ORA, which must contain `sqlnet.authentication_services = (NTS)`.

Once the authentication services have been set to NTS, Windows NT global groups and users can then be brought over to Oracle as "external" type users, which means that they are defined and controlled outside of Oracle.

In general, unless the operating system administrator and the database administrator work well together, using "external" users instead of normal users is not recommended.

Unix and Oracle Integration

Oracle also supports integration with Kerberos and Radius, as well as SecurID, CyberSafe, and Identix. Installing Kerberos or Radius support on Unix and Oracle is beyond the scope of this book.

If you want to use just the regular Oracle user name and password to connect to Oracle, change the setting to `sqlnet.authentication_services=(NONE)`.

Summary

In this chapter, you learned about the robust security model that has been designed into Oracle. You learned about the default users and their passwords and privileges, as well as how to create new users using Security Manager.

A new user needs a name, password, and default and temporary tablespaces assigned at a minimum. Once a user is created, you can grant additional system or object privileges to them using Security Manager.

Select rights allow users to read data, Insert rights allow users to add new rows of data, Update rights allow users to modify existing data, Delete rights allow users to delete entire rows of data, and Execute rights allow users to run procedures.

If more than a few people need a particular right, you should create a role, assign rights to the role, and put the appropriate people in the role. Roles can contain other roles, as long as there is no circular nesting.

Oracle can integrate with NetWare, Windows NT, and Unix so that users don't have to reenter a name and password in order to connect.

Key Terms

Before you take the exam, make sure you're familiar with the following terms:

DELETE permission

EXECUTE permission

INSERT permission

profile

role

Security Manager

SELECT permission

UPDATE permission

With Grant option

Review Questions

1. You should grant permissions on individual columns in a table, as this is much more efficient than granting permissions on a view. Select the most appropriate option.

   A. True, as long as the columns are small

   B. True, as long as the number of rows is small

   C. True, as long as you only grant the SELECT permission

   D. False

2. What keyword allows a user to grant their rights to others when using SQL syntax?

   A. With Admin

   B. With Grant

   C. With DBA

   D. With Administer

3. When can roles be nested?

   A. Never

   B. Always

   C. Ten levels deep

   D. As long as there are no circular assignments

4. Which of the following can the System DBA (Sysdba rights) do?

   A. Stop and start an Oracle instance

   B. Create new datafiles

   C. Create new tablespaces

   D. Create new users

5. Which of the following can the System DBO do?

    A. Stop and start an Oracle instance

    B. Create new datafiles

    C. Create new tablespaces

    D. Create new users

6. Which right do you need on a procedure to run it?

    A. Select

    B. Update

    C. Insert

    D. Execute

7. What is the default password for the SYS user?

    A. manager

    B. change_on_install

    C. sys

    D. oracle

8. What is the default password for the Internal user?

    A. Manager

    B. Change_on_install

    C. SYS

    D. Oracle (or the password created on installation)

9. What is the default password for the SYSTEM user?

    A. Manager

    B. Change_on_install

    C. SYS

    D. Oracle

10. Which of these accounts has Sysdba privileges by default?

    A. SYS

    B. System

    C. Demo

    D. Scott

11. Which of the following statements is false?

    A. The owner of an object has all rights on an object.

    B. If you are not the owner of an object, all rights have to be granted from the owner.

    C. Once rights are granted to a user, the user can immediately grant those rights to another user.

    D. Once rights are granted to a user, the user can grant those rights to another user only if they have been given the appropriate right.

12. Which of the following commands would create the new user Bob?

    A. `NEW USER "Bob" ...`

    B. `ALTER USER "Bob" ...`

    C. `CREATE USER "Bob"...`

    D. `ADD USER "Bob" ...`

13. Which of the following commands would modify Bob's existing user account?

    A. `SWITCH USER "Bob" ...`

    B. `ALTER USER "Bob" ...`

    C. `CREATE USER "Bob"...`

    D. `CHANGE USER "Bob" ...`

14. If you don't specify default tablespaces for a user when you create one, what will happen?

    A. The user will not be created.

    B. The System tablespace will be set as the default.

    C. The User tablespace will be set as the default.

    D. They won't have a default tablespace assigned to them.

15. What command will make Bob a Sysdba?

    A. `ALTER SYSDBA TO "Bob";`

    B. `PUT "Bob" IN SYSDBA;`

    C. `GRANT "Bob" IN SYSDBA;`

    D. `GRANT SYSDBA TO "Bob";`

16. What can you assign to users to set default password lengths?

    A. Roles

    B. Profiles

    C. Security settings

    D. System privileges

17. How many profiles can a user have assigned to them at any given time?

    A. One

    B. Two

    C. Four

    D. Unlimited

18. Which of the following rights allow you to read data?

    A. Read

    B. Select

    C. Update

    D. Execute

19. Which of the following rights allow you to modify data?

    A. Read

    B. Select

    C. Update

    D. Execute

20. Which of the following rights allow you to delete entire rows of data?

    A. Delete

    B. Purge

    C. Discard

    D. Drop

Answers to Review Questions

1. D. Granting rights to individual columns is almost never a better solution than creating a view and granting appropriate rights to the view.

2. B. The With Grant option allows users to grant their rights to others when using SQL syntax.

3. D. You cannot have circular assignments when nesting roles.

4. A, B, C, D. A System DBA can do basically anything in Oracle.

5. A, D. A System DBO can manage an existing instance, including stopping and starting it, as well as manage users.

6. D. The Execute right is needed to run procedures.

7. B. The default password for the SYS user is change_on_install.

8. D. The default password for the Internal user is Oracle or whatever password that was entered during the original installation.

9. A. The default password for the SYSTEM user is manager.

10. A. Only the SYS account has Sysdba privileges by default.

11. C. Users must be granted special permission to grant their rights to others before they can do so.

12. C. The CREATE USER command is used to create new users.

13. B. The ALTER USER command is used to modify existing users.

14. B. The System tablespace is the default tablespace unless you specify one for the user.

15. D. The GRANT SYSDBA TO X command is used to give Sysdba privileges.

16. B. Profiles are used to set password properties.

17. A. A user can have only one profile assigned to them at any one time.

18. B. The Select right allows you to see data.

19. C. The Update right allows you to modify data.

20. A. The Delete right allows you to delete entire rows of data.

Chapter

7

Installing and Managing Applications

ORACLE8i DBO EXAM OBJECTIVES OFFERED IN THIS CHAPTER:

✓ **How to Create Objects to Store Application Data**

- Use SQL*Worksheet to run scripts that create the objects of an application
- Use Oracle Schema Manager to list the objects created by each schema for the applications
- Use Storage Manager to control the space used by the objects in the database

✓ **How to Implement the Logical and Physical Structure for New Applications**

- Define the components of an application in an Oracle database
- Create the logical and physical structure to set up a new application
- Use Storage Manager to manage the applications
- Define the use of tablespaces
- Create and manage rollback segments

Exam objectives are subject to change at any time without prior notice and at Oracle's sole discretion. Please visit Oracle's Training and Certification Web site (http://education.oracle.com/certification/index.html) for the most current exam objectives listing.

he major reason people install an Oracle server is to support some type of application. An *application* consists of one or more tables of data and usually other objects as well, including views, procedures, synonyms, and indexes. Every object in an Oracle database has an owner, which is the user account that was connected to the instance when the object was made. The owner of an object has all rights on the object—in fact, the owner of the object is the only one who initially has rights to the object, and it's the owner who must grant rights to the other users in the database.

In this chapter, we will look at some application database design issues, as well as how to prepare the Oracle database for a new application. We will then cover issues that pertain to choosing and creating the user account that owns the application. We will also look at creating various database objects and how to best secure the new application. Although we have covered Security, Storage, and Schema Managers before, we will go over how to use these utilities to manage an application.

Although there are literally thousands of different applications that run on an Oracle database server, there are some basic steps you should follow in order to help ensure a smooth installation and implementation. The basic steps to installing an application on an Oracle server include the following:

- Designing or acquiring a database design

- Ensuring adequate resources

- Creating and managing a tablespace for the application

- Setting up a schema account

- Creating and managing database objects

- Planning, implementing, and managing database security

You can use graphical tools for your implementation of the application. Enterprise Manager can do the basic functions of Storage Manager, Schema Manager, Instance Manager, and Security Manager. We will use the individual tools (instead of Enterprise Manager) because of the advanced tools and viewing options that these individual tools make available.

Designing or Acquiring a Database Design

Although many database operators won't have anything to do with the application database design, there are several basic terms and principles that need to be learned in order to be a successful database operator.

Bad database design is a common performance problem. As an Oracle operator, if you are using a prepackaged application, you will probably not have any input into the logical design of the database, although you will probably have control over the physical placement of the application.

About the only way you can overcome a bad logical database design is by throwing more hardware at it. Take, for instance, a database implementation of a third-party application where a four-CPU server is required for a relatively small database because of the overuse of indexes (there are 14 multiple-column indexes on the main OLTP table). The old saying "Garbage in, garbage out" applies to database designs, as database operators over bad databases all know. There is nothing as frustrating as being in charge of a poorly designed and implemented database.

There are several principles of logical database design that you should understand to better realize exactly how a database works.

Logical Database Design

Logical database design deals with designing the tables, columns, rows, indexes, views, and other objects used to support the application. There are many books available on database design and programming, which are beyond the scope of the Oracle Internet database operator certification exam and this book. A good database designer and programmer is an invaluable part of the database team. Nonetheless, there are several cornerstones of database design, including primary keys, foreign keys, indexes, and views, that you should know about.

Putting a limitation or restriction on data can be done using various methods, including constraints, which Oracle uses to enforce column and row restrictions, triggers, which are used to enforce business logic, and client application coding, which can check data for errors before it is sent to Oracle. Most database applications use a combination of these methods to be as efficient as possible.

Primary Keys

Relational data is organized into tables, which each hold data about a single type of object. For example, in a database designed to track online orders, you would probably have a table for customers, one for products, one for orders, and one for order details.

A *primary key* is a column on a table used to track a row. Primary keys must be unique in that no duplicate or NULL values are allowed.

The primary key column should be chosen on an existing attribute guaranteed to be unique (such as e-mail addresses or part numbers). If no existing column exists, a new column should be generated (such as customer_id or Book_id) (see Figure 7.1).

FIGURE 7.1 Primary keys in an Order Entry database

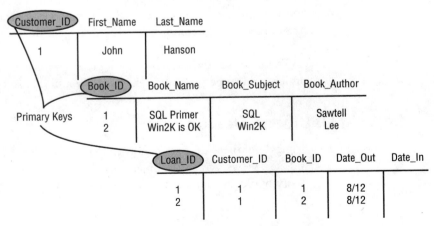

Although most tables will have a primary key, it is not required. For example, you may have a table that contains the two-letter abbreviation for states, as well as the entire state name for use in reporting. Because the table is small and you can guarantee there are no duplicates, a primary key is not necessary.

Primary keys are not only useful for keeping data clean and consistent in the table in which they reside, they are also useful for guaranteeing the consistency of data in other tables by means of a foreign key.

Foreign Keys

A *foreign key* is used for referential integrity and points to an existing primary key. For example, the Loan table should have a field for the customer and that field should have a foreign key constraint that points to the primary key of the Customer table (see Figure 7.2).

FIGURE 7.2   Foreign keys in an Order Entry database

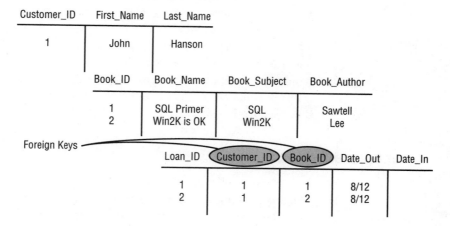

Foreign keys work by ensuring that there is a matching entry in the primary key field of another table. For example, if your customers only went up to number 700, and you tried to enter customer 701 into the Foreign Key field, an error would be generated.

Indexes

Indexes are objects used to greatly speed up data retrieval. Without indexes, data is stored in natural order, in other words, the order in which it is entered. When you need to find a row without any indexes, Oracle has to look at every row in order to find matches.

Indexes on a database work much like a phone book; they organize the data so that searches don't have to examine every row. Indexes can be very simple or can get very complex. Complex indexes are beyond the scope of this book, but planning and creating basic indexes are covered later in this chapter.

Creating appropriate indexes is key to fast data retrievals. You should create indexes on columns that get searched; don't create indexes that won't get used.

Views

A view is a subset of columns in a database. Views can contain columns from one or more tables and can also be restricted by any column criteria (such as SALARY > 50,000). A view does not contain a copy of the data, but is basically a stored SELECT statement. Views are handy for organizing complex data, allowing you to easily run the same query over and over again, and providing a simple security method.

Once a view is created, data is selected from the view just as it would be from the table. The security advantage is that columns not listed in the original view definition won't be seen by anyone using the view.

For example, you may have a table that contains employee information along with salaries. If you hire a temp to make changes to the address columns, you wouldn't want the temp to also see the salary column. By creating a view that does not contain the salary column, you can limit the temp to just the columns they need to change.

Instance Parameters

A database application may require changes to the Instance Parameter file. The most common change is increasing the size of the System Global Area (SGA), which is the amount of RAM used. You may also need to increase the number and size of various buffers, and even change the way the redo log is archived. Remember that instance parameters affect every application running in a particular database. If certain applications need conflicting parameters, the best solution would be to run separate instances.

The schema owner will not have enough rights to make parameter changes, unless they are also the system database administrator (System DBA). Coordinating requests to the System DBA from various application owners should be done in a formal method so that problems can be avoided.

Physical Database Design

Once you get the logical database design, you can start on the physical design, which deals with what files go where, and which tables go on what files.

Chapter 5, "Creating and Managing Databases," goes into detail on fault tolerance and performance issues when designing the physical structure of a database, but the main issues to keep in mind for the majority of sites are how to eliminate bottlenecks and contention for resources while maintaining fault tolerance (while also staying on budget).

Oracle really doesn't care where you place your physical files, but for clarity's sake you should probably install each database application on a different set of files. Tablespaces are the method you use to do this. Creating and managing tablespaces is covered later in the chapter.

Ensuring Adequate Resources

Once the logical and physical designs are done, you need to evaluate whether or not your existing resources are adequate for the new application. If you are buying a third-party application, the application should come with recommended hardware and software requirements.

Appendix B, "Performance and Tuning," goes into more detail on tuning an Oracle database and getting the most out of existing resources.

The major areas for which you need to ensure that adequate hardware resources exist are as follows:

- Hard drive space

- RAM

- CPU speed and number

- Network bandwidth

Hard drive space is relatively easy to forecast if you know the size and number of rows in the application. For example, if you anticipate 100,000 rows and your rows are 500 bytes long, the table will take 50,000,000 bytes, or 50MB of space. Simply add up the sizes of all the tables and make sure your server has enough room. You also need to ensure adequate redo logs and rollback segments. Redo logs are heavily dependent on the type of application you use, as are rollback segments. Sizing and increasing these is covered in Appendix B, "Performance and Tuning."

The amount of RAM is harder to estimate, but more is always better. Appendix B, "Performance and Tuning," covers various tuning tools you can use to determine if you have adequate RAM.

CPU speed and number for optimal performance can also be determined using tools covered in Appendix B, "Performance and Tuning."

Network bandwidth can be a bottleneck, especially if your servers are on 10Mbps or you have slow WAN connections. You can use various tools covered in Appendix B, "Performance and Tuning," as well as network monitoring tools in order to determine if your network is a bottleneck.

You should also realize that a database is an ever-changing application and that a resource that was adequate yesterday can easily become a bottleneck tomorrow. Monitoring and tuning a database is a constant operation.

Creating and Managing a Tablespace

A tablespace is a group of one or more system files where Oracle data will reside. Objects must be created on a tablespace. There must be at least a System tablespace when a database is created.

Normally, you want to have the application data stored on a different tablespace than the system tablespace.

You can create new tablespaces using SQL syntax or Storage Manager. In Exercise 7.1, you create two tablespaces, one using SQL syntax and one using Storage Manager.

EXERCISE 7.1

Creating New Tablespaces

1. To create a tablespace called payroll_app from SQL syntax, start the SQLPlus Worksheet application, using a Sysdba user to connect to the ORCL instance.

2. Enter the command CREATE TABLESPACE "PAYROLL_APP" DATAFILE 'd:\oracle\oradata\payroll.dbf' SIZE 10M AUTOEXTEND ON NEXT 500K MAXSIZE UNLIMITED.

3. To create a tablespace using Storage Manager, start Enterprise Manager and connect to the ORCL instance.

4. Start Storage Manager from the Tools ➤ Database Applications menu.

5. Highlight the Tablespace folder, right-click, and choose Create.

6. Enter Sales_app for the name.

7. Select the Add button to add a datafile to the tablespace.

8. Enter sales_app.dbf for the name, and make it 10MB in size.

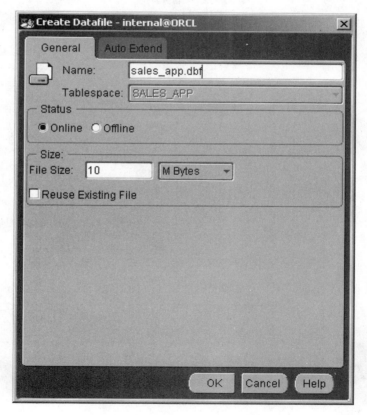

9. Go to the Auto Extend tab.

10. Set the datafile to extend 500KB as needed with unlimited space.

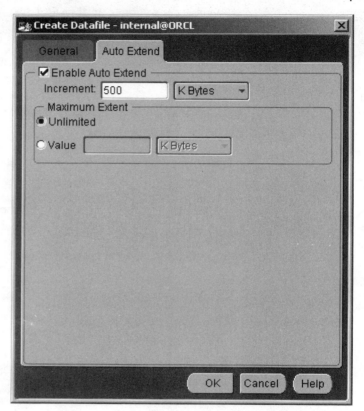

11. Choose OK, then Create, and then OK when it is successfully created.

Creating and managing tablespaces and datafiles is covered in more detail in Chapter 5, "Creating and Managing Databases."

Creating a Schema Account

A *schema account* is simply a user account that owns one or more objects in the database. You can have a single schema account for every application in the database or many separate accounts—one for each application.

Since an application must have someone who owns the objects in the application, your major decision is whether to use the same user account for all applications or to create a separate account for each application.

The main advantage of using the same account is ease of administration, especially when the same person is in charge of all the applications. The disadvantage is that if different people are using the same account, it is virtually impossible to secure the applications from the other administrators.

The advantages of using separate schema accounts, one for each application, is that you can have different people managing different applications on the same server, and they cannot interfere with each other. The disadvantage is that there is more work for the system operator, as separate accounts must be set up and managed.

When different people manage different applications on the same server, creating separate schema accounts should always be done. Using different schema accounts for different applications allows you to delegate management in the future, even if the same person is currently in charge of both applications.

Database Accounts and Schemas

As covered previously, there are basically three types of user accounts in Oracle. They are as follows:

- System DBA and System DBO
- Schema accounts (object owners)
- Users

The System DBA and System DBO have special privileges that extend to the entire database (all applications) and include the ability to stop and start the database, as well as perform backups and restores. Object owners are users who own some type of object in the database. The most common sort of object owner is one who owns a common set of tables, indexes, views, and other objects that are all tied into a single application. All objects must have an owner, which is usually the user account that was used to create the object.

For ease of administration, a unique user account should be created for the sole purpose of creating application objects. This user then becomes the schema for that particular set of objects. For example, the Sales application may require 10 tables, 20 indexes, 30 views, and 40 procedures. For best practices, you should first connect as the SYS or Internal user and create a user such as sales_owner and provide appropriate privileges. You would then connect as sales_owner and run the sales application database creation scripts. For the Sales application, the user used to run the initial database creation script would be the owner of the Sales application in Oracle.

You should use a generic account, such as sales_owner instead of a particular user (such as Linda), in case the original person leaves the company. In this example, if Linda was the schema user, you couldn't delete her account when she left the company without all of her objects being deleted too.

Creating and Managing Schema Accounts

As was shown in Chapter 6, "Oracle Users and Security," creating accounts is relatively straightforward. You can create an account using a tool such as SQLPlus Worksheet and SQL syntax, or you can use the graphical tool Security Manager. In Exercise 7.2, you create accounts using both SQL syntax and Security Manager.

EXERCISE 7.2

Creating a Schema Account

1. To create an account using syntax, start SQLPlus Worksheet and connect to the ORCL instance with a Sysdba account.

2. Enter the following commands:

   ```
   CREATE USER "PAYROLL_OWNER"

   IDENTIFIED BY "password"

   DEFAULT TABLESPACE "PAYROLL_APP"

   TEMPORARY TABLESPACE "TEMP";

   GRANT "CONNECT" TO "PAYROLL_OWNER";

   GRANT "DBA" TO "PAYROLL_OWNER";
   ```

3. Choose the Execute button (or F5). The account should be created.

4. Start Security Manager to create an account using graphical tools.

5. Create an account called Sales_owner with a password of password.

6. Make sure to assign the user to the Sales_app tablespace, and grant them the connect and DBA rights.

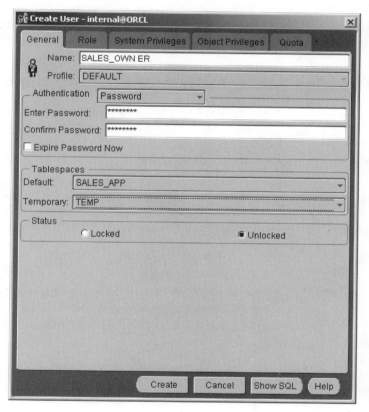

7. Choose Create to make the user.

Creating and Managing Database Objects

Once the tablespace and application owners are created, you can begin to create the various database objects. Most of the time, installing a third-party application will automatically create all of the objects for you. You may need to modify objects or create new ones, however, even in third-party applications. An example of that would be a new view you create that lets a manager easily query certain tables.

If you designed the application yourself, you will need to create all of the objects by hand, unless you are using some sort of database design program that will create the objects after you have designed them.

Creating Schemas Using SQL Syntax and Schema Manager

A *schema* is a group of one or more objects owned by the same user. In our example, once the payroll_owner makes some objects, there will be a schema called payroll_owner. In order to create new schemas, simply connect as the newly created schema owner and make some objects using Schema Manager (or SQLPlus Worksheet).

You can use *Schema Manager* to manage schemas, as well as create, modify, and delete objects. The most common types of objects are tables, indexes, views, procedures, and synonyms, all of which you will learn how to create.

SQLPlus Worksheet lets you input SQL syntax or run scripts provided by third-party vendors, while Schema Manager is a graphical tool that lets you easily see the schemas that have been created. You can create objects from either tool—it just depends on whether you like syntax or graphical utilities.

Creating Tables

Since data is stored in tables, you will need to have at least one table for your application. *Tables* consist of a name for the table itself, as well as names and characteristics for each of the columns. Creating tables is relatively easy—you should spend the majority of the time in planning the tables, columns, primary keys, and foreign keys.

If you have foreign keys, make the tables that contain the primary keys before you make those with the foreign keys.

You can create tables using SQL syntax or Schema Manager. In Exercise 7.3, you create tables using both methods.

EXERCISE 7.3

Creating Tables

1. Start SQLPlus Worksheet, and connect as the sales_owner account to the ORCL instance.

2. Run the following command:

```
CREATE TABLE "SALES_OWNER"."CUSTOMERS" ("CID" NUMBER,
       "FNAME" VARCHAR2(30), "LNAME" VARCHAR2(30),
       "ADDRESS1" VARCHAR2(30), "ADDRESS2" VARCHAR2(30),
       "CITY" VARCHAR2(20), "STATE" VARCHAR2(10),
       "COUNTRY" VARCHAR2(20), "ZIP" VARCHAR2(15),
       CONSTRAINT "PKEYCID" PRIMARY KEY("CID"));
```

3. Start Schema Manager.

4. Open the Tables folder. You should see the Customers table.

5. Create a new table by right-clicking Sales_owner and choosing Create.

EXERCISE 7.3 *(continued)*

6. Create a new table called Orders with the columns OID (number), CID (number), Date_of_order (date), and Salesperson (varchar2,30). Don't choose Create yet.

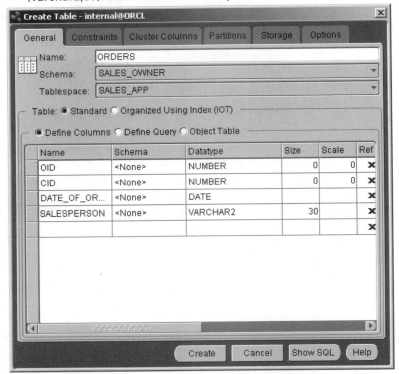

7. Go to the Constraints tab.

8. Add a primary key constraint called Pkeyoid to the OID column.

EXERCISE 7.3 *(continued)*

9. Add a foreign key constraint called Fkeycid to the CID column that references the CID column of the Customers table, then choose Create.

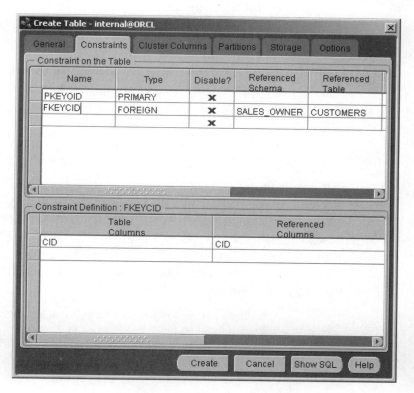

10. Select OK after the table is created successfully.

Creating Indexes

Indexes are used for fast data retrieval. You want enough indexes to help in searches, but because maintaining indexes requires overhead on the Oracle server, you don't want too many indexes. Creating indexes is relatively easy using Schema Manager. Just as with tables, the majority of your time should be spent on planning indexes. Appendix B, "Performance and Tuning," covers tools you can use to see which indexes are being used, as well as tools that can help you decide when more indexes may be of use. In Exercise 7.4, you create indexes using SQL syntax, as well as Schema Manager.

EXERCISE 7.4

Creating Indexes

1. To create an index using SQL syntax, start SQLPlus Worksheet and connect using the sales_owner account.

2. To create an index called index_names based on the last and first name columns of the Customers table, enter the following command:

```
CREATE INDEX "SALES_OWNER"."INDEX_NAMES"

     ON "SALES_OWNER"."CUSTOMERS"

     ("LNAME", "FNAME") TABLESPACE "SALES_APP";
```

3. To use Schema Manager to create an index called index_sales based on the salesperson column of the Sales table, start the utility and go to the Indexes folder. Right-click, and choose **Create**.

4. Enter Index_sales for the name.

5. Choose sales_owner for the schema and sales_app for the tablespace.

6. Choose the Orders table from the sales_owner schema.

7. Click the Salesperson row so that a *1* appears.

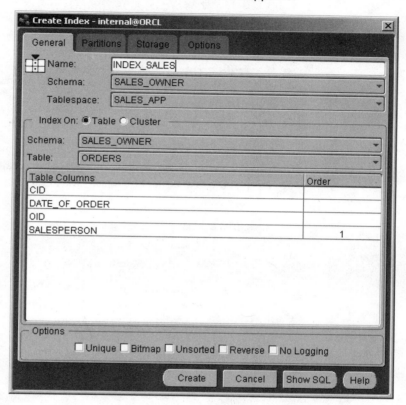

8. Choose Create to make the index.

9. Choose OK after the index is successfully created.

Creating Views

A *view* is a stored SQL query. Views can contain columns from one or more tables and are very useful when the same query is run over and over. Views are also useful for hiding columns of tables, because when you use a view, you only see the columns designated for the view, not all of the columns in the table. In Exercise 7.5, you create views using SQL syntax and Schema Manager.

Some people mistakenly think views contain copies of the data. The actual data only resides in tables. Views are simply stored queries that access the data from the tables when run.

EXERCISE 7.5

Creating Views

1. Start SQLPlus Worksheet, and connect to the ORCL instance as the sales_owner account.

2. To create a view on the Customers table called view1 that shows just the last name, first name, and state of the customers, enter the following command:

```
CREATE VIEW "SALES_OWNER"."VIEW1" AS

    SELECT LNAME, FNAME, STATE
    FROM SALES_OWNER.CUSTOMERS;
```

3. To use Schema Manager to create a view called view2 that shows the salesperson, date of order, and order id from the Sales table, go to the Index folder, right-click, and choose Create.

4. Enter View2 for the name, choose sales_owner for the schema, and enter "select salesperson, date_of_order, oid from sales_owner.orders" for the code.

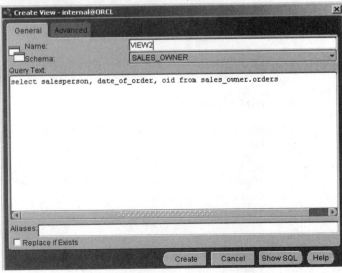

5. Choose Create to make the view.

6. Select OK after the view is made successfully.

Creating Procedures

Procedures are SQL codes that have been grouped together, given a name, and stored as part of the database. Advantages to using procedures include speed, consistency, and ease of use.

Procedures are precompiled, which means they run faster than raw SQL code. They also make the network faster since just the name of the procedure is sent across the network instead of potentially hundreds of lines of code. Procedures can be used by anyone who has rights to the procedure, which makes running the same queries from different programs and different computers much easier. Procedures can be given names that describe their function, which makes using them much easier to remember and use. In Exercise 7.6, you create procedures using SQL syntax and Schema Manager.

EXERCISE 7.6

Creating Procedures

1. To create a procedure called proc1 that updates the database for the salesperson who gets credit for the order, start SQLPlus Worksheet and connect to the ORCL instance with the sales_owner account.

2. Run the following command:

```
CREATE OR REPLACE PROCEDURE "SALES_OWNER"."PROC1"

        (p_salesperson in char)
           p_oid in number)

           as
        begin
        update orders set salesperson=p_salesprerson
        where p_oid=old;

        commit;
        end proc1;
```

3. To create a procedure using graphical tools, start Schema Manager.

4. Highlight the Procedures folder, right-click, and choose Create.

5. Make sure the sales_owner schema is selected.

6. Enter Proc2 for the name, choose sales_owner for the schema. In the window, enter the following code:

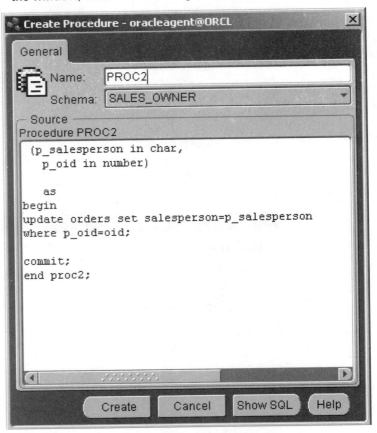

7. Choose Create and then OK after the creation.

Creating Synonyms

Object names can get very complex, especially if a formal naming convention is used and you have many applications in the same database. A *synonym* is a simple name you can use to point to an object so that you only have to refer to the simple synonym name instead of the original object name.

Synonyms can be created using SQL syntax or the graphical tool Schema Manager. In Exercise 7.7, you create two synonyms, one for each table in the sales_owner schema.

Creating Synonyms

1. To create a synonym called all_customers that points to the Customers table using SQL syntax, start SQLPlus Worksheet and connect to the ORCL database as the sales_owner account.

2. Enter the following command:

```
CREATE SYNONYM "SALES_OWNER"."ALL_CUSTOMERS"

    FOR "SALES_OWNER"."CUSTOMERS";
```

3. To graphically create a synonym called current_sales that points to the Orders table, start Schema Manager.

4. Go to the Synonyms folder, right-click, and choose Create.

5. Enter current_sales for the name, choose sales_owner for the schema, table for the type of object, and then the sales_owner schema and the Orders table.

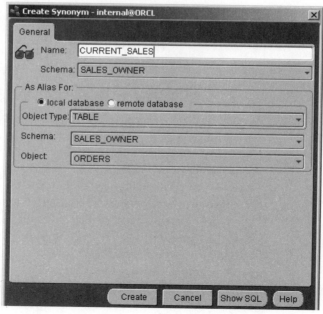

6. Choose Create and then OK after the synonym is created.

Planning, Implementing, and Managing Database Security

Once the new application is installed, you will need to design and maintain the security for the application. Chapter 6, "Oracle Users and Security," covers security basics, including who should have what type of rights and how to grant those rights. To be more specific, users should only have rights to the tables and other objects they need to perform their jobs, and they should have just the minimum rights they need in order to help secure the application.

Spending time on planning application security is vital, as there is a lot more data damaged by users (both innocently and maliciously) than that destroyed by viruses and system failures.

Ensuring Adequate Tablespace Sizing

Creating tablespaces was covered earlier in the chapter. Maintaining tablespaces is also done with Storage Manager. If your tablespaces need more room, you can increase the size of current datafiles or add new datafiles to the tablespace.

Appendix B, "Performance and Tuning," has more details on watching for and fixing tablespaces that are out of room.

Summary

The major reason for installing an Oracle server is to run applications on it. Successfully installing an application involves planning steps, implementation steps, and ongoing maintenance.

Some planning items include purchasing the application or designing it in-house. Even if you purchase the application, you should be aware of the primary and foreign keys in your tables, as well as the major tables, views, and indexes the application uses. If you design and program your own application, you need to be very aware of relational database design and how to use primary and foreign keys to ensure data reliability.

Once the application is purchased, you need to make sure the Oracle server and network have sufficient resources for the application. Remember that the server needs to not only support your current needs, but should be adequate for the foreseeable future.

A separate tablespace should be created for the application, possibly even on a different set of drives than other data. The tablespace should be monitored for space issues and expanded if you start running out of room.

You should create a schema owner, which is a user account that will own all of the objects of the application. Once you create the user, connect to Oracle as that user when you create any and all objects associated with the application.

User accounts may need to be created, if they haven't been already. Once the accounts are created, use the Schema Manager to grant rights to the ordinary users. Remember to grant just those rights that the users need, so that your data isn't unnecessarily at risk.

Ongoing maintenance includes performing backups, checking for adequate storage, and tuning. Backups and tuning are covered in Chapter 10, "Backups and Restorations," and Appendix B, "Performance and Tuning," respectively.

Storage Manager can be used to make sure tablespaces have sufficient room in them for the objects and data of the database.

Key Terms

Before you take the exam, make sure you're familiar with the following terms:

application

foreign key

index

primary key

procedure

schema

schema account

Schema Manager

synonym

table

view

Review Questions

1. Which of the following tools can be used to create a new table? (Select all that apply.)

   A. Object Manager

   B. Enterprise Manager

   C. SQLPlus Worksheet

   D. Schema Manager

2. Which of the following is the correct SQL syntax to use to create a new table?

   A. CREATE TABLE "SALES_OWNER"."CUSTOMERS"
   ```
           ("CID" NUMBER,"FNAME" VARCHAR2(30),
           "LNAME" VARCHAR2(30), );
   ```

   B. CREATE TABLE CALLED "SALES_OWNER"."CUSTOMERS"
   ```
           ("CID" NUMBER, "FNAME" VARCHAR2(30),
           "LNAME" VARCHAR2(30), );
   ```

   C. ADD TABLE "SALES_OWNER"."CUSTOMERS"
   ```
           ("CID" NUMBER,"FNAME" VARCHAR2(30),
           "LNAME" VARCHAR2(30), );
   ```

   D. ADD TABLE CALLED "SALES_OWNER"."CUSTOMERS"
   ```
           ("CID" NUMBER,
           "FNAME" VARCHAR2(30),
           "LNAME" VARCHAR2(30), );
   ```

3. Which of the following objects hold the data inside a database?

   A. Table

   B. View

   C. Procedure

   D. Primary Key

4. Which of the following is the correct SQL syntax to use to create a new view?

A. CREATE VIEW "SALES_OWNER"."VIEW1" AS Select lname, fname, state from sales_owner.customers;

B. CREATE DATA VIEW "SALES_OWNER"."VIEW1" AS Select lname, fname, state from sales_owner.customers;

C. ADD VIEW "SALES_OWNER"."VIEW1" AS Select lname, fname, state from sales_owner.customers;

D. ADD DATA VIEW "SALES_OWNER"."VIEW1" AS Select lname, fname, state from sales_owner.customers;

5. Which of the following tools is used to run third-party scripts?

A. Object Manager

B. Enterprise Manager

C. SQLPlus Worksheet

D. Schema Manager

6. Which of the following is the correct SQL syntax to use to create a new synonym?

A. CREATE SYNONYM "SALES_OWNER"."ALL_CUSTOMERS" EQUALS "SALES_OWNER"."CUSTOMERS";

B. CREATE SYNONYM "SALES_OWNER"."ALL_CUSTOMERS" AS "SALES_OWNER"."CUSTOMERS";

C. CREATE SYNONYM "SALES_OWNER"."ALL_CUSTOMERS" ON "SALES_OWNER"."CUSTOMERS";

D. CREATE SYNONYM "SALES_OWNER"."ALL_CUSTOMERS" FOR "SALES_OWNER"."CUSTOMERS";

7. How many owners can you have for a particular schema?

A. One

B. Two

C. Four

D. Unlimited

8. How do you create a new schema?

    A. Create a new tablespace.

    B. Create a new user.

    C. Have a user create an object.

    D. Create a new datafile in a tablespace.

9. Where will objects in a particular schema be stored by default?

    A. In the SYS tablespace

    B. In the TEMP tablespace

    C. In the USER tablespace

    D. In the default tablespace of the schema account

10. Which of the following best describes a view?

    A. A group of related objects owned by the same account

    B. Objects used to greatly speed up data retrieval

    C. A stored SQL query

    D. A simple name you can use to point to an object so that you only have to refer to the simple name instead of the original object name

11. Which of the following best describes a primary key?

    A. A group of related objects owned by the same account.

    B. A column on a table used to track a row. They must be unique, in that no duplicate or NULL values are allowed.

    C. A primary key is used for referential integrity and usually points to a column in another table.

    D. A simple name you can use to point to an object so that you only have to refer to the simple name instead of the original object name.

12. Which of the following best describes a synonym?

    A. A group of related objects owned by the same account

    B. Objects used to greatly speed up data retrieval

    C. A stored SQL query

    D. A simple name you can use to point to an object so that you only have to refer to the simple name instead of the original object name

13. Which of the following best describes a foreign key?

    A. A group of related objects owned by the same account.

    B. A column on a table used to track a row. They must be unique, in that no duplicate or NULL values are allowed.

    C. A foreign key is used for referential integrity and points to a column in another table.

    D. A simple name you can use to point to an object so that you only have to refer to the simple name instead of the original object name.

14. You have a database that is going to hold three different applications that will be managed by three different departments. How many schema accounts should you create?

    A. None—use the Sysdba account

    B. One

    C. Two

    D. Three

15. Which instance parameter are you most likely to change because of the addition of a new application to a database?

    A. Block size

    B. ARCHIVELOG mode

    C. Name of the database

    D. Size of the SGA

16. Who should be allowed to make changes to the parameter file? (Select all that apply.)

    A. System administrator

    B. System operator

    C. Schema owner

    D. Database user

17. When should you optimize performance of your application?

    A. When you first install the application

    B. After the application has run for a while

    C. When you have performance problems

    D. All of the above

18. What do you call a group of one or more system files where Oracle data will reside?

    A. Index

    B. Table

    C. Tablespace

    D. Redo logs

19. Which user has the most rights over their objects?

    A. System DBA

    B. System DBO

    C. Schema owner

    D. Database users

20. When creating or editing a tablespace, which button allows you to add a new datafile?

    A. Add

    B. New

    C. Create

    D. Edit

Answers to Review Questions

1. B, C, D. There is no such thing as Object Manager, and the other tools can all be used to create and manage objects.

2. A. The CREATE TABLE command is used to create a new table.

3. A. Tables hold the data inside a database.

4. A. The CREATE VIEW command is used to create a new view.

5. C. SQLPlus Worksheet is used to run scripts.

6. D. The CREATE SYNONYM...FOR command creates a new synonym.

7. A. There is only one account labeled as the owner of any particular object, and thus the schema.

8. C. To create a new schema, simply create an object for a user that doesn't already have objects of its own.

9. D. The default tablespace of the schema account is where objects for that schema are stored by default.

10. C. A view is simply a stored SQL query.

11. B. A primary key is used to ensure uniqueness of rows.

12. D. A synonym is a new, usually shorter and simpler name you can use to refer to other objects.

13. C. A foreign key points to a primary key on another column and helps ensure referential integrity.

14. D. Since there are three different applications with different administrators, you should create three different schema accounts.

15. D. The SGA (System Global Area) will probably need to be increased when adding a new application to an existing database.

16. A, B. Although the system administrator and operator should be allowed to make changes to the parameter file, schema owners and plain users shouldn't. They might not understand the ramifications of doing so with respect to other applications running in that database and instance.

17. D. Optimizing performance of the application is appropriate at any time.

18. C. A tablespace is a group of one or more system files where Oracle data will reside.

19. C. The schema user has the most rights over their objects.

20. A. The Add button from within the tablespace editor allows you to add a new datafile to a tablespace.

Chapter

8

Importing and Exporting Data

ORACLE8i DBO EXAM OBJECTIVES OFFERED IN THIS CHAPTER:

✓ **How to Load Non-Oracle Data**

- List the types of constraints of a table
- Disable table constraints by using Schema Manager
- Load data into a table by using Oracle Data Management Tools
- Re-enable constraints after loading data, using Schema Manager
- Automate periodic data loads using Job service

Exam objectives are subject to change at any time without prior notice and at Oracle's sole discretion. Please visit Oracle's Training and Certification Web site (http://education .oracle.com/certification/index.html) for the most current exam objectives listing.

he responsibilities involved in managing your data will be reflected in many different areas of your Oracle Server administration duties. This includes the migration of data from other sources, as well as working with data from your local Oracle Server. There are many different activities that you can perform when it comes to managing data. These include adding new records to a table through the *INSERT statement* or doing a direct load. You can add data from a flat file or move Oracle data to a flat file using the various data manager utilities.

The other major activities that involve your data are backup and restoration, which are covered in detail in Chapter 10, "Backups and Restorations."

In this chapter we will cover the following topics:

- The INSERT statement

- The Data Manager Utility

    - *Exports*

    - *Imports*

    - *Loads*

- Conventional versus direct loads

- Scheduling data jobs

Let's begin by looking at the INSERT statement and how it's used to add data to your Oracle Server.

The INSERT Statement

When you use the INSERT statement, you add a single row of data to your table. There are variations of the INSERT statement that allow you to add multiple rows of data by selecting data from another table. You can also use the SELECT INTO statement to copy data from one location to another.

The INSERT command was introduced in Chapter 4, "Introduction to SQL and PL/SQL."

Before you can use the INSERT statement, you must know a little about the structure of the table you wish to insert data into. You should know the number of columns in the table, the data type of these columns, the column names, and any defaults or *constraints* that are on a particular column. INSERT statements can add one or more rows and are generally logged in the redo log files in case of a crash. Any indexes you have will automatically be updated when the new row is inserted, and you have to have appropriate permissions to INSERT new rows.

To gather this information, you can use the *Schema Manager*, Enterprise Manager, or various procedures. To use Schema Manager (which is probably the easiest way), simply navigate through the console tree to the desired tablespace. Open the tablespace, and the tables will be displayed in the right pane. Highlight the table, and the right pane will show its schema. You are now looking at the table properties. Figure 8.1 shows Scott's tablespace and the EMP table.

FIGURE 8.1   The EMP table of Scott's tablespace

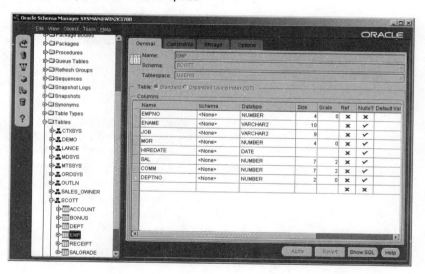

Notice the names, number, and position of the columns. If you go to the Constraints tab, you will notice there is a *primary key constraint* on EMPNO and a foreign constraint that references the department number of the Department table. That means that any new employee you add will have to have a unique employee number and a valid department.

When you are inserting character data, you must enclose the characters in single quotation marks. When you are inserting numeric data, you do not use quotation marks.

You need to specify the employee number, name, job, manager, hire date, salary, commission, and department number when you add a new employee. If a column happens to be blank, you can use quotation marks, " ", as placeholders. You can add a new record to the EMP table by running the code shown in Exercise 8.1.

EXERCISE 8.1

Using the INSERT Statement

1. Open SQLPlus, and connect as Scott with a password of tiger by choosing Start ➤ Program Files ➤ <Oracle_Home> ➤ Application Development ➤ SQL Plus.

2. In the query analyzer, add the following code and run it with the Return key:

```
INSERT into emp values (7986,'MASTERS','Clerk',
7902,sysdate,900,NULL, 20);
```

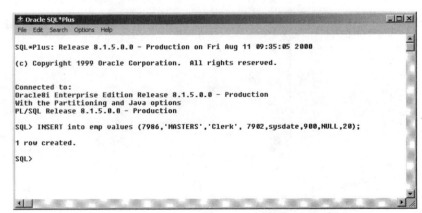

3. This will add a single row to the table. To verify your new row of data, run the following query:

```
SELECT * FROM emp;
```

4. You should now see employee number 7986 in the output list.

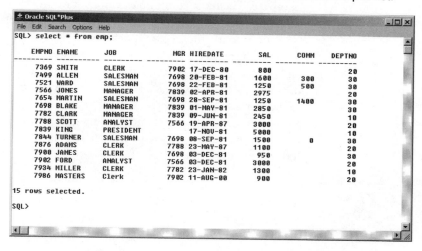

There is much more information about the INSERT statement that could be covered, but it is related much more to the Oracle developer than to the operator. As an operator, you really need to know when it is appropriate to use the INSERT statement to import data versus doing so via Schema Manager, etc.

Remember these facts about the INSERT statement:

- It generally adds a single record at a time.

- The inserted record IS a logged transaction.

- If there is an index, it will be updated as well.

- You must have INSERT permission on the table you wish to add records to.

Data Management Tools

Schema Manager and Enterprise Manager are the utilities that come with Oracle that can import and export data to and from tables. These tools collectively are referred to as the Data Management tools. Schema and Enterprise Managers also support loading of non-Oracle data into an Oracle database. The most common example of non-Oracle data is ASCII data that may have been exported from another type of database.

Import, load, and export functions all have Wizards that help walk you through the process, making data manipulation relatively easy. Imports, loads, and exports can also be scheduled to run on a regular basis. An example would be a weekly load from a *datafile* supplied by a different division.

To import, load, or export data, you need to log in as a user who has enough rights to do the particular function. For example, to import or load data, you must have at least Insert rights, and to export data, you need to have at least Select rights.

Importing and exporting also rely on the *Oracle Intelligent Agent,* which is covered in Chapter 9, "Proactive Management of an Oracle Server." The Agent is in charge of running jobs, and importing and exporting are just a few of the many types of jobs you can create.

To get to the data import and export functions within Enterprise Manager, open the database and then the Schema Objects folder until you get to the tables. Right-click the tables, and a Data Management option will appear. To get to the Data Management option from Schema Manager, open the Tables folder and right-click a table.

Import and export functions in Oracle8 were provided by a separate utility called Data Manager. Data Manager functionality has been included in Schema and Enterprise Manager in Oracle8i.

Exporting Oracle Data

Schema Manager (and Enterprise Manager) can be used as a quick way to copy parts of one database to another by using the export function. You can export the entire database, selected tables, or selected user information. To make copies of the data, simply export one or more tables from the source database to a file, copy the file to the destination Oracle server, and import the data into the destination database.

We will use Schema Manager throughout the rest of the chapter for data exports and imports because it is more focused on data manipulation than is Enterprise Manager.

Because the data is copied and not moved (the data on the source server is not modified in any way), you can revert back to your old copy if there is a problem with the new data.

Schema Manager allows you to not only copy the table schema and data, you can also copy users, groups, and rights to the new database. In Exercise 8.2, you export a database to a file.

EXERCISE 8.2

Exporting Oracle Data

1. Start Schema Manager, and connect to the ORCL database as Scott with a password of tiger (unless you have changed it). If Scott cannot connect and you get an error stating he has no rights to view the data dictionary, he needs additional rights. For this exercise, put him in the DBA role and then reconnect.

2. Go to Tools ➢ Data Management ➢ Export to start the Export Wizard. You should see the Introduction screen. Choose Next to go to the next screen.

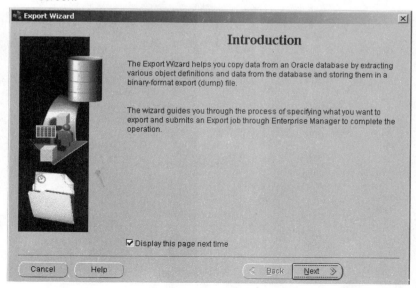

3. The Export File screen allows you to specify the name of the Export file. Use the default name by choosing Next.

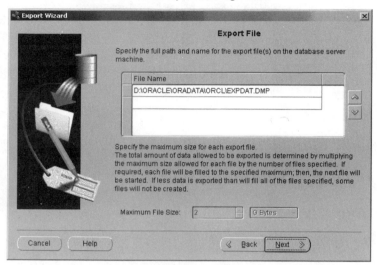

4. The Export Type page allows you to export the entire database, choose to export a certain user's object, or select certain tables. The default is to export the entire database, which is what we want for this exercise. Choose Next to continue.

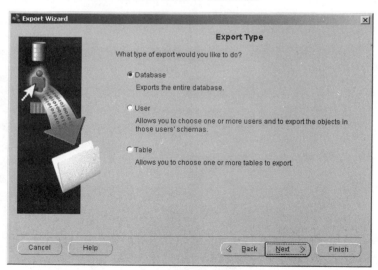

5. The Associated Objects screen allows you to export the security, indexes, constraints, and data associated with selected tables. Leave all of the options selected, and choose Next.

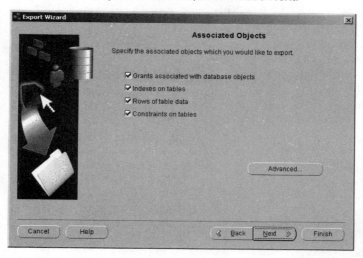

6. The Schedule screen allows you to schedule the export. By default, the job runs immediately and only once. To make a repeating job, you would select an ongoing schedule for when you want the job to run. Note that scheduled jobs rely on the Agent, which is covered in Chapter 9, "Proactive Management of an Oracle Server." Leave the export to run immediately, and select Next to continue.

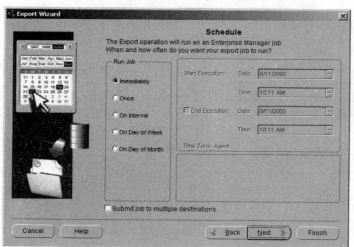

EXERCISE 8.2 *(continued)*

7. The Summary page summarizes the export, and allows you to submit the job now and/or save the job in the Job Library for later use. Change the selection so that the job is submitted immediately as well as saved in the Job Library (for later use). Select Finish to continue.

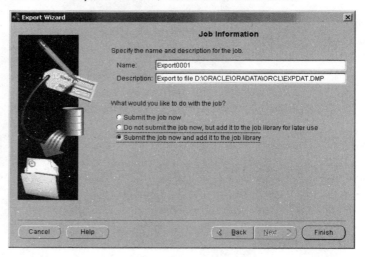

8. You should see a Summary screen. Choose OK to close the Summary screen.

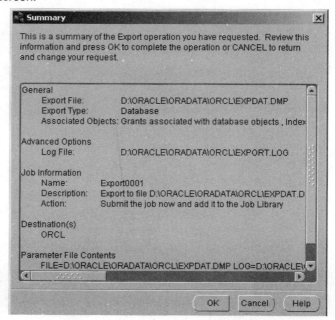

The export itself may take a while to complete, depending on how large the database is. Of course, if you scheduled the export for a later time, the export will not happen when you click the Finish button. We will use the Export file in the next section on importing data.

Importing Data

Data Manager can also be used to import previously exported data. In order to import data, you must have enough rights, room in the database, and a previously exported file. In Exercise 8.3, we will import the file created in Exercise 8.2.

EXERCISE 8.3

Importing Oracle Data

1. Make sure you have completed Exercise 8.2 successfully (exporting the ORCL database).

2. Start Schema Manager, connect as system with a password of manager, and delete the DEPT table from Scott's tablespace by right-clicking and choosing Remove. Answer Yes to the prompt. See Chapter 7, "Installing and Managing Applications," for more information on Schema Manager.

3. Start the import by choosing Tools ➢ Data Management ➢ Import. You should see the Introduction screen. Choose Next to continue.

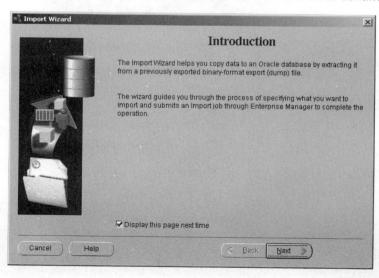

4. The Import File screen allows you to select the Export file you wish to import. The Wizard will select the file you made in Exercise 8.2. Choose Next to continue.

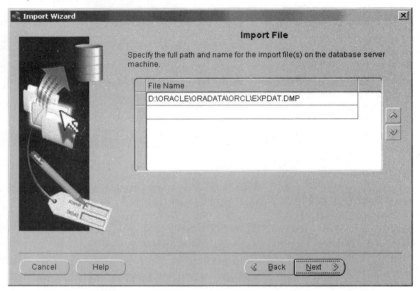

5. The Import file will be processed. Once the file has been processed, you will automatically go to the Import Type screen.

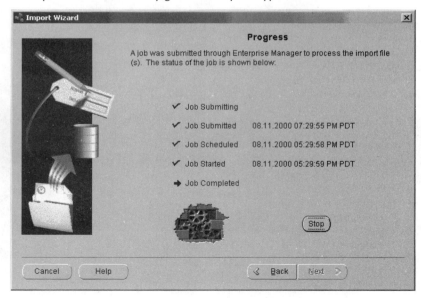

6. From the Import Type screen, you should select Table for this exercise so that you can import the DEPT table back into the database. Select Next to continue.

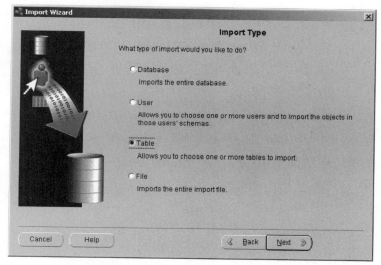

7. The Table Selection screen allows you to select which objects will be imported to which tablespaces and tables. On the left pane, open the Scott folder and move the DEPT table to the right pane. Select Next to continue.

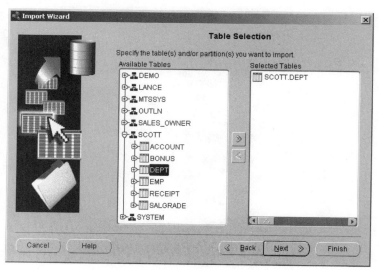

EXERCISE 8.3 *(continued)*

8. The Associated Objects screen allows you to select whether security, indexes, and data will be imported. Leave the default options, and select Next to continue.

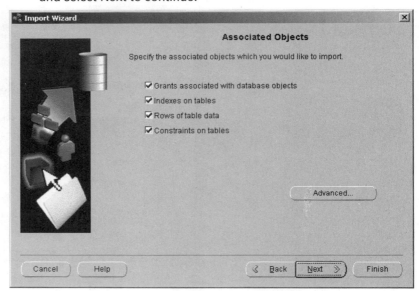

9. The Schedule screen allows you to specify when to run the import. Choose Immediately, and select Next to continue.

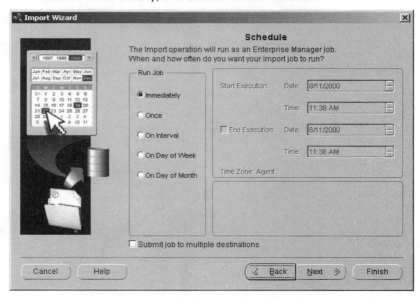

10. The Job Information page allows you to change the name of the job and to specify whether or not to save the job in the Job Library. Select to both submit and save the job, and choose Next to continue.

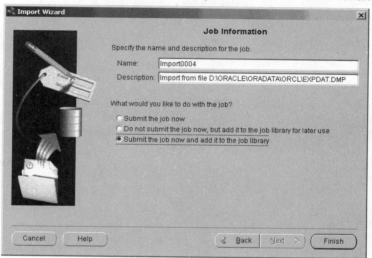

11. The last screen is a Summary page. Select OK to start the import.

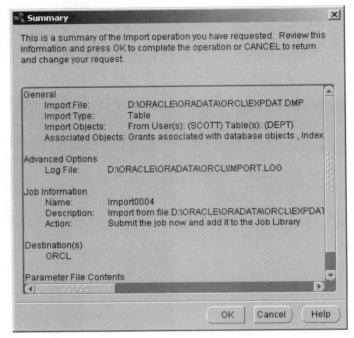

12. You can check the job status to make sure the import completed successfully. You can also go back to Schema Manager and confirm that the DEPT table got re-created by doing a refresh.

Loading Non-Oracle Data

Besides copying data from one database to another, the data manager utilities also work well for loading non-Oracle data. To load such data, you will need to make a *control file* that contains the formatting and location of the datafile.

There are two kinds of loads you can perform with Oracle:

- Conventional Loads
- Direct Loads

Conventional loads act like the normal INSERT statement. Conventional loads can run simultaneously with other database users and processes and are slower than direct loads. Conventional loads must follow all check constraints and primary and *foreign key constraints*. Conventional loads also update any indexes dynamically during the load.

Direct loads can be used when large amounts of rows (10,000+ as a quick rule of thumb) must be imported into the database. The data is formatted into blocks of data that match the storage structure of the database and is then inserted into the database structure, thus making it much faster.

Constraint Issues

Because direct loads bypass the normal checking done on data when it is inserted, constraints on the table to be loaded must be disabled before the load. Of course, you would want to enable the constraint immediately after the load. You can use Schema Manager to disable and enable constraints. In Exercise 8.4, you disable and enable constraints.

EXERCISE 8.4

Disabling and Enabling Constraints

1. Start Schema Manager, and connect with a SYSDBA account.

2. Open Scott's objects, and click the DEPT table. You should see the properties of the table.

3. Go to the Constraints tab.

4. Disable the primary key constraint by selecting the Disable box until it is checked (instead of a red X).

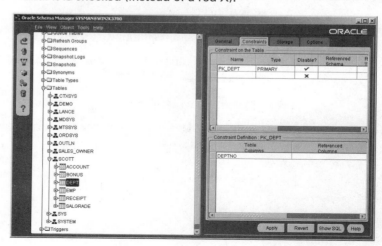

EXERCISE 8.4 *(continued)*

5. Choose Apply to save your changes.

6. To enable the constraint, simply check the Disabled box again until you get a red X (instead of a check). Go ahead and enable the constraint, and select Apply to save your changes.

Non-Oracle Data and Control Files

Non-Oracle data may be stored in a variety of formats. In order for Schema Manager to know the field and row delimiters, a control file must be created. A control file also points to the location of the datafile. If there is only a small amount of data, the data can also be included in the control file. Comments are designated by two hyphens, --.

More examples of control files can be found in the <Oracle root>\RDBMS\ DEMO\SQLLDR folder.

The key words of a control file are as follows:

Load Data This is required at the beginning of the control file.

Infile * This designates that the data is contained at the bottom of the control file. If an external file contains the data, the path and name of the file is given.

Into table This shows the location of the table that the data will go into.

Fields terminated by "," This shows which character designates the ends of fields.

Insert This inserts data into an empty table.

Replace or Truncate This deletes all rows in the table and then inserts the new rows.

Append This appends new rows without deleting old ones.

Begindata This is required when data is stored in a control file. It shows where data starts.

If the imported data doesn't have as many columns as the table, the row will be rejected. Data with too many columns, however, will just lose the extra columns, and the rest of the columns will be successfully loaded into the table.

In Exercise 8.5, you create control and data files and load the data into an Oracle database.

EXERCISE 8.5

Loading Non-Oracle Data

1. Start SQL Plus, and connect as Scott with a password of tiger.

2. Run Select * from dept;. Your results should look like this. Minimize SQL Worksheet.

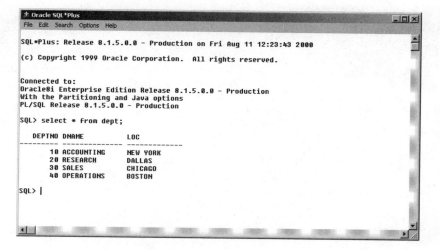

3. Start Notepad.

4. Load the ULCASE1.CTL file from the <oracle root>\RDBMS\ DEMO\SQLLDR folder.

5. Add **APPEND** above the INTO TABLE line, and add **SCOTT** with a period in front of the DEPT table name.

6. Change 10, "Accounting", Cleveland to 31, "Accounting", Cleveland. Add the term extra_data at the end of dept 13, and take off the city for dept 21. The file should look like this:

   -- Copyright (c) 1991 by Oracle Corporation

```
--    NAME

--       ulcase1.ctl - <one-line expansion of the name>

--    DESCRIPTION

--       <short description of component this file
declares/defines>

--    RETURNS

--

--    NOTES

--       <other useful comments, qualifications, etc.>

--    MODIFIED    (MM/DD/YY)

--       cheigham    08/28/91 -  Creation

--

-- $Header: ulcase1.ctl,v 1.1 1991/09/02 14:50:39
CHEIGHAM Stab $ case1.ctl

--

LOAD DATA

INFILE *

APPEND

INTO TABLE SCOTT.DEPT

FIELDS TERMINATED BY ',' OPTIONALLY ENCLOSED BY '"'

(DEPTNO, DNAME, LOC)

BEGINDATA

12,RESEARCH,"SARATOGA"

31,"ACCOUNTING",CLEVELAND

11,"ART",SALEM
```

Data Management Tools **279**

    13,FINANCE,"BOSTON", extra_data

    21,"SALES

    22,"SALES",ROCHESTER

    42,"INT'L","SAN FRAN"

7. Save the file, and exit Notepad.

8. Start Schema Manager, and connect as Scott with a password of tiger.

9. Go to the DEPT table, highlight it, right-click, and select Load. The Load Wizard should start. Select Next to continue.

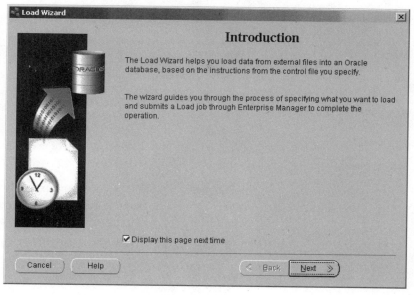

EXERCISE 8.5 *(continued)*

10. Enter the path to the file you just saved (in my case D:\Oracle\
    Ora81\RDBMS\DEMO\SQLLDR\ULCASE1.CTL). Select Next to continue.

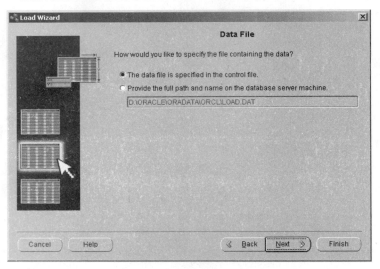

11. Page 2 allows you to select the datafile path. Because the data is
    included in the control file, leave all of the paths blank. Select Next to
    continue.

12. Page 3 allows you to do a conventional or direct load. You can also
    specify rows to be skipped from the advanced options. Leave the
    default settings, and choose Next to continue.

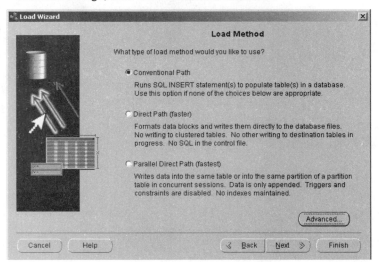

EXERCISE 8.5 *(continued)*

13. The Schedule screen allows you to set when the load will happen. Specify that the load should happen immediately, and choose Next.

14. The Job Information screen allows you to change the name of the job, as well as submit it to the Job Library. Go ahead and select it to be submitted, as well as save it to the Library. Select Finish to continue.

15. You should see a Summary screen. Select OK to submit the job.

16. After the load finishes, you can check the job from Enterprise Manager. Go to the history of the import, highlight the Completed step, and choose Show Output. Scroll up a little to see how many rows were added successfully. (You should have gotten six, with one rejected.) Close the log.

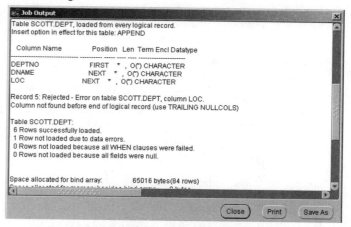

17. Go to SQL Worksheet. Rerun the query (Select * from dept) to see if all the rows are there (except dept 21).

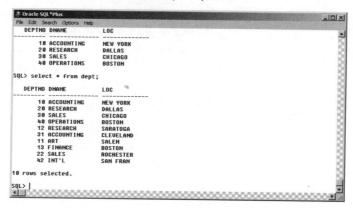

Scheduling Data Jobs

The Import, Export, and Load Wizards can all be used to schedule *jobs* on an ongoing basis. When data jobs are created, they are the same as any other job, and their history can be viewed from the History tab of the Jobs window. Once the job is created, it will show up in Enterprise Manager and can be managed like any other job. You can also create a data management job using the Job ➢ Create Job menu.

Creating and managing jobs is covered in more detail in Chapter 9, "Proactive Management of an Oracle Server."

Summary

In this chapter, many different aspects of managing your data in Oracle were covered. You looked at using the INSERT statement, as well as using Schema and Enterprise Managers to do data imports, exports, and loads.

When you use the INSERT statement, you must know something about the layout and design of the table you are inserting data into. The INSERT statement is generally used to add one record at a time. Inserts are logged transactions. To use the INSERT statement, you must have INSERT permission on the table you are trying to add data to.

Schema Manager can be used to export one or more tables of data. The schema, security information, and indexes can also be exported. The file can then be imported into an Oracle database, which re-creates the schema, data, and indexes.

Non-Oracle data can also be loaded by Schema Manager. A control file must be created that holds the formatting information for the data. The data can reside in a separate file or at the end of the control file.

A conventional load treats the data as a series of INSERT statements, while a direct load formats the data and loads it directly into the database. While a direct load is faster, all constraints on the table must be disabled to perform a direct load.

Key Terms

Before you take the exam, make sure you're familiar with the following terms:

constraint

control file

datafile

export

foreign key constraint

import

INSERT statement

job

load

Oracle Intelligent Agent

primary key constraint

Schema Manager

Review Questions

1. Which of the following are true regarding the INSERT statement? (Select all that apply.)

   A. You must have SELECT permissions in the table you wish to add records to.

   B. INSERT statements add only one record at a time.

   C. An INSERT is usually logged.

   D. You must have INSERT permissions in the table you wish to add records to.

2. What program can be used to export data from tables?

   A. Data Manager

   B. Export Manager

   C. Instance Manager

   D. Schema Manager

3. What program can be used to load non-Oracle data?

   A. Data Manager

   B. Export Manager

   C. Instance Manager

   D. Schema Manager

4. What program can be used to disable constraints?

   A. Data Manager

   B. Export Manager

   C. Enterprise Manager

   D. Schema Manager

5. What program has to be running to schedule imports?

   A. Data Manager

   B. Export Manager

   C. Oracle Agent

   D. Schema Manager

6. What are the advantages of conventional loads? (Select all that apply.)

   A. They're the fastest method for loading data.

   B. Constraints can be left as is.

   C. Non-Oracle data can be loaded.

   D. They can be started from the graphic tools of Schema Manager.

7. What are the advantages of direct loads? (Select all that apply.)

   A. They are the fastest method of loading data.

   B. Constraints can be left as is.

   C. Non-Oracle data can be loaded.

   D. They can be started from the graphic tools of Schema Manager.

8. Which of the following would specify that the data for a load would reside in the control file?

   A. Infile *

   B. Infile ()

   C. Infile null

   D. Infile Begindata

9. Which of the following needs to come before the beginning of the data in a control file?

   A. DataStartsHere

   B. −

   C. Infile Below

   D. Begindata

10. How many tables can be exported at once?

    A. One

    B. Five

    C. Twenty

    D. All of them

11. Which keyword is used when loading rows to an empty table?

    A. Insert

    B. Replace

    C. Truncate

    D. Append

12. Which keyword, when used, will delete all existing rows before loading new rows? (Select all that apply.)

    A. Insert

    B. Replace

    C. Truncate

    D. Append

13. What tab do you go to in order manage constraints in Schema Manager?

    A. General

    B. Enforcement

    C. Enabling

    D. Constraints

14. You have a table with three columns: department number (numeric), department name (character), and department city (numeric). Which of these rows would not be loaded? (Select all that apply.)

    A. `12,"RESEARCH","SARATOGA"`

    B. `13,FINANCE,"BOSTON", "MA"`

    C. `21,"SALES"`

    D. `22,"SALES",ROCHESTER`

15. What application is in charge of data loads once the job has been submitted?

   A. Oracle Agent

   B. Enterprise Manager

   C. Schema Manager

   D. Storage Manager

16. Where do you go to see if an import completed successfully?

   A. The Job Library

   B. The history of a job

   C. The history of Schema Manager

   D. The active job log

17. What should you disable before doing a direct load?

   A. Defaults on columns

   B. Constraints

   C. Data types

   D. Column lengths

18. What ensures uniqueness among rows?

   A. Defaults

   B. Indexes

   C. Primary keys

   D. Foreign keys

19. What ensures relational integrity among tables?

   A. Defaults

   B. Indexes

   C. Primary keys

   D. Foreign keys

20. Which would you perform to bring an ASCII data file into your Oracle database?

   A. Import

   B. Export

   C. Insert

   D. Load

Answers to Review Questions

1. B, C, D. You do not need SELECT permissions to run an INSERT command, although you do need INSERT rights. INSERTs add one row at a time and are usually logged transactions.

2. D. Schema Manager is used to export data.

3. D. Schema Manager is used to load data.

4. D. Schema Manager can be used to disable constraints.

5. C. The Oracle Agent must be running to schedule imports or exports.

6. B, C, D. Conventional loads act like INSERTS and are used to load non-Oracle data from Data Manager.

7. A, C, D. Direct loads affect the data directly and are very fast, but they require constraints to be disabled. Direct loads are used to load non-Oracle data from Schema Manager.

8. A. Only Infile * is a valid option and specifies that the data resides at the end of the control file.

9. D. The Begindata keyword shows where the data in a control file starts.

10. D. All of the tables of a database can be designated to be exported in the same operation.

11. A. The Insert keyword assumes you are loading data into an empty table.

12. B, C. Both the Replace and Truncate key words will delete all of the rows in the table before loading the new rows.

13. D. You enable and disable constraints from the Constraints tab.

14. B, C. Option B would not work because the character field is not enclosed in quotes, and option C would not work because there is an extra column.

15. A. The Oracle Agent manages jobs once they are submitted.

16. B. You can tell if a job completed successfully by going to the History tab of the Jobs window.

17. B. You should disable constraints when doing direct loads.

18. C. Primary keys ensure uniqueness among rows.

19. D. Foreign keys ensure relational integrity among tables.

20. D. Loads are how you bring non-Oracle (in this case ASCII) data into your Oracle database.

Proactive Management of an Oracle Server

ORACLE8i DBO EXAM OBJECTIVES OFFERED IN THIS CHAPTER:

✓ **How to Anticipate Administration Issues**

- Anticipate and know administration issues: database down, lack of space for tablespaces or segments, over-consumption of archive and trace files
- Automate detection by using: Job Service, Event Service

Exam objectives are subject to change at any time without prior notice and at Oracle's sole discretion. Please visit Oracle's Training and Certification Web site (http://education.oracle.com/certification/index.html) for the most current exam objectives listing.

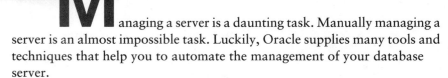

Managing a server is a daunting task. Manually managing a server is an almost impossible task. Luckily, Oracle supplies many tools and techniques that help you to automate the management of your database server.

The core piece in the management of the server is the *Oracle Intelligent Agent*, which is a piece of software that acts as a middleman between Oracle and the operating system.

The other pieces of the management puzzle are *events*, which you can use to watch for things that may happen in the database, and *jobs*, which can be set to automatically do something in the database.

In this chapter, I will cover the most common types of management issues you will probably face as a database operator. I will also cover how to install and configure the Oracle Agent, and how to configure all of the pieces you need for proactive management, including building and managing events and jobs.

Common Problems in Oracle

As an operator, there are common problems you will probably face on an ongoing basis due to the nature of database engines. The most common problems you will face include the following:

- Database down

- Out of room in datafiles

- Out of extents in datafiles

- Out of rollback segments

- Over consumption of hard drive space by archive and/or log files

- Undersized server (hardware) for the database

There are several ways to detect and fix these and other problems. I will cover some of the various methods, as well as the advantages and disadvantages of administering your Oracle database.

Detecting Problems

The first step in fixing a problem is detecting that you have a problem. Many times, the first indication that you have a problem is when you get calls from angry employees who are calling to let you know that the database is down. The idea behind proactive management is to detect and resolve issues before the phone ever rings.

There are generally two methods of detection: manual and automatic. Manual methods include having users call when a problem arises or checking certain items (such as the amount of hard drive space open on your server) on a regular basis. Automatic methods include creating events that monitor items (such as free hard drive space) and will alert you when an item drops below a certain threshold that you have set.

Manually Detecting Problems

Many administrators have a list of items they perform on a regular basis, such as checking the free space on servers, backing up and deleting old trace files, checking tablespaces for free space, backing up the database, and deleting old archive files.

The advantage of doing manual administration is that you get very familiar with your servers and can see how they are performing from day to day and learn about their characteristics.

There are several disadvantages to doing manual database administration, especially if there is only one operator with no one to cover for him in case of illness or emergencies. For example, if the operator is manually backing up the database, what happens when the operator gets sick? Does the database still get backed up properly? Probably not. Another problem with manual administration is consistency. Do tablespaces get extended the same way every time? Is there any rhyme or reason to how old archive files are deleted from the system?

If you have multiple operators, you need to maintain good communication between them, especially if manual administration is being performed. For instance, if one operator is deleting archive files older than one week, but the operator in charge of backing them up only backs them up when they are older than two weeks, you have a serious problem in case restorations need to be done.

Because of all of the problems with manual administration, you might want to consider automating your maintenance by using events and jobs.

Using Events to Detect Problems

An event is a set of circumstances that Oracle can watch for. Events can be designed to not only log that an event triggered, but events can also start jobs, which can be designed to fix the circumstances that triggered the initial event.

The advantage to using events is that, if properly configured, the event is always watching the database, even when the operator or administrator is not there. If an event is set to trigger a job (called a fix-it job), problems in the database can be automatically detected and fixed with no intervention needed on the part of the operator.

The disadvantage of using events is twofold. First, the event or fix-it job may be misconfigured and may not fix the problem at all. Second, not all problems can be anticipated ahead of time. Smart operators will still check on the status of their databases occasionally, although using events and jobs will certainly minimize the time spent doing routine functions.

Creating and configuring events is covered later in this chapter.

Responding to Problems

Once a problem is found, it should be responded to. Again, the two main methods for responding to problems are manually fixing the problem and automatically fixing the problem.

Manually Responding to Problems

Most problems are fixed manually. When a problem is found, the reason for the problem should be diagnosed, and the problem should be fixed. You should try to find the cause of the problem so that similar problems can be avoided in the future. For example, at the end of the month, when the monthly report is run, all users (aside from the one running the report) are basically locked out of the database while the report runs. You diagnose the problem as a lack of redo log segments. The solution is to add more redo log segments, but if you didn't know the cause of the problem (a lack of redo log segments caused by the running of the report), you wouldn't be able to successfully fix the problem.

Using Jobs to Respond to Problems

You can automate most (if not all) of the routine maintenance of a database by using jobs. You can also create jobs that run if a particular event triggers (called fix-it jobs). By automating the routine maintenance, you can give yourself more time to devote to the higher level items such as performance and tuning of the database.

There are two types of jobs: those scheduled to run on a regular basis and those scheduled to run only under a particular set of circumstances.

Examples of jobs set to run on a regular basis include jobs for backing up the database, deleting old archive and trace files, importing or exporting data, and checking the database for errors.

Examples of jobs that only run when needed include jobs for restarting the database, Listener, or Data Gatherer and jobs to extend tablespaces or datafiles and to add redo log segments.

Creating and managing jobs is covered later in this chapter.

Oracle Intelligent Agent

The Oracle Intelligent Agent (Agent) is the software that communicates with the instances so you can schedule various jobs (such as backups) and events (such as checking the up/down status of an instance). The Agent gets installed during a normal Oracle server installation.

After installation, the Agent will need to be loaded. By default, the Agent won't load until you tell it to. You can, however, set the Agent to load automatically when the operating system (or Oracle) starts.

The first time the Agent is loaded, it creates the following three files: $ORACLE_HOME/network/admin/snmp_ro.ora; $ORACLE_HOME/network/admin/snmp_rw.ora; and $ORACLE_HOME/network/agent/services.ora. If you change items about your server such as the instance name, the server name, or the TCP/IP address, or if the agent refuses to communicate with the server, it may be because these files contain obsolete information. You might want to try deleting these files (after backing them up) and restarting the Agent so that it can rediscover servers and instances as contained in the TNSNAMES.ORA file.

The Agent has to be loaded before Enterprise Manager can automatically find servers and databases. The Agent also needs to be loaded before events and jobs will work. The Agent loads a bit differently depending on which operating system you are using. Loading the Agent on Windows NT, NetWare, and Unix is covered in Exercises 9.1, 9.2, and 9.3, respectively.

Loading the Windows NT Agent

There are several steps that must be taken to get the Agent to load successfully on a Windows NT computer. The steps are as follows:

1. Install the Intelligent Agent.

2. Configure NET8 to communicate with the instance.

3. Give a user account the Log On as a Batch Job right.

4. Set the account as the preferred account in Enterprise Manager.

5. Provide the user who creates a job with read and write rights in the Oracle Home and Temp directories.

Installing the Agent

The Oracle Agent is installed by default as part of the normal Oracle installation. If you initially choose not to install the Agent but later change your mind, you must rerun the installation from the Oracle CD-ROM and select to install the Agent. Installing Oracle is covered in Chapter 2, "Installing and Configuring Oracle8i."

Configuring NET8

The Agent communicates with the Oracle database engine using parameters defined for NET8. In other words, you must successfully configure NET8 in order for the Agent to work. Configuring NET8 is covered in Chapter 2, "Installing and Configuring Oracle8i."

Configuring the Agent Account

There are several steps involved in configuring the account for the Agent to use when running Oracle on Windows NT. The steps are detailed in the following sections.

Configuring the Account for the Agent

You must either create a new account for the Agent to use or identify an existing account. The account must be given the Log On as a Batch Job right, which is done from the Advanced User Rights option inside User Manager. You should also make sure that the User Must Change Password at Next Logon box is not checked.

If the preferred account doesn't have the Log On as a Batch Job right, you will get a message indicating that the user can't be authenticated.

Changing the Agent Account Password

Occasionally, you may want to change the password assigned to the Agent account (for example, after an employee who had access leaves). You'll need to change the password in two places:

- Change the password using the Windows NT User Manager for Domains utility.
- Change the password assigned to the Agent in Enterprise Manager.

In the Windows NT User Manager for Domains utility, you can change the password through the user's Properties dialog box. You'll need to replace the old password with a new one and then confirm the new password.

Passwords, unlike usernames, are case sensitive in Windows NT.

Once you have changed the password, you need to tell Enterprise Manager about the changed password. Change the password exactly how you would assign one to the original user, from the Preferences menu.

Setting the Agent to Start Automatically

You can set the Agent to start automatically by choosing this option either during installation or later, through Control Panel ➤ Services. If you set the Agent to auto start, it will start when the server boots; no one needs to be logged in in order to make things happen.

It makes sense that if you have Oracle set to start automatically, then you should also set the Agent to start automatically. However, if you set the Oracle Instance Service to start manually, you may want the Agent set to start manually as well. Of course, you would then need to manually start both of them to get full functionality from Oracle.

Configuring the Agent in Enterprise Manager

Once you have configured the account for the Agent to use, you must configure Enterprise Manager to use that account when submitting jobs to the Agent. To configure Enterprise Manager, go to the Preferences menu and enter the account name and password for the preferred account for the utilities.

In Exercise 9.1, you configure and load the Windows NT Agent.

EXERCISE 9.1

Configuring and Loading the Windows NT Agent

1. In User Manager (or Computer Management in Windows 2000), create a new user called oracleagent with a password of password.

2. Deselect User Must Change Password at Next Logon, and select Password Never Expires. Choose Create to make the user.

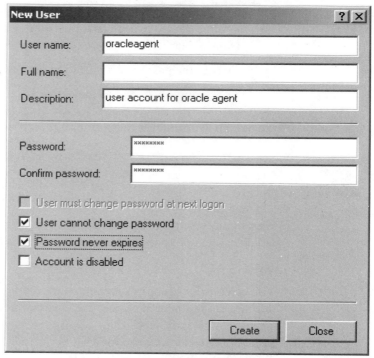

3. Assign Log On as a Batch File to the account by going to User Rights ➤ Advanced (or Local Security Settings in Windows 2000).

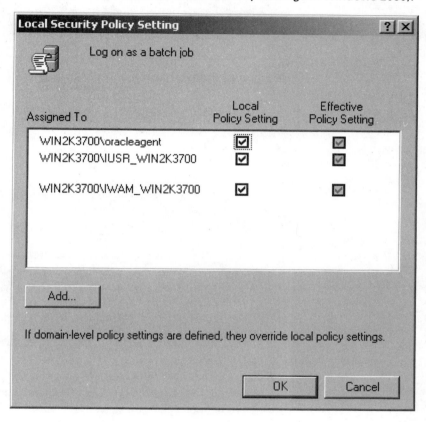

4. Start the Enterprise Manager Console, and connect as an administrator.

5. Set the preferred account for the Agent by going to System ➤ Preferences ➤ Preferred Credentials.

6. Enter **oracleagent** and **password** for the ORCL database.

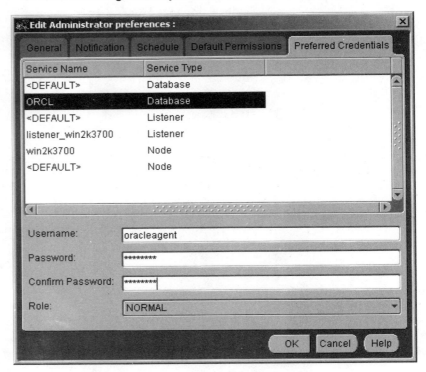

7. Enter an administrator user account and password for the node. Note that the account you use for node jobs needs to have the Log On as a Batch File right, as well as the normal rights it needs to run the commands you intend to give it.

8. Choose OK to save your changes.

Loading the NetWare Agent

The NetWare Agent is an NLM (NetWare Loadable Module) and is installed but not loaded by default. The Agent is called DBSNMP.NLM. To automate the loading of the Agent, put the command LOAD DBSNMP in the

AUTOEXEC.NEF file after the Oracle NLMs load. There are just a few steps involved in configuring the Agent for NetWare.

1. Configure NET8 on the server for the instance.

2. List each instance in the DB_SNMP section of SQLNET.ORA, with the case matching that in NET8 if more than once instance is run.

3. Correctly configure the HOSTS file or DNS for servers the Agent communicates with.

Configuring NET8 for NetWare

Use the EASYCFG program to configure the NET8 setting on the NetWare server. EASYCFG edits the TNSNAMES.ORA file to include service names and parameters. Any server that the Agent communicates with must be in the file.

Configuring SQLNET.ORA

In order for the Agent to communicate with more than one instance, the SQLNET.ORA file must contain the names of the instances. The case (upper or lower) must exactly match the names of the instances as contained in the TNSNAMES.ORA file.

Configuring the HOST file or DNS

As the SNMP Agent is TCP/IP based, it needs to be able to find the TCP/IP address of the server it is communicating with. Either setup DNS name resolution on the server, or edit the HOSTS file so that you have an entry for each server.

In Exercise 9.2, you load the Oracle Agent for NetWare.

EXERCISE 9.2

Loading the NetWare Agent

1. Go to the NetWare server and, from the console prompt, type **DISPLAY ORACLE STATUS**.

2. If Oracle is not loaded, type **ORALOAD**.

3. To load the Agent, type **DBSNMP**.

4. After the Agent loads, type **LSNCTL80**.

5. From the Listener prompt, type **DBSNMP STATUS**. You should get a message that the SNMP Agent has started.

6. If the Agent has not started, enter the command DBSNMP START.

7. Exit the Listener Control utility by typing **EXIT**.

Loading the UNIX Agent

There are several steps involved to install and configure the UNIX Agent. The Agent installs as part of the Enterprise Manager program. You should make sure you have the latest version of Oracle in order to make the Agent install and perform at its best.

EXERCISE 9.3

Loading the UNIX Agent

1. Insert the Oracle installation CD-ROM, and install the Agent by making sure it is selected during the Enterprise Manager installation.

2. Run the root.sh shell script, which will create or update the oratab file.

3. Put an entry for each database in the oratab file with the following format: <SID>:<$ORACLE_HOME>:[Y/N]

4. To confirm that the Agent installed successfully, do a directory ls -al dbsnmp from the Oracleroot\bin directory.

5. To start the Agent, run the command lsnrctl dbsnmp_start.

6. To check the status of the Agent, run the command lsnrctl dbsnmp_status.

7. To stop the Agent, run the command lsnrctl dbsnmp_stop.

Oracle Events

Managing an Oracle server can be a complex task. Oracle provides many tools to help with management, including pre-built events that you can enable for your database. The pre-built events that you can enable include the following:

- Up/Down status of a database
- Up/Down status of a Listener
- Up/Down status of the entire node
- Up/Down status of the Data Gatherer

You can set the frequency with which the event checks against the database, node, Listener, or Data Gatherer, as well as the response if the event happens. If an event happens, the administrator will get notified. You can also have a certain type of job run, called a fix-it job. Fix-it jobs may do such things as restart the Listener, which you can have automatically run, using a Listener event.

Once you create an event, you need to submit it to the Agent. Only servers that have an active Oracle Agent running can have events submitted and run on them. See the preceding section for information on installing and configuring the Agent.

You can choose to save the event in the *Event Library*, which allows you to quickly look at the status of the event, as well as make modifications and resubmit the event.

Creating Events

Creating events is done from the Events menu, using Enterprise Manager. In Exercise 9.4, you create a couple of events, and in Exercise 9.5, you edit and resubmit the events.

EXERCISE 9.4

Creating Events

1. Make sure the Agent is installed and configured correctly (see Exercise 9.1–9.3).

2. Start Enterprise Manager, and connect with an administrator account.

3. Go to Event ➤ Create Event.

4. On the General tab, enter the name Check DB Up/Down.

EXERCISE 9.4 *(continued)*

5. Highlight your instance in the Available Destinations pane, and select the Add arrow (or double-click it) to move it to the Monitored Destinations pane. If your instance is not listed, the Agent probably has not been started.

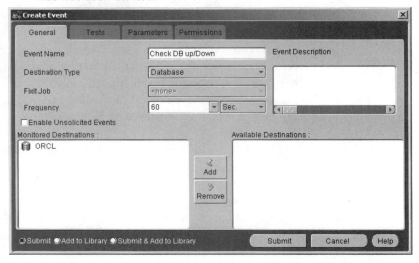

6. Go to the Tests tab.

7. Highlight the Database UpDown test in the Available Tests pane, and select the Add button (or double-click it). It should then be listed in the Selected Tests pane.

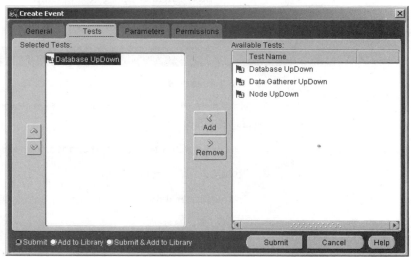

8. Choose Submit to save the event.

9. Go to the bottom right of the Enterprise Manager console.

10. Go to the Registered tab. You should see the event.

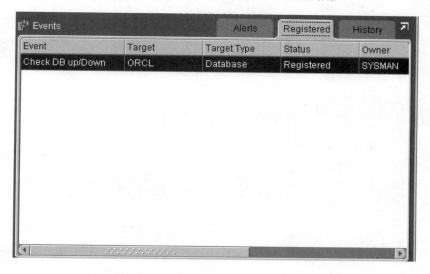

Events			Alerts	Registered	History	
Event	Target	Target Type	Status		Owner	
Check DB up/Down	ORCL	Database	Registered		SYSMAN	

Modifying Events

More than likely, you will want to or need to edit and change events that you have created. Common reasons to edit events include changing the timing of the events and adding or subtracting databases or nodes to monitor.

You can edit the event by going to the Event Library. Once you have edited the event, you can resubmit it. If you choose to resubmit it with the same name, you should delete the old registration before you resubmit it. In Exercise 9.5, you modify an existing event.

Modifying Events

1. Start Enterprise Manager, and connect with an administrator account.

2. Go to Event ➤ Event Library.

3. If you don't see the event from Exercise 9.4 or another event you want to edit, close the library, highlight the event in the bottom left pane, choose Event ➢ Copy to Library, then go to Event ➢ Event Library.

4. In the Event Library, highlight the event and choose Edit.

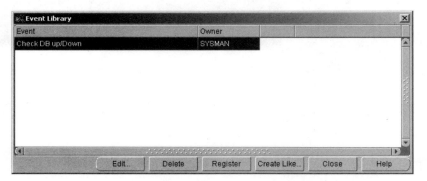

5. On the General tab, change the frequency to every 90 seconds.

6. Select the Submit and Save to Library radio button, then click Save.

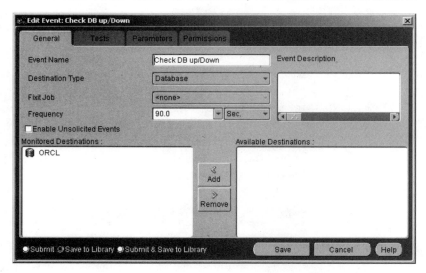

Oracle Jobs

An Oracle job is a set of code or one or more actions scheduled to run at a certain time or under certain conditions. Creating jobs is key to proactive management of the server and can save you from many off-hour maintenance tasks. Jobs are very flexible and can be designed to do the following:

- Run commands at the operating system level. These jobs literally open a command prompt and run some sort of batch file or executable file.

- Stop or start the instance. This job can start or stop an instance. The start instance job is particularly useful for events that watch the status of instances.

- Import, export, or load data. These jobs are very useful when automating routine data imports or exports.

- Back up or recover the database. This is the most common job, essential for ensuring data recoverability.

- Broadcast a network message. This job is useful for linking with other jobs such as scheduled instance downs.

- Cancel a running job. This job is useful if some error is detected during the running of a job.

- Run a SQL command or script. These jobs are written using SQL commands. They are often used to back up the database, rebuild indexes, and perform other various routine maintenance on the database.

- Stop or start the Listener. Another very useful job when combined with an event that monitors the status of the Listener.

Since jobs are just an automated way to run commands, the actual contents of the job are only limited by your ability to program.

Creating Jobs

The required elements of a job are the name, schedule, and the type and actual command to be executed during one or more steps.

Note that a job may contain many tasks, and you can designate the sequence of tasks, as well as designate that tasks always operate, operate only on failure of another task, or operate only on success of another task. For instance, you may wish to do a cold backup task, which means you would need to do a stop instance task first. You should make the cold backup task dependent on the stop instance task, so you don't attempt to backup a database that is not closed.

Exercise 9.6 will create a job that will execute an operating system command. The command given is appropriate for Windows NT. Change the command (in step 8) as appropriate for your operating system. Exercise 9.7 will create a job that executes a SQL command.

EXERCISE 9.6

Creating an Operating System Job

1. Start Enterprise Manager, and connect with a user that has administrator rights.

2. Create a new job by going to Job ➢ Create Job.

3. On the General tab, enter the job name Dir of C:

4. Change the destination type to Node, then select the node in the Available Destinations pane and either click Add or double-click the node. It will then appear in the Selected Destinations pane.

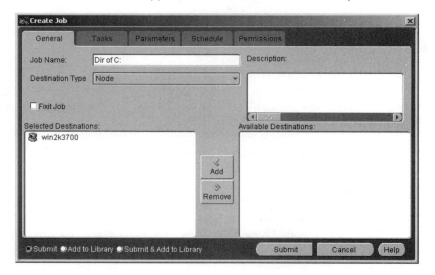

5. Go to the Tasks tab.

6. Highlight the Run OS Command in the Available Tasks pane, and double-click or choose the Add button to move it to the Job Tasks screen.

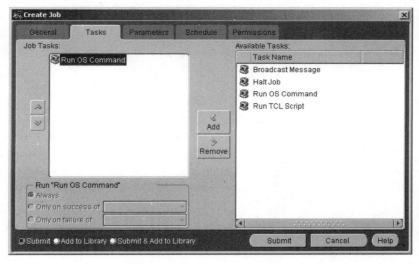

7. Go to the Parameters tab.

8. Enter **dir c:** for the command.

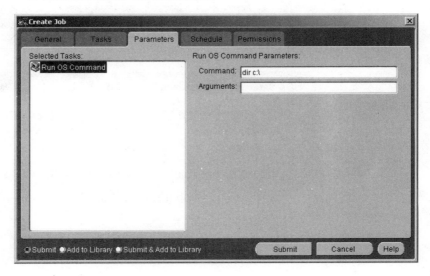

EXERCISE 9.6 *(continued)*

9. Change the radio button at the lower left to Submit and Add to Library, and then click on Submit.

10. Go to the Jobs window (the lower left window of the Enterprise Manager Console). On the History tab, you should see that the job completed successfully.

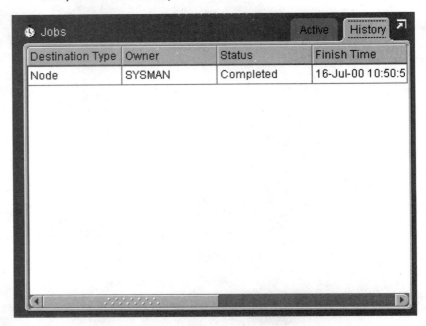

Destination Type	Owner	Status	Finish Time
Node	SYSMAN	Completed	16-Jul-00 10:50:5

EXERCISE 9.7

Creating a SQL Job

1. Start Enterprise Manager, and connect with an administrator account.

2. Create a new job by going to Job ➤ Create Job.

3. On the General tab, enter Run SQL Command for the job name.

4. Highlight the ORCL instance in the Available Destinations pane, and right-click or choose the Add button to move the ORCL instance to the Selected Destinations pane.

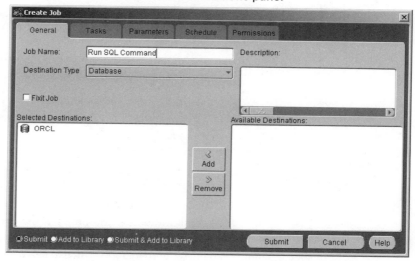

5. Go to the Tasks tab, and choose Run SQL*Plus Script.

6. Go to the Parameters tab.

7. Enter **select * from scott.emp;** in the Script Text pane.

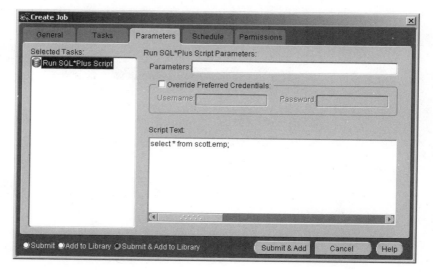

EXERCISE 9.7 *(continued)*

8. Select the Override Preferred Credentials box if the user account created earlier for the Agent doesn't have enough rights to perform the operation.

9. Go to the Schedule tab. Note the default is Immediate, but you can change the schedule as needed.

10. Change the selection at the bottom left to Submit and Add to Library, and choose Submit and Add.

11. Look at the Jobs window in the lower left of the Enterprise Manager console. The job should have completed successfully. If it didn't, you may want to resubmit it with different credentials.

Modifying and Running Jobs Manually

You can modify jobs to change their name, type, command, or schedule. In order to modify a job it must be contained in the *Job Library*. You can also use the Create Like button so that the original job will not be overwritten.

Even if you have scheduled a job, you can run it manually at another time. To run a job manually, it must have first been saved in the Job Library. To run a job manually, simply open the Job Library (select Job ➢ Job Library from within Enterprise Manager), highlight the job you want to run, right-click it, and then click Submit (see Figure 9.1).

FIGURE 9.1 The Job Library

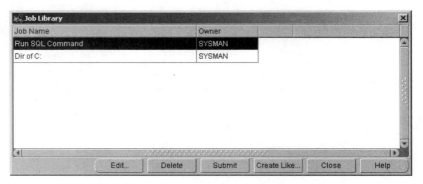

Viewing Job Details, Output, and History

A very helpful feature of SQL Enterprise Manager is that it keeps a record of each job's time of execution, as well as whether the job was successful or not. You can also see the output of a job. In Exercise 9.8, you examine the history of the job that we ran in Exercises 9.6 and 9.7 to see if they successfully completed.

EXERCISE 9.8

Viewing Job Details, Output, and History

1. Start Enterprise Manager, and connect with an administrator account.

2. Go to the Jobs window (the bottom left window), then go to the History tab.

3. Double-click the Node job (created in Exercise 9.6) to open the Progress window. Note when the job started and completed.

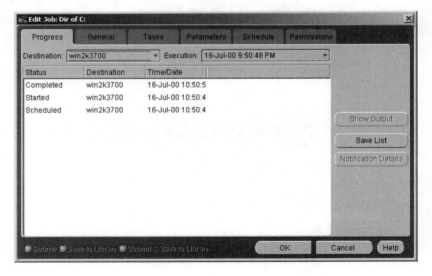

EXERCISE 9.8 *(continued)*

4. Double-click the Completed step (or highlight it and choose Show Output) to see the output.

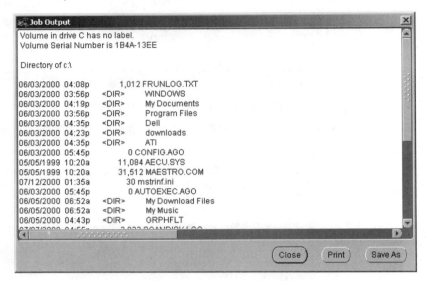

```
Job Output                                                              ×

Volume in drive C has no label.
Volume Serial Number is 1B4A-13EE

Directory of c:\

06/03/2000  04:08p              1,012 FRUNLOG.TXT
06/03/2000  03:56p      <DIR>        WINDOWS
06/03/2000  04:19p      <DIR>        My Documents
06/03/2000  03:56p      <DIR>        Program Files
06/03/2000  04:35p      <DIR>        Dell
06/03/2000  04:23p      <DIR>        downloads
06/03/2000  04:35p      <DIR>        ATI
06/03/2000  05:45p                  0 CONFIG.AGO
05/05/1999  10:20a             11,084 AECU.SYS
05/05/1999  10:20a             31,512 MAESTRO.COM
07/12/2000  01:35a                 30 mstrinf.ini
06/03/2000  05:45p                  0 AUTOEXEC.AGO
06/05/2000  06:52a      <DIR>        My Download Files
06/05/2000  06:52a      <DIR>        My Music
06/05/2000  04:43p      <DIR>        GRPHFLT

                                        Close      Print      Save As
```

5. Choose Close and then Cancel to close that job.

6. Double-click the Run SQL Command job (created in Exercise 9.7) to see details of the job.

EXERCISE 9.8 *(continued)*

7. Double-click the Completed step (or highlight it and choose Show Output) to see output of the SQL command.

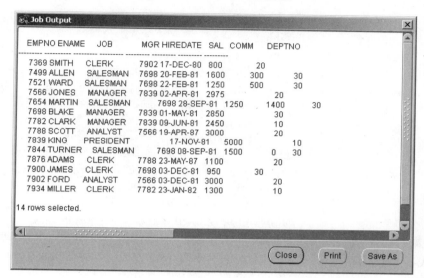

EMPNO	ENAME	JOB	MGR	HIREDATE	SAL	COMM	DEPTNO
7369	SMITH	CLERK	7902	17-DEC-80	800		20
7499	ALLEN	SALESMAN	7698	20-FEB-81	1600	300	30
7521	WARD	SALESMAN	7698	22-FEB-81	1250	500	30
7566	JONES	MANAGER	7839	02-APR-81	2975		20
7654	MARTIN	SALESMAN	7698	28-SEP-81	1250	1400	30
7698	BLAKE	MANAGER	7839	01-MAY-81	2850		30
7782	CLARK	MANAGER	7839	09-JUN-81	2450		10
7788	SCOTT	ANALYST	7566	19-APR-87	3000		20
7839	KING	PRESIDENT		17-NOV-81	5000		10
7844	TURNER	SALESMAN	7698	08-SEP-81	1500	0	30
7876	ADAMS	CLERK	7788	23-MAY-87	1100		20
7900	JAMES	CLERK	7698	03-DEC-81	950	30	
7902	FORD	ANALYST	7566	03-DEC-81	3000		20
7934	MILLER	CLERK	7782	23-JAN-82	1300		10

14 rows selected.

Close   Print   Save As

8. Choose Close and then Cancel to close the job.

Deleting Jobs

If you no longer need a job, you can easily delete it in Enterprise Manager. Make sure you check the Active tab for jobs that are scheduled to run. Note that if you delete a job, all of its steps and history are also deleted.

You may want to save a job to the library before you delete it so that you can easily resubmit the job in the future.

Summary

Managing a server is a daunting task. Having to manually manage a server is an almost impossible task. Luckily, Oracle supplies many tools and techniques that you can use to help automate the management of your database server.

The most common problems you will face include databases that are down, a shortage of room in datafiles, a shortage of extents in datafiles, lack of sufficient rollback segments, and over consumption of hard drive space by archive and/or log files. There are several ways to detect and fix these and other problems.

You have to first detect a problem before you can fix it. You can manually manage your server, hoping to detect problems before they occur, or you can create events and jobs to detect problems automatically.

Events are automatic processes that can monitor instances, Listeners, and nodes and can be set to notify the operator, as well as start a fix-it job.

Jobs can be defined that can not only run SQL statements, but can also run command-prompt commands and replication jobs. Jobs can be run on a regular basis, on demand when an event triggers, or only once.

In order for events or jobs to work, you need to correctly install and configure the Oracle Agent. The Agent installs differently depending on which operating system you are using. For Windows NT, the Agent is a service; for NetWare, it is an NLM (NetWare Loadable Module); for Unix, it is a configurable service.

Key Terms

Before you take the exam, make sure you're familiar with the following terms:

event

Event Library

job

Job Library

Oracle Intelligent Agent

Review Questions

1. In Enterprise Manager, where do you set the account for the Agent?

    A. System ➤ Preferences ➤ Preferred Credentials

    B. System ➤ Security ➤ Preferred Credentials

    C. Security ➤ Preferences ➤ Preferred Credentials

    D. Security ➤ Preferences ➤ Agent Account

2. What command starts the Agent in Unix?

    A. `lsnrctl dbsnmp_stop`

    B. `lsnrctl dbsnmp_start`

    C. `lsnrctl dbsnmp_status`

    D. `lsnrctl agent_start`

3. What command shows the status of the Agent in Unix?

    A. `lsnrctl dbsnmp_stop`

    B. `lsnrctl dbsnmp_start`

    C. `lsnrctl dbsnmp_status`

    D. `lsnrctl agent_status`

4. Which of these is not an option when you create an event?

    A. Submit the Event

    B. Add to the Library

    C. Submit and Add to the Library

    D. Reregister the Event

5. What is the default schedule for a job?

    A. Never

    B. Immediate

    C. Tonight at midnight

    D. Every night at midnight

6. What kinds of jobs can be created? (Choose all that apply.)

   A. SQL

   B. OS Command (Command Prompt)

   C. Broadcast

   D. Backups

7. How many tasks can a job have?

   A. One

   B. Five

   C. Ten

   D. Limited only by your resources

8. Tasks within a job can be set to run when? (Choose all that apply.)

   A. Always

   B. Only on success of a different task

   C. Only on failure of a different task

   D. Never

9. What must be running before you can register an event? (Choose all that apply.)

   A. Oracle Intelligent Agent

   B. Oracle Systems Management Server service

   C. Enterprise Manager

   D. Security Manager

10. You can target an event to which of the following? Select all that apply.

   A. Node

   B. Database

   C. Listener

   D. Table

11. In order to modify jobs, they must be what?

    A. Created with the Edit option

    B. Stored in the Job Library

    C. Tagged with Administrator rights

    D. Named names that start with SYS_

12. How can you see the output of a job?

    A. Select the job, select the completed task, and then choose Output

    B. Select the job, select the completed task, and then choose Print Results

    C. Select the job, select the completed task, and then choose Details

    D. Select the job, select then the completed task, and then choose Show Output

13. An operating system job runs with the security of what account?

    A. The user who made the job

    B. The account specified in the preferred credentials for the node

    C. The owner of the system management database

    D. The account specified in the preferred credentials for the database

14. How do you override the preferred credentials for a job?

    A. You can't

    B. Select the New Credentials button, and fill in the details

    C. Select the Override Preferred Credentials button, and fill in the details

    D. Select the Account Details button, and fill in the details

15. The name of the NetWare Oracle Agent is what?

    A. NETAGENT.NLM

    B. DBSNMP.NLM

    C. NETAGENT.AGT

    D. DBSNMP.AGT

16. Who is in charge of manual database maintenance?

   A. The System DBO

   B. Oracle jobs

   C. Oracle events

   D. Procedures

17. Which of the options can be detected by an event?(Choose all that apply.)

   A. Out of rollback segments

   B. Large trace files

   C. Full tablespaces

   D. Security rights problems

18. What button do you select to see the results of a job within Enterprise Manager?

   A. Show Output

   B. Results

   C. Details

   D. Properties

19. What service allows the Oracle Intelligent Agent to communicate with servers by using their fully qualified domain names?

   A. Enterprise Manager

   B. WINS

   C. DHCP

   D. DNS

20. Under Windows NT, what right does the account assigned to the Agent require?

   A. Domain Admin

   B. Logon Locally

   C. Create a Process

   D. Logon as a Service

Answers to Review Questions

1. A. To set the account for the Agent, you must go to System ≻ Preferences ≻ Preferred Credentials.

2. B. The `lsnrctl dbsnmp_start` command starts the Agent in Unix.

3. C. The `lsnrctl dbsnmp_status` command shows the status of the Agent in Unix.

4. D. You cannot reregister the same event—you have to delete the old one and submit a new one.

5. B. The default schedule for a job is Immediate.

6. A, B, C, D. All of the types of jobs listed can be created.

7. D. A job can have an unlimited number of tasks, as long as you don't run out of system resources.

8. A, B, C. Tasks can be set to always execute, as well as on success or failure of other tasks.

9. A, B, C. Security Manager is not necessary to register events.

10. A, B, C. Tables cannot be a target of events.

11. B. Jobs have to be in the library before they can be edited.

12. D. The Show Output button shows the output of tasks from within a job.

13. B. The account specified for the node is the one used to run operating system jobs.

14. C. The Override Preferred Credentials button allows you to set new credentials for a job.

15. B. The Agent in NetWare is DBSNMP.NLM.

16. A. The System DBO is in charge of manual administration.

17. A, B, C. You can detect common problems with events, except for security issues.

18. A. The Show Output button allows you to see the results of a job.

19. D. DNS provides host name resolution, which allows the Agent to communicate with servers using the servers' names.

20. D. The user account assigned to the Agent in Windows NT needs the Logon as a Service right.

Chapter 10

Backups and Restorations

ORACLE8i DBO EXAM OBJECTIVES OFFERED IN THIS CHAPTER:

✓ **Why and When to Back up Databases**

- Define the frequency of database backups
- Back up a database by using Oracle Backup Management Tools
- Perform a full database backup
- Define how to automate periodic database backups

✓ **Recover a Crashed Database**

- Identify different crash scenarios
- Perform a complete recovery in NOARCHIVELOG mode
- Archive redo log files to avoid loss of data and reduce recovery time
- Set a database in ARCHIVELOG mode
- Perform a complete recovery in ARCHIVELOG mode

Exam objectives are subject to change at any time without prior notice and at Oracle's sole discretion. Please visit Oracle's Training and Certification Web site (http://education.oracle.com/certification/index.html) for the most current exam objectives listing.

his chapter looks at various options for protecting your data, an area of crucial importance. It discusses the reasons for backing up data and planning and choosing appropriate backup strategies. It shows you how to perform various types of backups and how to restore databases when necessary.

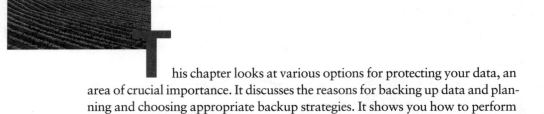

For more details on performing backups and recoveries, see *OCP: Oracle8i DBA Architecture and Administration and Backup and Recovery Study Guide* (Sybex, 2000) and *OCP: Oracle8i DBA SQL and PL/SQL Study Guide* (Sybex, 2000).

Why Backup

Having fault-tolerant disk drives doesn't mean you don't have to do backups. Data can be corrupted by a variety of problems, including those that follow:

- Hard disk drive failure
- Hard disk controller failure
- Motherboard failure
- Power outage or spike
- Virus attack
- Accidental change or deletion of data
- Malicious change or deletion of data

Creating (and testing) regular backups is an integral part of any good operator's maintenance plan. The words you never want to hear are "The hard drive is dead and the backups are bad."

Developing a Backup Plan

Because you will probably be the one in charge of scheduling and verifying backups, there are several issues beside those associated with doing the routine backups that must be looked at before a backup plan can be designed and properly implemented. To this end, consider the following:

- How often will the backups occur?
- To what medium will the backups be made?
- Who is responsible for the backups?
- How will the backups be verified?
- Will Windows NT, NetWare, or Unix capabilities (such as clustering, drive mirroring, or RAID 5) be used to help protect data?

How Often Will the Backups Occur?

A backup is much like a spare tire—you may never need it, but it is a lifesaver when you do. The frequency with which you back up is directly related to how much data you will lose if the system suffers a major catastrophe. If you only back up once a week on the weekends, any crash suffered late in the week could mean many days of data will be lost. Conversely, if you back up the redo logs every hour, the most data you will lose will be an hour's worth.

Full backups should be done at least weekly, and redo logs should be backed up nightly, unless the database can be easily reconstructed. Of course, the more critical the data, the more often you should back it up.

To What Medium Will the Backups Be Made?

Oracle can back up to a tape ora file. If a tape drive is used, it must be installed in the computer running Oracle, unless a third-party backup solution is used.

If you back up to a file, you should store the file on a different volume and drive than the database to guard against losing both your database and your backups.

Who Is Responsible for the Backups?

The scariest thing in the world is when two co-administrators both think that the other one is taking care of the backups. Have a plan in place for the person in charge, and detail what is to happen on that person's day off.

You should also carefully label your tapes and plan a rotation method that periodically retires older tapes for both archival purposes and so that new tapes can be introduced into the rotation.

How Will the Backups Be Verified?

Trusting the backup you've made without verifying it is like trusting your spare tire to be in good condition without ever checking it—it *probably* is, but... The purpose of a backup is not simply to have something backed up, but to be able to restore it in a reasonable manner.

One of the best ways to verify if your backups are working is to restore them to a separate computer. Not only does this verify the integrity of your backups, it helps prepare you in case you have to bring up a spare server quickly.

Protecting Your Data with Various OS Options

The ultimate goal of designing and implementing a disaster recovery plan is to plan for and protect the data in case of a major catastrophe. Most operating systems have several options that can be used to protect data in case of hard drive failure, effectively keeping Oracle from knowing that there has been a problem.

You can learn about the options available through the various operating systems by referring to a number of other chapters in this study guide. For instance, refer to the discussion in Chapter 5, "Creating and Managing Databases," for a detailed discussion on the different RAID levels and their various advantages and disadvantages.

Backup and Recovery Scenarios

There are several different scenarios to consider when planning your backups (and thus your restores). The first decision you have to make is whether to back up the database while it is in use or to kick all of the users out of the database while you back it up. Another issue is whether to put the database in ARCHIVELOG mode, and if so, what parameters to use.

In order to best prepare for recovery scenarios, you should start by understanding how Oracle can fail. You should also be aware of the different backup options available to you, including backing up a closed database and backing up a live database.

Instance Failures versus Media Failures

There are two basic types of crash scenarios. They are as follows:

- Instance failures

- Media failures

An instance failure occurs when the instance stops unexpectedly or when the SHUTDOWN ABORT command is issued.

When an instance fails, the database is no longer available for users. When the instance is restarted, Oracle will recover committed (completed) transactions from the redo log files. Of course, if the instance failed because of hardware issues, you will have to fix the hardware before you can restart the instance.

To recover from an instance failure, simply restart the instance, and Oracle will use the redo log files to roll complete transactions into the database while incomplete transactions will be discarded.

When a media failure occurs, you should first fix the media, next restore the database, and then restore any archived log backups that were created after the last full backup.

Cold versus Warm Backups

There are two basic ways to back up an Oracle database: cold backups and warm backups. Each is defined as follows:

- Cold backups are backups that occur after the instance is shut down, the users are all disconnected, and the database files are closed. All of the files associated with the database are then backed up.

- Warm backups are backups that occur when the database is still in use, the instance is still running, and the users are still connected to the database.

The advantage of a cold backup is that the database is in a guaranteed consistent state, and you know exactly when the backup was performed and what transactions were completed before the backup started.

The disadvantage of cold backups is that you must shut the instance down in order to perform one, which means that all users must be disconnected from the instance and that the database will be unavailable until the backup is completed and the instance restarted.

The advantage of a warm backup is that the database can be backed up while it is in use. A disadvantage of warm backups is that you may not know exactly what is in the backup, as user transactions get backed up only if they are finished before the backup starts.

In order to do warm backups you should first convert the database to ARCHIVELOG mode, which is discussed later.

NOARCHIVELOG Mode versus ARCHIVELOG Mode

The redo logs of an Oracle database are designed to hold transactions that may not be in the database at the time of a system or instance failure. Redo logs hold transactions until they are flushed to the database, which happens on a regular basis but not immediately after transactions are completed. When you create a database, the database (by default) is in *NOARCHIVELOG mode*, which means that the redo logs autowrap as needed. As stated in Chapter 5, "Creating and Managing Databases," a database must have at least two redo log files, as Oracle will switch between them as one or the other gets full. In NOARCHIVELOG mode, any changes in the log are lost when Oracle switches back to that log file.

You may want to capture the changes that are held in the log file before the changes are overwritten. Setting the database to *ARCHIVELOG mode* changes the redo logs so they get backed up to a system file before they get overwritten.

The biggest problem with ARCHIVELOG mode is that there has to be enough room on the hard drive for the redo log file to create its backup. If there is not, the log file cannot be overwritten, the switch from the previous log file, therefore, fails, and the instance, consequently, locks and stops.

NOARCHIVELOG mode protects against instance failure, but doesn't protect against media failure. ARCHIVELOG mode protects against both instance and media failure (but only if you consistently back up the redo logs).

Production databases should be run in ARCHIVELOG mode, unless the database can be easily re-created.

Backing Up in NOARCHIVELOG Mode

Backing up a database in NOARCHIVELOG mode implies only doing full backups of the database. If the instance is started, the database files are locked by Oracle and cannot be copied. In order to do a full database backup, you will have to stop the instance, copy all of the database files to a safe location, and then restart the instance.

Of course, any changes that took effect since the last full database backup will be lost when you restore the database. For example, if you back up the database on Sunday and lose the hard drive on Tuesday, all of Monday's and Tuesday's data will be lost when you restore the Sunday backup.

Because you are backing up the database so you can recover from a media failure, you should copy your database files to a physical drive that's separate from the one you stored your database files on.

EXERCISE 10.1

Performing a Full Database Backup in NOARCHIVELOG Mode

1. Stop the instance (using Server Manager or Instance Manager).

2. Make a backup directory (call it OR8I.BAK) on a volume and physical drive that's different from those where the live database files are.

3. Copy all of the database files, the redo log files, the control files, the password file, and the parameter file to the new directory.

4. Restart the instance.

Converting a Database to ARCHIVELOG Mode

There are basically two steps involved in running a database in ARCHIVELOG mode. They are as follows:

1. Modify the parameter file to support ARCHIVELOG mode.

2. Modify the database to run in ARCHIVELOG mode.

Once you have edited the parameter file and converted the database to ARCHIVELOG mode, the database will run in ARCHIVELOG mode every time you start the instance.

Editing the Parameter File for Automatic ARCHIVELOG Mode

There are three key commands to enter in the INIT file to support ARCHIVELOG mode once ARCHIVELOG mode has been enabled for the database. The commands are the following:

```
log_archive_start = true
log_archive_dest_1 =
"location=d:\Oracle\oradata\<SID>\archive"
log_archive_format = "%%<SID>%%T%TS%S.ARC"
```

You should edit the INIT file before converting the database to ARCHIVELOG mode; otherwise, Oracle will use the default path for the redo log backups, and logs will have to be manually backed up (instead of automatically by Oracle).

The `log_archive_start=true` command tells the instance to back up the redo logs before they are overwritten. The `log_archive_dest_1` command tells Oracle the path to the logs. The `log_archive_format` command tells Oracle the filenames to put on the backups of the redo logs.

Earlier versions of Oracle (Oracle8) were limited to 8.3 names on Novell servers.

In Exercise 10.2, you edit the INIT.ORA file to support automatic archiving in the ORCL database.

EXERCISE 10.2

Editing the INIT.ORA File to Support Automatic Archiving

1. Go to the `<Oracle Home>\ADMIN\<SID>\pfile` directory.

2. Edit the INIT.ORA file with Notepad.

3. Go to the Log Archive section (about two-thirds of the way down).

4. Remove the # characters to unremark the Log Archive commands. If there is no log archive section, enter the commands as shown above, substituting the path to the database files.

```
db_block_size = 8192

remote_login_passwordfile = exclusive

os_authent_prefix = ""

distributed_transactions = 10
compatible = 8.0.5
sort_area_size = 66560

log_archive_start = true
log_archive_dest_1 =
"location=d:\Oracle\oradata\Sales2k\archive"
log_archive_format = "%%Sales2k%%T%TS%S.ARC"
```

5. Save the file.

Modifying the Database to Run in ARCHIVELOG Mode

You can convert a database to ARCHIVELOG mode by issuing the ALTER DATABASE ARCHIVELOG command. To convert the database back to NOARCHIVELOG mode, issue the command ALTERDATABASE NOARCHIVE command. To convert the database to start in ARCHIVELOG mode when the instance is started, you will need to issue this command:

```
ALTER DATABASE ARCHIVELOG;
```

Once the database is running in ARCHIVELOG mode, you can cause the redo log files to switch by issuing the command:

```
ALTER SYSTEM SWITCH LOGFILE;
```

You can also use Instance Manager to do the conversion and switch log files, which is what you do in Exercise 10.3.

EXERCISE 10.3

Converting a Database to ARCHIVELOG Mode Using Instance Manager

1. Start Enterprise Manager, and connect to the ORCL database.

2. Start Instance Manager by going to Tools ➤ Database Applications ➤ Oracle Instance Manager. You can also start Instance Manager directly if you do not want to run Enterprise Manager. Note that you will need to connect with a user account that has Sysdba rights in order to change modes.

3. Go to the Information tab. Notice that the database is running in NOARCHIVELOG mode.

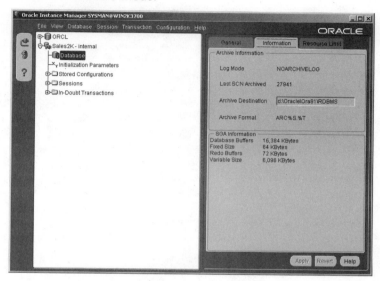

4. Go to the Database menu in Instance Manager, and check the Archive Log box.

5. You will be prompted as to how to shut the database down. Choose Transactional (30 seconds), and choose OK to make the change.

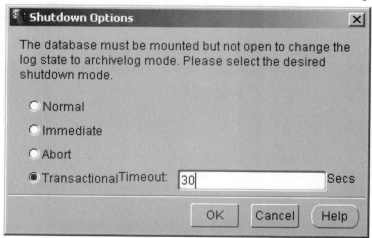

EXERCISE 10.3 *(continued)*

6. You will be prompted to choose whether or not you want auto-matic archiving enabled. To make it permanent, you will need to edit the INIT file for the database (which you did in Exercise 10.2). Choose Yes.

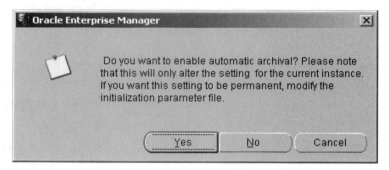

7. After the database restarts, go to the General tab. The database should be running in ARCHIVELOG mode.

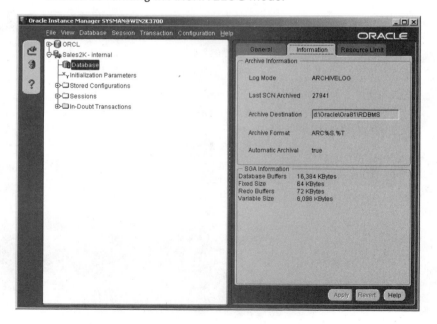

EXERCISE 10.3 *(continued)*

8. To make sure the redo logs are automatically archiving, go to Database ➤ Manually Archive ➤ Current in Instance Manager. Choose OK to take the default path for the archive log.

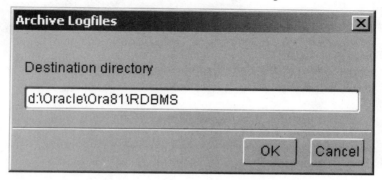

9. Go to the directory shown in step 8. You should see a file called ARC00XX.001. If you cycle the redo log again, you will see another file that increments by one. You can also switch redo log files (and thus create the automatic log backup) by issuing the command ARCHIVELOG SWITCH from SQLPlus Worksheet or Server Manager.

Creating Backup Jobs

Once you have enabled ARCHIVELOG mode, you can create backup jobs to automate database backups. In Exercise 10.4, you create a backup job that will back up the database.

EXERCISE 10.4

Creating a Backup Job

1. Start Enterprise Manager.

EXERCISE 10.4 *(continued)*

2. Start the Backup tools by highlighting a database, right-clicking, and choosing Backup Management ➤ Backup.

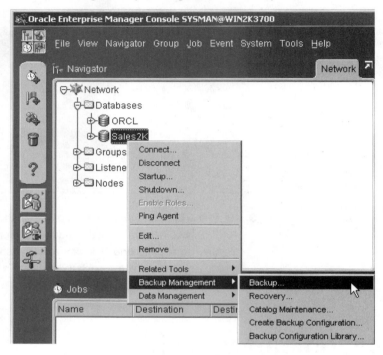

3. The Backup Wizard should start. Choose Next to continue.

EXERCISE 10.4 *(continued)*

4. Choose your backup strategy on the next screen. For most databases, you can use the Predefined Backup Strategy option (the default). Select Next to continue.

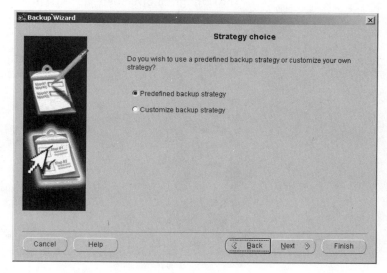

5. The Backup Frequency screen allows you to choose how often the database will be backed up. If your database is small, you may choose to back up the database daily (the second option). Choose to back up the database daily, and select Next to continue.

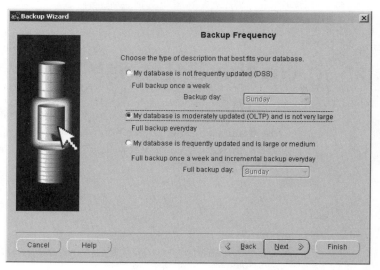

EXERCISE 10.4 *(continued)*

6. The Backup Time screen allows you to choose when the database will be backed up. Leave it at 12:00 A.M., and choose Next.

7. The Configuration screen shows a summary of the backup. Choose Finish to save the backup configuration.

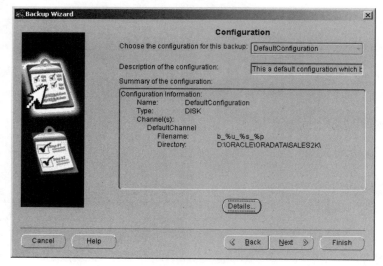

8. You should see a Summary screen. Choose OK to save the backup job.

Backing Up the Database Immediately

When you run the Backup Wizard, you can also choose to back up the database immediately. You may wish to back up the database immediately (instead of waiting for the nightly backup) after major maintenance or just before making major changes. In Exercise 10.5, you back up the database immediately.

EXERCISE 10.5

Backing Up the Database Immediately

1. Start Enterprise Manager.

2. Start the Backup tools by highlighting a database, right-clicking, and choosing Backup Management ➢ Backup.

3. The Backup Wizard should start. Choose Next to continue.

4. Choose your backup strategy at the next screen. To back up the database immediately, select Customize Backup Strategy and select Next to continue.

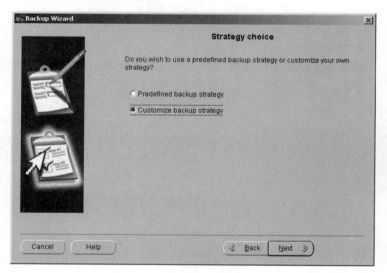

5. From the Backup Selection screen, you can choose to back up the entire database, tablespaces, datafiles, or archive logs. Choose Entire Database, and select Next to continue.

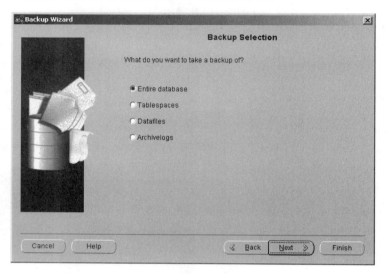

6. In the Archived Logs screen, you can choose to back up the logs along with the database. Choose Yes, All of the Archived Logs, and also choose the Delete the Archived Logs after They Have Been Backed Up box (the default setting). Choose Next to continue.

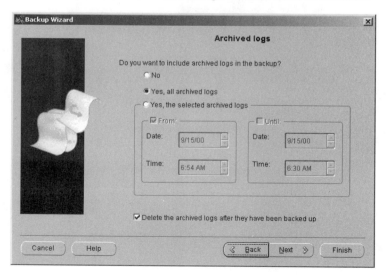

7. In the Backup Options screen, choose to back up the full database. Select Next to continue.

8. You should see a Configuration screen that shows a summary of the backup. Choose Next to continue.

9. The Schedule screen allows you to choose when to run the backup. Leave the job to run immediately, and choose Next to continue.

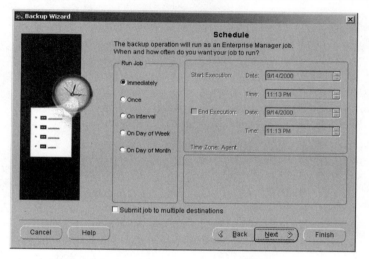

EXERCISE 10.5 *(continued)*

10. The Job Information screen allows you to submit the job and/or store the job in the Job Library. Select the Submit the Job Now and Add it to the Job Library option, then select Finish. On the Summary screen, click OK to start the job.

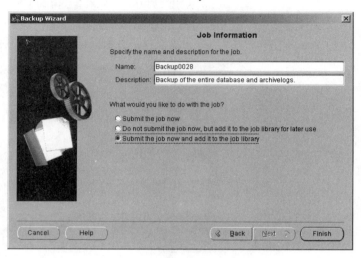

11. Go to the history of the job that was created from the Jobs screen of Enterprise Manager. The job should have completed. Open the Job Output screen for the completed step to see the details of the backup.

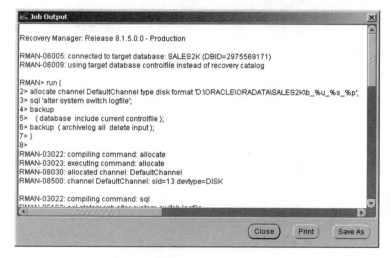

Restoring Databases

The process of restoring Oracle databases can be summed up in the following steps:

1. Find and fix the cause of the failure.

2. Delete the database (in case of media failure).

3. Restore the database from the last full database backup.

4. Restore any archived redo logs that were created since the last full backup.

Restoring Data from a Cold Backup

To restore a database from a cold backup, simply stop the instance (if it is running), copy all of the files from the backup folder or tape to the database directory, and restart the instance.

Because restoring from a cold backup is simple and straightforward, many Oracle operators do cold database backups at least weekly.

When restoring from a cold backup, the key to success is making sure you both back up and restore every file that makes up the database.

Restoring Data from a Full Backup

To restore the database from a previous backup, you will need to start the Recovery Wizard from within Enterprise Manager. To restore the full database, the database must be in MOUNT mode; however, tablespaces and datafiles can be restored while the database is in OPEN mode. In Exercise 10.6, you restore the User tablespace from the full backup that was created in Exercise 10.5.

EXERCISE 10.6

Restoring a Database Using A Full Backup

1. Start Enterprise Manager.

2. Start the Backup tools by highlighting a database, right-clicking, and choosing Backup Management ➤ Recovery.

3. The Backup Wizard should start. Choose Next to continue.

4. In the Recovery Selection screen, choose to recover tablespaces (the default). Select Next to continue.

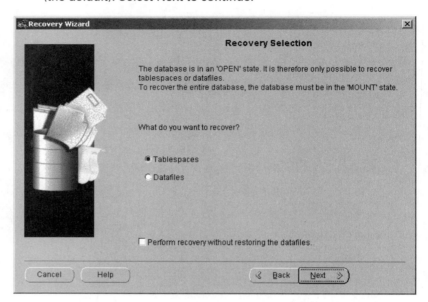

5. Select to recover the Users tablespace. Select Next to continue.

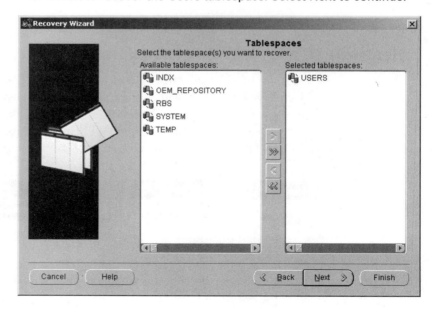

6. The Rename screen allows you to choose a new path and filename for the tablespace files. Leave the new name blank (so that the original name is used), and select Next to continue.

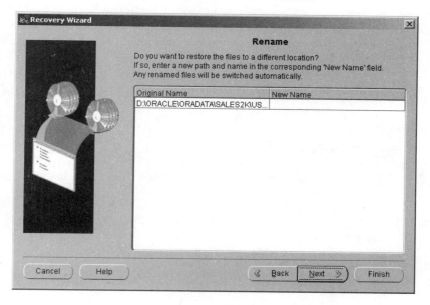

7. The Configuration screen shows a summary of the restoration. Choose Finish and then OK to start the restoration.

8. After a few minutes, go to the Jobs screen of Enterprise Manager and check the history of the job. The job should have completed successfully. If not, read the output of the job to determine why it didn't work.

Summary

Preserving data under less than ideal circumstances is one of the primary responsibilities of a database operator. There are several options to consider when trying to protect your data.

Cold backups imply stopping the instance and backing up all of the database files, while a warm backup allows you to keep the instance running. NOARCHIVELOG mode (the default) allows only cold backups, while ARCHIVELOG mode allows both cold and warm backups.

To switch a database to ARCHIVELOG mode, you need to issue the command ALTER DATABASE ARCHIVELOG MODE.

Because Oracle database files are locked when Oracle is running, normal file backups will not back up any data. The solution is to back up the database to a local file. After the backup process is complete, the file is closed by Oracle and can be backed up normally by the operating system.

Restoring a database deletes all of the previous data and objects. You can also choose to restore individual tablespaces or datafiles. Restoring databases successfully depends mostly on the quality of backups.

Automating backups is done by creating jobs. The history of backup jobs should be periodically reviewed to make sure that the jobs are completing successfully.

Key Terms

Before you take the exam, make sure you're familiar with the following terms:

ARCHIVELOG mode

NOARCHIVELOG mode

Review Questions

1. What program allows you to do backups graphically in Oracle8i?

   A. Transfer Manager

   B. Backup Manager

   C. Security Manager

   D. Enterprise Manager

2. What would happen if the power was suddenly lost on the Oracle server?

   A. Media failure

   B. Volume failure

   C. Database failure

   D. Instance failure

3. How do you edit a recurring (scheduled) backup?

   A. You can't—you have to delete and re-create it

   B. From the Jobs screen

   C. From the Events screen

   D. From the Management/Database Maintenance Plan screen

4. What happens in ARCHIVELOG mode when the hard drive is full?

   A. The instance stops

   B. The instance continues normally

   C. The redo logs automatically grow

   D. The redo logs switch to NOARCHIVELOG mode

5. Choose the correct syntax to use in the INIT file to start ARCHIVELOG mode.

   A. `log_archive_mode start = yes`

   B. `log_archive_start = yes`

   C. `log_archive_mode start = true`

   D. `log_archive_start = true`

6. Which type of backup requires the database to be shut down?

   A. Cold

   B. Warm

   C. Hot

   D. Online

7. Which of these modes allow you to back up live databases? (Select all that apply.)

   A. ARCHIVELOG

   B. NOARCHIVELOG

   C. ONLINE

   D. OFFLINE

8. What is the minimum number of redo log files that are needed?

   A. zero

   B. one

   C. two

   D. three

9. What utility can be used to change from NOARCHIVELOG mode to ARCHIVELOG mode?

   A. Enterprise Manager

   B. Schema Manager

   C. Instance Manager

   D. Storage Manager

10. What command will switch to the next redo log?

    A. ALTER SYSTEM SWITCH LOGFILE;

    B. ALTER DATABASE SWITCH LOGFILE;

    C. ALTER SYSTEM SWITCH LOGS;

    D. ALTER DATABASE SWITCH LOGS;

11. If you are in OPEN mode, which of these can you restore? (Select all that apply.)

    A. Database

    B. Tablespace

    C. Datafile

    D. Redo logs

12. What utility can be used to change the INIT file to support ARCHIVELOG mode?

    A. Instance Manager

    B. Enterprise Manager

    C. Storage Manager

    D. Schema Manager

13. You are in automatic ARCHIVELOG mode and the database suddenly stops. What is the probable cause?

    A. The volume is full.

    B. You are out of RAM in the instance.

    C. The redo logs are corrupt.

    D. The user tablespace is full.

14. Who has to switch redo logs in manual ARCHIVELOG mode?

    A. It happens automatically.

    B. A job is automatically created to do it.

    C. An event is automatically created to do it.

    D. The administrator must take care of it.

15. Which of these files is critical for a database backup? (Select all that apply.)

    A. Parameter (INIT) file

    B. Control file

    C. Database files

    D. Password file

16. What command enables ARCHIVELOG mode for a database?

A. ALTER DATABASE ARCHIVELOG ENABLE;

B. ALTER DATABASE ARCHIVELOG SET;

C. ALTER DATABASE ARCHIVELOG SWITCH;

D. ALTER DATABASE ARCHIVELOG;

17. How do you recover from an instance failure? (Select all that apply.)

A. Restart Oracle.

B. Restore the entire database.

C. Restore the redo logs.

D. Reinstall Oracle.

18. If you are running in NOARCHIVELOG mode, which of these can you do?

A. Full database backup

B. Redo log backup

C. Tablespace backup

D. Datafile backup

19. How many times do you have to run the command ALTER DATABASE ARCHIVELOG;?

A. Every time you start the instance

B. Every time you want to back up the redo logs

C. Every time you want to back up a tablespace

D. Once to convert the database to ARCHIVELOG mode

20. Which mode should production databases be run in?

A. ARCHIVELOG mode

B. NOARCHIVELOG mode

C. REDO LOG mode

D. BACKUP LOG mode

Answers to Review Questions

1. D. The Backup Manager is started from Enterprise Manager.

2. D. Instance failure occurs when the server or instance stops without being shut down properly.

3. B. You can edit jobs from the Jobs screen of Enterprise Manager.

4. A. If there isn't enough room for the redo logs to back up so they can switch, the instance stops.

5. D. `Log_archive_start=true` tells the instance to start in ARCHIVELOG mode (if it was previously enabled).

6. A. A cold backup implies that the instance and, thus, the database is shut down first.

7. A, C. ARCHIVELOG mode allows you to keep the database online, which allows you to back up a live database.

8. C. You have to have at least two redo log files so that Oracle can switch between them as it logs transactions.

9. C. Instance Manager can be used to convert a database to ARCHIVELOG mode.

10. A. The ALTER SYSTEM SWITCH LOGFILE; command will switch to the next redo log file.

11. B, C. You can only restore tablespaces and datafiles when you are in OPEN mode.

12. A. Instance Manager can be used to edit parameters for when you start an instance.

13. A. If there is no room for the archive logs, the instance will stop.

14. D. Manual ARCHIVELOG mode means that archiving of redo logs will not happen automatically—the administrator must do it.

15. B, C. You can always re-create the parameter and password files, but the control files and datafiles are critical.

16. D. The ALTER DATABASE ARCHIVELOG; command converts the database to ARCHIVELOG mode.

17. A. Restarting Oracle is all that is needed to recover from an instance failure, as long as there are no other issues such as hardware.

18. A. When you are running in NOARCHIVELOG mode, you can only do full database backups.

19. D. The ALTER DATABASE ARCHIVELOG; command converts the database to ARCHIVELOG mode.

20. A. Production databases should be run in ARCHIVELOG mode to protect against media.

Introduction to WebDB

ORACLE8i DBO EXAM OBJECTIVES OFFERED IN THIS CHAPTER:

✓ **How to Install Oracle WebDB**

- Describe the use of Oracle WebDB
- Install Oracle WebDB
- Build database objects and components
- Learn how to start and exit Oracle WebDB

✓ **Administer with WebDB**

- Describe WebDB Administer
- List the WebDB key features
- Manage users, privileges, and roles
- Monitor Oracle WebDB by using WebDB Administer

✓ **Set Up the Listener with WebDB**

- Select the PL/SQL Gateway Setting to configure the listener
- Set up the Database Access Descriptor
- Set up the global settings
- Change directory mappings
- Change Multipurpose Internet Mail Extensions types

Exam objectives are subject to change at any time without prior notice and at Oracle's sole discretion. Please visit Oracle's Training and Certification Web site (http://education .oracle.com/certification/index.html) for the most current exam objectives listing.

ebDB is Oracle's Internet development solution that allows you to quickly develop and manage Internet applications. *WebDB* is a browser-based Web publishing and development package that uses the Oracle8i database as the main data storage engine. WebDB must be installed after Oracle8i is installed, and it comes with its own set of tools and utilities to create and manage a Web site.

Key Features of WebDB

ebDB allows you to build an Internet application so that users can get to the data stored in the Oracle database via an Internet browser, such as Netscape Navigator or Internet Explorer. Since users only need a browser, support costs should be lower, since Net8 and Oracle clients don't have to be installed on every client. The major features of WebDB include the following:

- It's entirely Web based.

- You can access data via TCP/IP and an Internet browser.

- It has integrated security with Oracle8i.

- It includes graphical administration tools.

- It includes graphical database design tools.

- It's designed to be easy to use.

- Knowledge of PL/SQL isn't needed.

- No Java or ActiveX is involved.

- The entire application is stored in the Oracle Database.

Although WebDB is designed to be used with Oracle8i, WebDB can be used with Oracle 7.3.4 or later.

The major utility that comes with WebDB is the *WebDB Administrator*, which allows for the creation and monitoring of the Internet application.

Installing WebDB

You must first install WebDB before you can use it. WebDB must be installed on a computer that can reach the Oracle8i server. WebDB is often installed on the Oracle server itself if the server has enough spare hardware. Before install, make sure you have enough free room in the database where WebDB will reside.

As of this writing, the current version of WebDB is 2.2 (which is used in this chapter). Version 3 is due in the relatively near future and will be renamed Oracle Portal. As always, check `www.oracle.com` for the latest information about WebDB.

In Exercise 11.1, you install WebDB.

EXERCISE 11.1

Installing WebDB

1. To install WebDB, go to the appropriate folder for your operating system under the version of WebDB that you have. For the purpose of this exercise, look for the Windows NT folder for version 2.2 of WebDB, folder E:\2.2.0.0.5\NT. Also, make sure that the Oracle database instance is started and reachable from the computer you will install WebDB on.

2. Start the ORAINST.EXE program. The Oracle Installer program should start.

3. Enter the company name, and change the Oracle Home Name to
WebDB, as well as the path. Choose OK to continue. You may get
prompted to confirm your choices. Choose OK again to move to
the next screen. Make sure that the ORACLE_HOME you choose for
WebDB is a different directory than the ORACLE_HOME for the
Oracle database (if you are setting up WebDB on the same physical
machine).

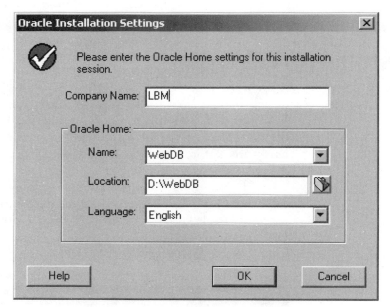

4. You will then be prompted to select between a Typical Install and
a Custom Install. Choose Custom Install and then OK.

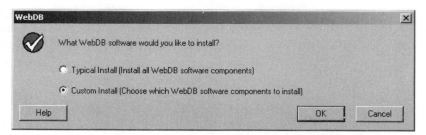

5. Highlight the two WebDB components by holding the Ctrl key and selecting them. Choose Install to continue.

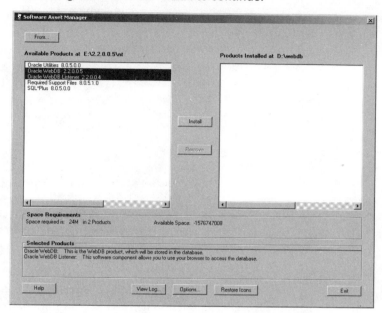

6. Confirm the name of the server where WebDB will reside, as well as the Data Access Descriptor and Schema (which are discussed later). Leave the default settings for those, as well as the default port of 80. Choose OK to continue.

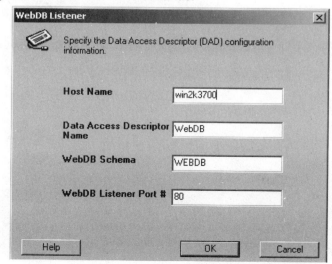

7. WebDB should start to install. After a while, you will get prompted to choose the version of Oracle that WebDB will run on. Choose the appropriate version (which should be Oracle8i). Select Next to continue.

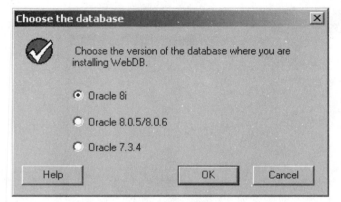

8. You should then be prompted to enter the SYS user password and alias to the database you wish to use. Enter the password (the default password for SYS is change_on_install) and alias (use the ORCL database if you don't have another sample database), and choose OK.

   If you enter a nonexistent alias, you will be prompted to start the Easy Configuration program so that you can create the alias. If you need to create the alias, go ahead and run through the program. If you simply mistyped the alias, go back and reenter the alias.

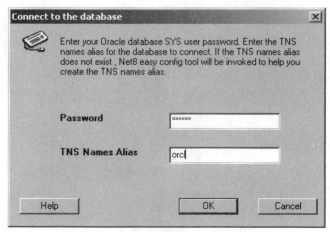

9. You will be prompted for the Web Toolkit user and location. Go ahead and designate OAS_PUBLIC (which will be created) as the user and the USERS and TEMP tablespaces as the default tablespace and the temporary tablespace, respectively. Choose OK to continue.

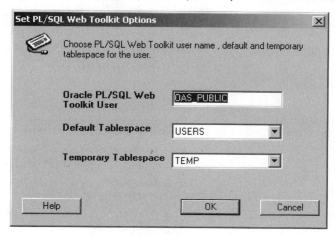

10. You should get a window that states that the Toolkit Packages installation completed. Choose OK to continue.

11. You will next be prompted for the schema and tablespace for the WebDB application. Use the default schema and tablespaces unless you have created new schema accounts and tablespaces where you want WebDB stored. Choose OK to continue.

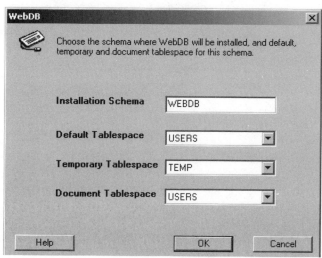

EXERCISE 11.1 *(continued)*

12. You should get a screen that states that the password of the WEBDB
    user is WEBDB. Take note of the password, and choose OK to continue.

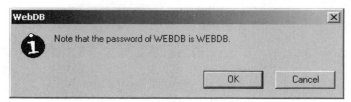

13. You can select additional languages from the next screen. Choose
    all of the additional languages you need, and choose OK to continue.

14. You will be prompted to start the actual WebDB installation. Note
    that the installation cannot be cancelled once it is started. If all of
    your information is correct, choose Yes to start the installation.

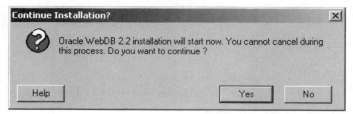

15. You may see an MS-DOS box start and various scripts run. The sta-
    tus box will show various tasks starting. When WebDB is done
    installing, you will see a status box to that effect. Choose OK to
    close the box. The Listener will then install.

16. When the Listener for WebDB finishes installing, you will see a sta-
    tus box indicating that the Listener completed. Note the path to the
    Listener. Select OK to close the box.

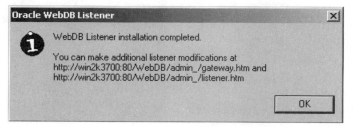

17. Choose Exit at the main Software Asset Manager screen to close
    the installation program. Choose Yes when asked to confirm the
    exit command.

Connecting to WebDB

Once WebDB is installed, you will need to connect to it to administer, create, and manage the site.

The installation program automatically starts the WebDB application and Listener after the installation. To stop or start the service manually on Windows NT, go to Services and stop or start the Oracle WebDB Listener service.

To connect to WebDB, simply start your browser application and enter the address for WebDB, which is HTTP://<server>/webdb:<port>. If you used the default port of 80, you do not have to specify the port. After you enter the address, you will be prompted for the user connection information, as shown in Figure 11.1.

FIGURE 11.1   Connecting to WebDB

Once you are connected, the WebDB Administration program appears by default. See Figure 11.2.

FIGURE 11.2 The WebDB Administration program

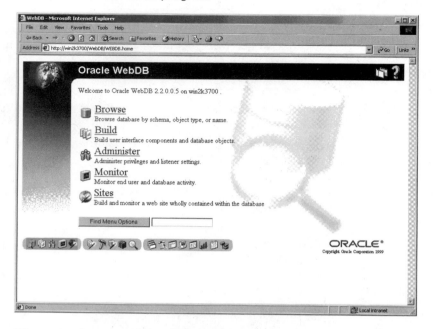

The major features of the WebDB Administration program include:

Browse   Used to see existing objects and schemas

Build   Used to create new objects and Web interfaces

Administer   Used to change WebDB and Listener properties

Monitor   Used to look at site statistics and database activity

Sites   Used to build Web sites

The following sections address each of these features in turn.

Browsing Database Objects

WebDB Administrator includes a robust database-browsing capability that allows you to easily look at your database. To browse objects, simply start the WebDB Administrator program and choose Browse.

In Exercise 11.2, you use WebDB Administrator to browse the ORCL database.

Browsing Objects with WebDB Administrator

1. Start an Internet browser (Netscape or Internet Explorer), and connect to WebDB by entering its address, http://<server>/webdb:<port>.

2. Enter the appropriate security information (WebDB and WebDB if you followed Exercise 11.1).

3. Select Browse from the main menu.

4. You will be able to choose the schema, type of object, and object name. To see all of the schemas and objects, simply leave the default wildcard entries, as shown below, then click Browse.

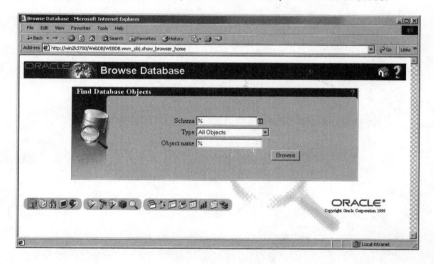

EXERCISE 11.2 *(continued)*

5. You will then see folders that represent the various schemas. To see the objects contained in the Scott schema, simply click the Scott schema once.

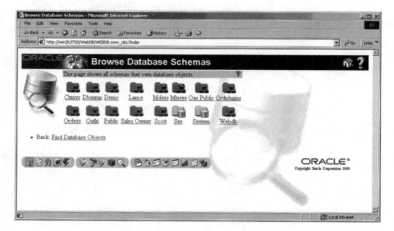

6. To see the actual objects of a particular schema, drill down by clicking the type of object. To see the tables of the Scott schema, click the Tables folder once.

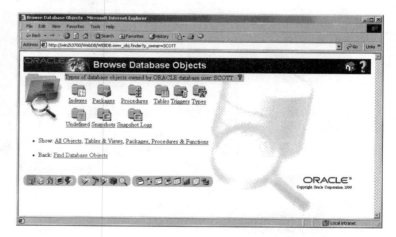

EXERCISE 11.2 *(continued)*

7. You will see each of the tables of the Scott schema. To open the Emp table, simply click the table once. You should see a Query and Update Table screen.

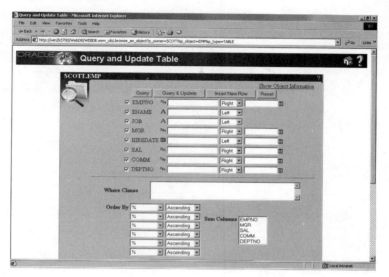

8. To see and be able to update all rows, leave the entries blank and choose Query and Update. You should see the data of the table with Update to the left of each row.

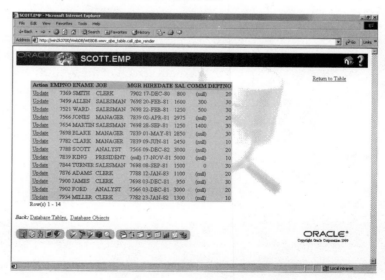

9. To update the first row (SMITH is the ENAME), simply choose the Update action item. You will be taken to an Update EMP screen that allows you to change the contents of the row.

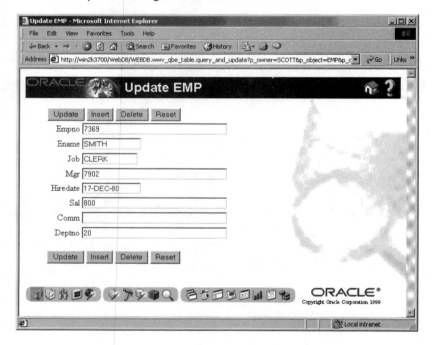

10. To save your changes, choose Update; to add a new row, choose Insert; to delete the row, choose Delete; to cancel your changes, choose Reset. For our purposes, choose the Back button until you are at the main screen of the WebDB Administration program (about seven times).

Building Database Objects

WebDB Administrator can be used to easily build database objects, including tables and views that you can later incorporate into the Web site. You can also build interface components that can be used in your Web site. The various components you can build include those that follow:

Forms   A component that allows access to tables, views, and stored procedures

Menus   Links to various Web pages

Frame Drivers   Queries based on a list of values

Dynamic Pages   Web pages that change as the data changes

Reports   A component that allows read-only access to tables and views

Charts   Graphical ways to view data

Calendars   A component that allows you to view date data in calendar form

Hierarchies   Web pages linked in a parent-child relationship

In Exercise 11.3, you build a new table, as well as look at some sample forms, reports, and calendars based on the ORCL database.

EXERCISE 11.3

Building and Running Database and Internet Objects

1. Start an Internet browser (Netscape or Internet Explorer), and connect to WebDB by entering its address http://<server>/webdb:<port>.

2. Enter the appropriate security information (WebDB and WebDB if you followed Exercise 11.1).

3. Select Build from the main menu.

4. To build a new table, choose Database Objects from the Build screen.

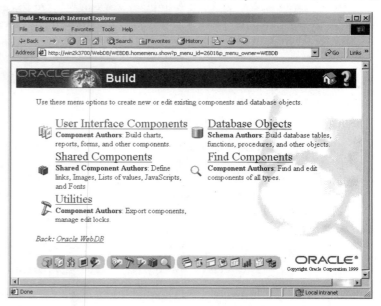

5. Choose Table from the Build Database Objects screen.

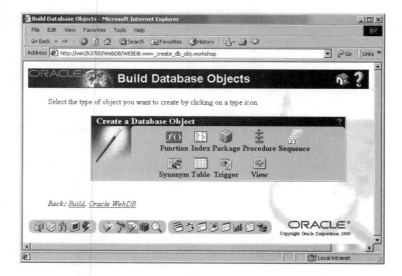

EXERCISE 11.3 *(continued)*

6. Choose SCOTT for the schema where the table will be built, and enter **Activities** for the name of the table. Click the yellow right-arrow to continue.

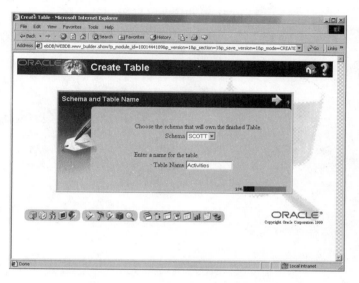

7. Enter **Activity_Date** for the first column and **Activity_Description** for the second column, with datatypes of DATE and VARCHAR2, respectively. The length of Activity_Description should be 100. Clear the Primary Key fields for Activity_Date and Activity_Description and the NULL boxes for both fields. Select the yellow right-arrow to continue.

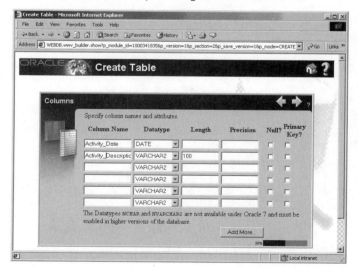

8. The Storage screen allows you to choose the tablespace (and properties of the extents) where the new table will be stored. Leave the default tablespace selection, and select the yellow right-arrow to continue.

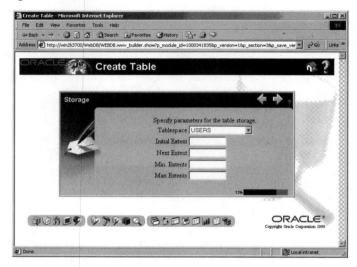

9. You will get a Create Table confirmation screen. Choose OK to create the table.

10. Choose the Back:Build option at the bottom of the screen to go to the main Build menu.

11. To build a Web component, choose User Interface Components.
You should see the User Interface Components screen.

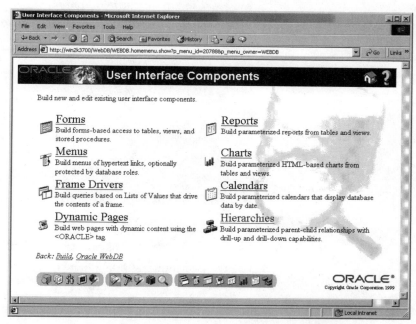

12. Choose Forms to look at the sample forms or to create new forms.

13. Choose Example Form and then Run.

14. To add a new employee, simply enter the data and click the Update button.

15. Use the Back button (three times) to go to the User Interface Components screen.

16. Choose Reports to look at example reports or to build new ones.

EXERCISE 11.3 *(continued)*

17. Select the Example Wiz RPT and then Run to see the example report. Note that the last names are hot links and by clicking them you are taken to the form for that record.

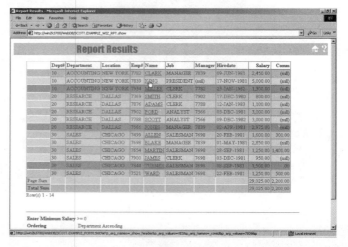

18. Use the Back button (three times) to go to the User Interface Components screen.

19. To look at calendar components, choose Calendars.

20. Choose the example calendar listed at the bottom of the screen.

21. To see what the calendar will look like, choose the Run command; you'll then see the Example Calendar Results screen.

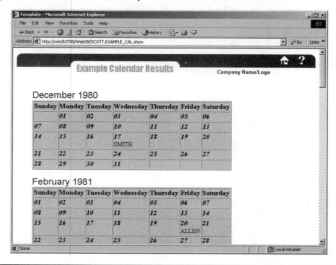

Administering Users, Privileges, and Roles

The Administer option allows you to manage users, roles, privileges, and WebDB log and Listener settings. The Administer option also allows users to change their Oracle passwords.

User Manager

With User Manager, you can create and manage users. User Manager is roughly equivalent to Security Manager. To create or manage users, simply choose User Manager from the main Administer screen. You can then enter a new user or look up an existing user. See Figure 11.3.

FIGURE 11.3   Creating and managing users with WebDB's User Manager

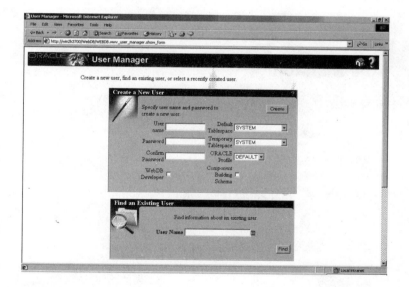

Grant Manager

Grant Manager allows you to grant privileges to users and roles to various objects. To use Grant Manager, simply select it from the main Administer screen and either enter the name of the object to which you wish to give users rights or use the % (wildcard) character to see all of the objects of a particular schema or type (see Figure 11.4). Grant Manager is also roughly equivalent to Security Manager.

FIGURE 11.4 Managing rights with Grant Manager

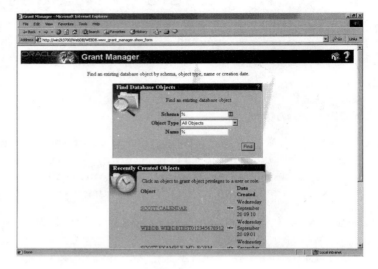

Role Manager

Role Manager allows you to create and manage roles and role memberships. To use Role Manager, simply select it from the main Administer screen. The top screen allows you to create new roles, while the middle screen lets you find and manage existing roles. The bottom screen shows you recently created roles (see Figure 11.5). Role Manager is roughly equivalent to Security Manager.

FIGURE 11.5 Managing roles with Role Manager

Changing Your Password

The Change Your Password screen, accessed from the Administer screen, allows you to quickly change your password using a graphical interface (see Figure 11.6). Remember that passwords are case sensitive in Oracle.

FIGURE 11.6   Changing your password with WebDB

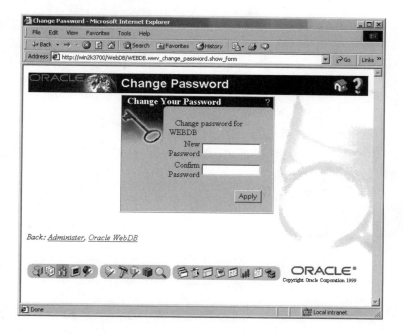

Reporting WebDB Privileges

One of the most requested features of a security management system is to be able to see which users have what rights. WebDB has an easy to use section called Report WebDB Privileges that can be used to show the rights of users and the roles that have been granted rights to database objects. To report on privileges, go to the Administer main menu and choose Report WebDB Privileges. You will see a list of users in the Current WebDB Privileges screen (see Figure 11.7).

FIGURE 11.7 Showing WebDB privileges

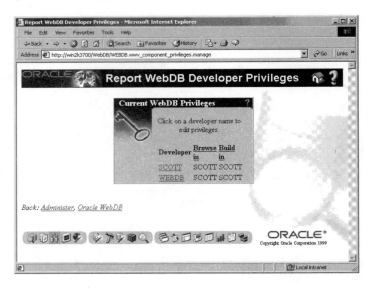

To edit a user's privileges, simply click the user. This will take you to the User Manager screen, as shown in Figure 11.8.

FIGURE 11.8 The User Manager screen in WebDB

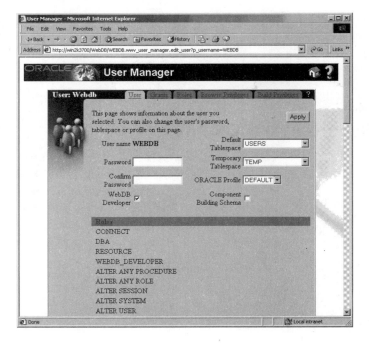

The User tab shows a summary of the user. Note that the data of a user may extend past the bottom of the screen. The Grants tab lets you see and grant rights. The Roles tab lets you see and grant roles. The Browse Privileges tab shows the schemas that the user can select from, while the Build Privileges tab shows the schema that the user can create objects and store data in.

Configuring WebDB Activity Logs

WebDB comes with built-in logging capabilities that are enabled by default. From the Configure WebDB Activity Log screen, you can change the various properties of logging, as well as look at the logs. To manage the logs, select Configure WebDB Activity Log from the Administer screen. The first screen, the Set Log Attribute screen, allows you to specify how often the log files are switched (see Figure 11.9), while the WebDB Database Based Logging System screen shows you exactly where the logging information is contained and how old the data is (see Figure 11.10).

FIGURE 11.9 Setting the Log Switch Interval for WebDB

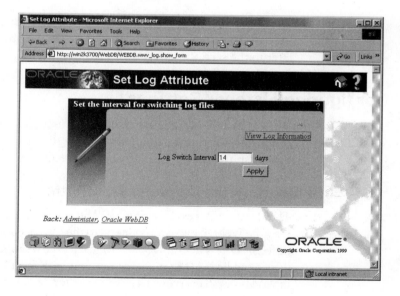

FIGURE 11.10 Viewing the WebDB Database Based Logging System

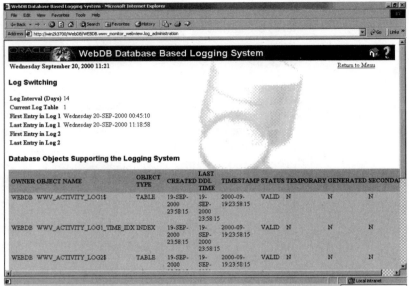

To view the actual log information, simply run a SELECT statement on the table that contains the current log or use the Monitor screens as discussed later in the section, "Monitoring WebDB."

Configuring Listener Settings

WebDB installs a Listener that connects user requests with the WebDB application. Although the default settings for the Listener usually work fine, you may wish to modify some settings for security or performance reasons.

Configuring the Database Descriptor

The Database Access Descriptor (DAD) is a named group of settings that specify how the WebDB gateway connects to the Oracle database. You can have many different DADs in WebDB, one for each type of access. For example, you may have a public DAD that uses an account with SELECT rights on only those tables you wish everyone to have access to. Another DAD can be set up for administration that doesn't involve a default user and password, one that will require you to log in to WebDB before you can access it (like the default DAD).

You can change the DAD connection information by selecting Listener Settings from the main Administer screen. From the main Oracle WebDB PL/ SQL Gateway Settings screen, you can change the name of the DAD as well as various DAD configurations (see Figure 11.11).

FIGURE 11.11   Changing global Listener settings

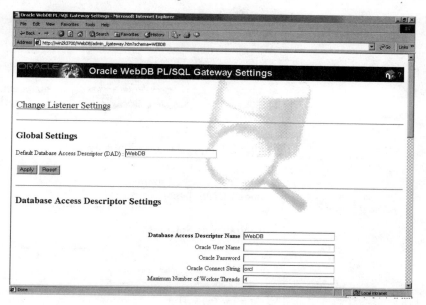

Items you may wish to consider changing include the account the gateway uses to access the Oracle database, as well as the password for the user. You can also set the connection string, which is the same as the database service name. A medium-sized application (about 200 users) should have the Maximum Number of Worker Threads set between 5 and 10. For the best performance, you should set the connections so that they are kept open between requests, although this will consume more system resources. The default (home) page for connections that use this DAD can also be set on the main Oracle WebDB PL/SQL Gateway Settings screen.

Changing Listener Settings

You can also change the Listener properties from the main Oracle WebDB PL/SQL Gateway Settings screen by choosing Change Listener Settings at the top of the page. Once at the Oracle WebDB Listener Settings screen (see Figure 11.12), you can change miscellaneous settings such as the number of threads the Listener uses, as well as the directory mappings and MIME file extension support.

FIGURE 11.12 The Oracle WebDB Listener Settings screen

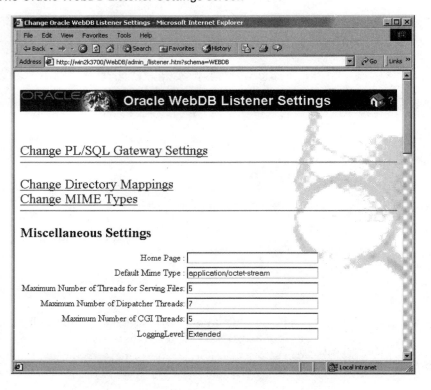

To save your changes, choose the Apply button. To discard your changes, choose Reset.

Configuring Directory Mappings

To change directory mappings, you need to move down the Listener Settings page. You'll see a section for directory mappings and CGI directory mappings. See Figure 11.13.

FIGURE 11.13   Directory Mapping settings

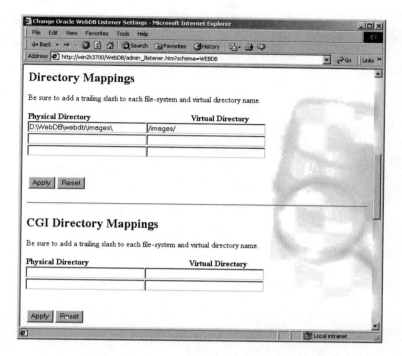

Configuring MIME connections

You can set the extension associations for Multipurpose Internet Mail Extension (MIME) types at the bottom of the Listener Settings screen. See Figure 11.14.

FIGURE 11.14 A list of the MIME extensions that are supported

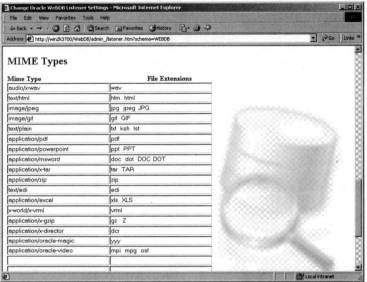

Monitoring WebDB

WebDB comes with sophisticated monitoring software built-in. Select Monitor from the main Administrator screen to see the various categories of items you can monitor (see Figure 11.15).

FIGURE 11.15 The main Monitor screen

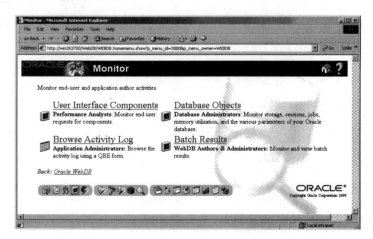

The various categories of items included on the Monitor screen are as follows:

User Interface Components   Used to monitor response times and requests for various objects and components

Browse Activity Log   Used to look at the WebDB log

Database Objects   Used to monitor locks, redo logs, rollback segments, and various storage structures

Batch Results   Used to monitor PL/SQL batch jobs

Building a Site

WebDB also comes with an intuitive Web site builder. To start building a site, chooses Sites from the main Administrator screen. The first page of the Create Site Wizard prompts you to choose between creating a new site or finding an existing one (see Figure 11.16).

FIGURE 11.16   Creating a new site and managing existing sites

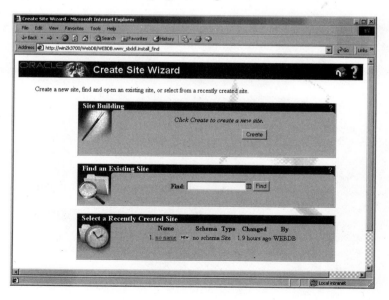

If you choose to create a new site, you can choose to accept the automatically generated name or give it your own name. You will then be prompted to designate a schema user for the site, as well as the language of the site. At

the end of the Wizard, you will see a Create Site summary screen, as shown in Figure 11.17.

FIGURE 11.17 The Create Site summary screen

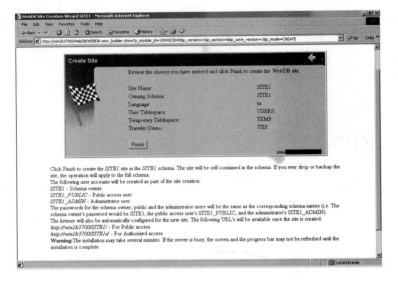

Note that three users will have been created:

- <Site Name> is the schema owner

- <Site Name_Public> is for public access users

- <Site Name_Admin> is for the administrator's use

Note the path to the new site for public use (`http://server/<site name>`), the path for administration of the site (`http://server/<site name>s`), and the password of the user chosen as the user account.

Once the new site has been created, you can connect to it using the browser and typing the path to the site. You should see something like that in Figure 11.18.

FIGURE 11.18 A WebDB site

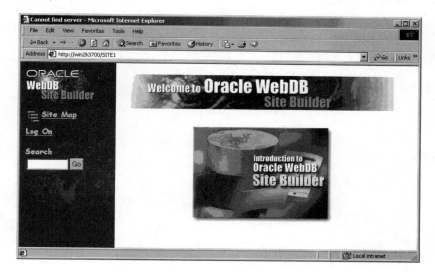

Summary

WebDB is a graphical, TCP/IP- and Web-based utility that not only allows you to manage your database, but also includes powerful Web-based application development and monitoring tools.

WebDB must be installed on a computer that can connect to the Oracle server. It supports Oracle version 7.3.4 or newer. WebDB also installs a mini-Listener that watches for incoming requests. WebDB doesn't require the use of NET8 or the Oracle client on workstations that need to get to data stored in an Oracle database. Clients can simply run an Internet browser, which connects to WebDB, which then connects to Oracle.

The WebDB Administration program is a powerful tool that allows you to manage database objects, as well as Web page components. You can also manage the users, roles, and security of a database.

WebDB is a great tool that makes using an Oracle database much easier and developing Web-based applications a snap.

Key Terms

Before you take the exam, make sure you're familiar with the following terms:

WebDB

WebDB Administrator

Review Questions

1. Which protocol do clients use to connect to WebDB?

   A. NetBEUI

   B. Net8

   C. TCP/IP

   D. All of the above

2. Where are Web sites that are created using WebDB stored?

   A. In the database

   B. In a folder called /SITES

   C. In a folder called /WEBDB

   D. They are created dynamically with PL/SQL code

3. What is the default password for the WebDB user account? (The account is WEBDB.)

   A. oracle

   B. change_on_install

   C. sys

   D. WebDB

4. Where should WebDB be installed?

   A. On the server running Oracle

   B. On each workstation

   C. On the workstation of the Oracle administrator

   D. On both the server and all workstations

5. What is the name of the main WebDB utility?

   A. WebDB Manager

   B. WebDB Administrator

   C. WebDB Site Builder

   D. WebDB Control

6. Which menu item do you pick to create a new tablespace?

A. Build

B. Browse

C. Administer

D. Monitor

7. Which menu item do you pick to change the password of the main administration user?

A. Build

B. Browse

C. Administer

D. Monitor

8. Which menu item do you pick to look at how many times a stored procedure has been run?

A. Build

B. Browse

C. Administer

D. Monitor

9. Which of these would connect you to the WebDB application if you installed on port 3500, on a server called WEBSERVER?

A. HTTP://webserver/webdb

B. HTTP://webserver/webdb:3500

C. FTP://webserver/webdb:3500

D. HTTP://webdb:3500

10. What program does the administrator of the site use to connect to WebDB?

A. Oracle Enterprise Manager

B. An Internet browser

C. SQLPlus Worksheet

D. Server Manager

11. If you set the port on WebDB to 800, which port should the client use?

   A. 800

   B. 280

   C. 1580

   D. The client will automatically find WebDB's port.

12. The Browse menu of WebDB Administrator allows you to do which of the following? (Select all that apply.)

   A. Create new objects

   B. See existing objects

   C. Change the security of objects

   D. Monitor the usage of objects.

13. Which of the following users would be the administrator for a site called SITE1?

   A. SITE1

   B. SITE1_Admin

   C. SITE1_SYS

   D. SITE1_SYSTEM

14. What would be the path to the administration section of a site called SITE1, on a server called SERVER1?

   A. http://SERVER1/SITE1

   B. http://SERVER1/WEBDB/SITE1

   C. http://SERVER1/SITE1s

   D. http://SERVER1/WEBDB/SITE1s

15. What would the password be for a WebDB-created user called SITE1_ADMIN?

   A. PASSWORD

   B. ORACLE

   C. Blank

   D. SITE1_ADMIN

16. What Net8 configurations does WebDB require on the clients?

   A. None

   B. The alias to WebDB must exist

   C. The alias to WebDB will be created the first time the browser is used to connect to WebDB

   D. TNSNAMES.ORA must have an entry for the public path to WebDB

17. Where would you go to change a MIME extension in WebDB Administrator?

   A. Build

   B. Browse

   C. Administer

   D. Monitor

18. What happens if you don't specify an account and password for the WebDB gateway to use?

   A. WebDB won't work.

   B. You will be prompted for a user name and password.

   C. WebDB will use the schema user.

   D. WebDB will give the user SELECT rights only.

19. What versions of Oracle does WebDB support? (Select all that apply.)

   A. Oracle 7.2

   B. Oracle 7.3.4

   C. Oracle8

   D. Oracle8i

20. When does WebDB get installed?

   A. As part of a normal Oracle8i installation

   B. When Oracle Enterprise Manager is installed

   C. When the Diagnostics and Tuning Packs are installed

   D. You have to install WebDB separately

Answers to Review Questions

1. C. WebDB is TCP/IP-based as clients use normal Internet browsers to connect to it.

2. A. Web sites created using WebDB are stored in the database.

3. D. The default password for users created with the WebDB installation is the same as the user name.

4. A. WebDB should be installed on the server running Oracle (or on another server that can connect to Oracle, but it shouldn't be installed on workstations).

5. B. WebDB Administrator is the name of the main WebDB utility.

6. A. You can create new database objects from the Build option.

7. C. You can manage users from the Administer option.

8. D. The Monitor option allows you to see the usage of various database objects.

9. B. To connect to WebDB, you need to use the HTTP protocol and specify the server/webdb along with the port.

10. B. Administrators and clients use an Internet browser to connect to WebDB.

11. A. If you set the port on WebDB for 800, you also have to make sure that the clients communicate on port 800.

12. B. The Browse option only allows you to see existing objects.

13. B. When you create a site, a user called <Site Name_Admin> is created and can administer the site.

14. C. The administration path to a site adds an *s* to the end of the path, which is //<server>/<site name>.

15. D. The password of a user created using the WebDB Wizard is the same as the user name.

16. A. WebDB doesn't require or use Net8 on the client.

17. C. You can manage the Listener and MIME extensions from the Administer screens.

18. B. If you don't specify a gateway account, you will be prompted for an account when you connect to WebDB.

19. B, C, D. WebDB supports Oracle 7.3.4 and higher.

20. D. You have to install WebDB separately from Oracle and Enterprise Manager after Oracle has been installed.

Appendix A

Practice Exam

1. Oracle8i is an example of what kind of database?

   A. Hierarchical

   B. Flat file

   C. Relational

   D. Three tiered

2. A database instance consists of which of the following? (Select all that apply.)

   A. Operating system files

   B. RAM

   C. Server processes

   D. Database files

3. What does a primary key ensure?

   A. Rows are unique

   B. Data can be found quickly

   C. Stored queries can be run by name

   D. Objects can be referred to by a simple name

4. Which of the following commands would create a report from the emp table sorted by manager?

   A. `Select * from emp, manager;`

   B. `Select * from emp order by manager;`

   C. `Select * from emp sort by manager;`

   D. `Select * from emp arrange by manager;`

5. What goes into the repository in Oracle?

   A. The data dictionary for system tables

   B. The data required by Enterprise Manager

   C. The installation log of Oracle

   D. The area of the instance that caches procedures

6. Which service is required to automatically discover databases and servers?

   A. Oracle repository

   B. Tablespace Manager

   C. Instance Manager

   D. Oracle Intelligent Agent

7. Which tool would you use to change startup parameters of a database?

   A. Instance Manager

   B. Schema Manager

   C. Storage Manager

   D. Backup Manager

8. Which of the following files are kept open when a database is in use? (Select all that apply.)

   A. Parameter file

   B. Control file

   C. Datafiles

   D. Redo log files

9. Which tool can be used to create a database?

   A. Enterprise Manager

   B. Instance Manager

   C. Database Configuration Assistant

   D. Easy Configure

10. What is the default folder that holds all of the <SID> folders for the datafiles of a database?

    A. \DATAFILES

    B. \DATABASE

    C. \ORACLE8I

    D. \ORADATA

11. Which users are contained in the password file? (Select all that apply.)

    A. System DBA

    B. System DBO

    C. Database DBA

    D. Ordinary Oracle users

12. When can you delete the database trace file?

    A. Only when the instance is running

    B. Only when the instance is stopped

    C. Anytime

    D. Only Oracle can delete the trace file

13. What is the Net8 configuration file called?

    A. LISTENER.ORA

    B. NET8.ORA

    C. TNSNAMES.ORA

    D. SQLNET.ORA

14. TNSNAMES.ORA can be edited using which program?

    A. Enterprise Manager

    B. Instance Manager

    C. Net8 Assistant

    D. Oracle Universal Installer

15. Which utility can be used to stop and start an instance?

    A. Instance Manager

    B. Schema Manager

    C. Storage Manager

    D. Backup Manager

16. Which of the following SHUTDOWN modes requires an instance recovery when the instance restarts?

    A. SHUTDOWN NORMAL

    B. SHUTDOWN TRANSACTIONAL

    C. SHUTDOWN IMMEDIATE

    D. SHUTDOWN ABORT

17. Which of these STARTUP modes allows users into the database?

    A. STARTUP MOUNT

    B. STARTUP OPEN

    C. STARTUP NOMOUNT

    D. STARTUP RESTRICT

18. The user APP_MANAGER owns a schema that contains the tables, indexes, and other objects for an application. Which of the following users can initially assign rights to other users?

    A. APP_MANAGER

    B. System DBA

    C. System DBO

    D. Plain users

19. Which utility would you use to create a new tablespace?

    A. Instance Manager

    B. Schema Manager

    C. Storage Manager

    D. Backup Manager

20. A tablespace is used for what purpose?

    A. To hold system variables

    B. To hold database objects and data

    C. To hold application code

    D. To hold security settings

21. How can you increase the size of a tablespace? (Select all that apply.)

    A. Add a new datafile to the tablespace

    B. Increase the size of existing datafiles in the tablespace

    C. Compress the data

    D. Increase the size of the instance

22. A tablespace has to have at least how many datafiles?

    A. One

    B. Two

    C. Three

    D. None

23. Rollback segments are used to hold what?

    A. System variables

    B. User variables

    C. Indexes as they are created

    D. Data modified by transactions before the transaction is committed

24. You have 400 users who will each have a single transaction open. How many rollback segments should you configure?

    A. 50

    B. 100

    C. 200

    D. 400

25. Which of the following users can start an instance?

    A. System DBA

    B. System DBO

    C. Schema User

    D. Database User

26. Which command does the parameter file need so that you can add additional System DBAs and System DBOs?

    A. remote_login_passwordfile=shared

    B. remote_login_passwordfile=exclusive

    C. administrators=shared

    D. administrators=exclusive

27. Which program would you use to make additional users System DBAs?

    A. Instance Manager

    B. Schema Manager

    C. Storage Manager

    D. Security Manager

28. You are given a script by a third-party vendor. Which program would you use to run the script?

    A. Instance Manager

    B. Schema Manager

    C. Storage Manager

    D. SQLPlus Worksheet

29. How can you view objects in Schema Manager? (Select all that apply.)

    A. By schema

    B. By object type

    C. By security context

    D. By creation date

30. Which of the following objects gets larger as you add more data to the database? (Select all that apply.)

    A. Synonym

    B. Table

    C. Index

    D. Procedure

31. Which rights do you need to run a procedure? (Select all that apply.)

    A. Select

    B. Execute

    C. Update

    D. Run

32. What rights do you need to edit an existing row? (Select all that apply.)

    A. Select

    B. Execute

    C. Update

    D. Delete

33. If Sue has Select rights on the Payroll table, a role called Accounting has Update rights on the table, and Sue is a member of the role, what rights does Sue have? (Select all that apply.)

    A. Select

    B. Update

    C. Insert

    D. Delete

34. What can Security Manager be used to do? (Select all that apply.)

    A. Grant rights to users

    B. Create objects

    C. Create roles

    D. Put users in roles

35. What is the main advantage of incremental backups?

    A. Fast to restore

    B. Fast to back up

    C. Most reliable

    D. Easy to restore

36. A cold backup implies that the instance is what?

    A. Running in NOMOUNT mode

    B. Running in OPEN mode

    C. Running in RESTRICT mode

    D. Closed

37. To back up a database while it is in use, you must first be running in which mode?

    A. LOG mode

    B. ARCHIVELOG mode

    C. NOARCHIVELOG mode

    D. LIVE LOG mode

38. When an instance fails because the server accidentally got rebooted, who does the database recovery?

    A. The Oracle database engine

    B. The System DBA

    C. The System DBO

    D. The schema user

39. Which command converts a database to ARCHIVELOG mode?

    A. CHANGE DATABASE ARCHIVELOG;

    B. ALTER DATABASE ARCHIVELOG;

    C. SWITCH DATABASE ARCHIVELOG;

    D. CONVERT DATABASE ARCHIVELOG;

40. To restore a database that was in NOARCHIVELOG mode when backed up, what STARTUP mode should the database be in?

    A. OPEN mode

    B. NOMOUNT mode

    C. MOUNT mode

    D. CLOSED mode

41. To do a direct load of data, what needs to be disabled? (Select all that apply.)

    A. Indexes

    B. Constraints

    C. Views

    D. Synonyms

42. What tool do you use to disable and enable constraints?

    A. Storage Manager

    B. Instance Manager

    C. Schema Manager

    D. Backup Manager

43. What kind of job would you create to respond to an event?

    A. On Demand

    B. Scheduled

    C. Fix-It

    D. Event Driven

44. Events can be created to monitor which of the following? (Select all that apply.)

    A. Overconsumption of hard drive space

    B. Database down

    C. Listener down

    D. Out of room in tablespaces

45. Clients connect to WebDB using which protocol?

    A. NetBEUI

    B. Net8

    C. TCP/IP

    D. All of the above

46. Which menu item do you pick to create a new tablespace in WebDB Administrator?

    A. Build

    B. Browse

    C. Administer

    D. Monitor

47. Which menu item in WebDB Administrator do you pick to look at how many times a table has been accessed?

    A. Build

    B. Browse

    C. Administer

    D. Monitor

48. Which of these would connect you to the WebDB application if you installed on port 7000 of a server with an IP address of 192.168.1.54?

    A. HTTP://192.168.1.54/webdb

    B. HTTP://192.168.1.54/webdb:7000

    C. FTP://192.168.1.54/webdb:7000

    D. HTTP://webdb:7000

49. Which of these users would be the administrator for a site called ORACLEDB?

    A. ORACLEDB

    B. ORACLEDB_Admin

    C. ORACLEDB_SYS

    D. ORACLEDB_SYSTEM

50. Where would you go to change Listener options in WebDB Administrator?

    A. Build

    B. Browse

    C. Administer

    D. Monitor

Answers to Practice Exam

1. C.   Oracle8i is a relational database. See Chapter 1 for more information.

2. B, C.   A database instance consists of the server processes and RAM used to open and cache a database. See Chapter 1 for more information.

3. A.   Primary keys ensure that rows are unique in the table. See Chapter 1 for more information.

4. B.   The ORDER BY command sorts rows returned from a query. See Chapter 1 for more information.

5. B.   Enterprise Manager creates the repository to contain settings and configurations. See Chapter 3 for more information.

6. D.   The Oracle Intelligent Agent allows you to automatically discover databases and servers. See Chapter 3 for more information.

7. A.   Instance Manager can be used to change startup parameters. See Chapter 3 for more information.

8. B, C, D.   The parameter file is only read at startup, while the others are all in use when the instance is running. See Chapter 2 for more information.

9. C.   The Database Configuration Assistant can be used to create new databases. See Chapter 5 for more information.

10. D.   The \ORADATA folder, located under the <Oracle Root> directory, is the default folder for database files. See Chapter 5 for more information.

11. A, B.   The password file only contains users that have System DBA or System DBO rights. See Chapter 2 for more information.

12. C.   You can delete the database trace files at any time. They will just be created anew by the instance. See Chapter 2 for more information.

13. C.   The Net8 configuration file is called TNSNAMES.ORA. See Chapter 2 for more information.

14. C.   TNSNAMES.ORA can be edited by the Net8 Assistant. See Chapter 2 for more information.

15. A.   Instance Manager is used to stop and start instances. See Chapter 3 for more information.

16. D.   SHUTDOWN ABORT stops the instance without doing a checkpoint in the database, and thus needs to go through the recovery process when the instance next starts. See Chapter 3 for more information.

17. B.   STARTUP OPEN starts the instance normally. See Chapter 3 for more information.

18. A.   Initially, only the schema owner can give rights to others. See Chapter 7 for more information.

19. C.   Storage Manager is used to create new tablespaces. See Chapter 7 for more information.

20. B.   A tablespace is used to hold database objects and data. See Chapter 7 for more information.

21. A, B.   To increase a tablespace either make the existing datafiles larger or add more datafiles. See Chapter 7 for more information.

22. A.   A tablespace has to have at least one datafile. See Chapter 7 for more information.

23. D.   Rollback segments are used to hold transactions. See Chapter 7 for more information.

24. B.   You should have approximately one rollback segment for every four active transactions. See Chapter 7 for more information.

25. A, B.   The System DBA and the System DBO can start an instance. See Chapter 6 for more information.

26. B.   The parameter file needs remote_login_passwordfile=shared so that you can add additional operators. See Chapter 6 for more information.

27. D.   You manage security with Security Manager. See Chapter 6 for more information.

28. D.   Scripts are run with SQLPlus Worksheet. See Chapter 7 for more information.

29. A, B.   You can view objects by type or by schema. See Chapter 7 for more information.

30. B, C.   Tables and indexes get larger; synonyms and procedures don't. See Chapter 7 for more information.

31. B.   You only need the Execute right to run a procedure. See Chapter 6 for more information.

32. C.   You only need the Update right to edit existing rows. See Chapter 6 for more information.

33. A, B.   Sue gets Select rights for being herself and Update rights for her role membership. See Chapter 6 for more information.

34. A, C, D.   Security Manager can be used to grant rights to users, create roles, and put users in roles. See Chapter 6 for more information.

35. B.   Incremental backups are fast to back up, as only changed information is backed up. See Chapter 10 for more information.

36. D.   Cold backups imply that the instance is stopped, and the database files are closed. See Chapter 10 for more information.

37. B.   You must be running in ARCHIVELOG mode to back up a database in use. See Chapter 10 for more information.

38. A.   Oracle performs the database recovery when an instance fails. See Chapter 10 for more information.

39. B.   The ALTER DATABASE ARCHIVELOG command switches the database to ARCHIVELOG mode. See Chapter 10 for more information.

40. D.   Since the database was closed when it was backed up in NOAR-CHIVELOG mode, the database needs to be closed when it is restored. See Chapter 10 for more information.

41. A, B.   Both indexes and constraints need to be disabled to do a direct load. See Chapter 8 for more information.

42. C. Schema Manager is used to enable and disable constraints. See Chapter 8 for more information.

43. C. Events can be set to start fix-it jobs. See Chapter 9 for more information.

44. A, B, C, D. Events can be created to monitor all of the conditions listed. See Chapter 9 for more information.

45. C. WebDB is TCP/IP based. See Chapter 11 for more information.

46. A. Database objects are created from the Build screens of WebDB Administrator. See Chapter 11 for more information.

47. D. The Monitor screens of WebDB Administrator allow you to see the usage of various database objects. See Chapter 11 for more information.

48. B. To connect to WebDB, use the HTTP protocol and specify <the IP address>/webdb along with the port. See Chapter 11 for more information.

49. B. When you create a site, a user called <site>_Admin is created to administer the site. See Chapter 11 for more information.

50. C. You can manage the Listener and MIME extensions from the Administer screens. See Chapter 11 for more information.

Appendix

B

Performance and Tuning

An Oracle database can be likened to a high performance sports car—initially it has incredible performance, but its performance will lessen over time without regular maintenance. Today's servers are powerful enough that you may be running at less than optimal performance and not notice any actual effect. The danger of not optimizing performance is that when circumstances do change (such as when adding a lot of data or more users), performance may degrade rapidly.

Databases can also encounter intermittent performance problems due to the way users are using the database. A poorly designed application will be more prone to having problems that a correctly designed one.

In this appendix, you will analyze just what the database is supposed to be doing and configure the database to best support its job. You will also look at two of the tools available from Oracle that are invaluable to analyzing performance issues in a database: the Diagnostics and Tuning Packs.

Analyzing Database Usage

Before you can accurately analyze and tune database performance, you need to know the primary purpose of the database. As stated in Chapter 1, there are two primary functions a database can perform.

- OLAP or online analytical processing

- OLTP or online transaction processing

OLAP databases tend to be historical databases, with little new data being added to the database. OLAP databases are also called data warehouses.

OLTP databases are designed for holding new, dynamic data such as an order entry system. OLTP databases are also called data marts.

OLAP and OLTP functions are hard to optimize on the same set of tables within a database. For the best performance, separate the two functions into two separate databases or, at least, two separate sets of tables within the same database.

Many performance problems can be traced to the complications that come with simultaneously running the OLAP and OLTP functions. For instance, a manager may run a weekly report on Friday afternoon, severely slowing down the 25 clerks who are online with customers, taking orders. In this case, solutions to the problem may include simply running the report after hours, adding bigger hardware to the server, or replicating the data to a different server for the manager's use. Keep the usage of the database in mind as you look at various other scenarios that affect performance.

Locking Issues

In the early days of databases, most databases were single user databases, which meant that only one person at a time could use the database. Newer, smarter databases were written to allow multiple people simultaneous access to the database. In general, there is one rule of thumb with multiple users accessing a database: *Many readers can simultaneously work in a database, but only one writer can work in a database at a time.*

Oracle tracks each user and what they are doing by using locks. A lock can be kept on various database objects by various users for various purposes, but all locks basically help avoid contention in the database. When more than one user attempts to edit the same data, you can get locking contentions. For example, if someone is reading a newspaper, you can look over their shoulder and read either the same article as the other person or a different article. If you want to read an article in a different section, you can grab that section and start reading. This is an example of multiple readers. The problem comes when both of you attempt to do the crossword puzzle at the same time. If both of you attempt to write in the same crossword entry, one person would fail. If both of you were to pick different crossword puzzle lines to fill in, you would be OK.

Contention problems also come in when there are just too many readers in one database or when someone who wants to write in the database is blocked by someone who wants to read the database. For example, if the crossword puzzle is on the back of the sports page, no one can read the sports page until the person is done doing the crossword puzzle.

One of the worst contention problems you can encounter is a deadlock where two connections are each trying to access a resource that the other one has (see Figure B.1).

FIGURE B.1 A deadlock situation

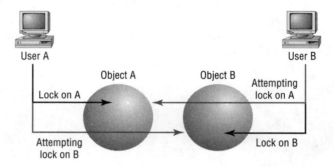

An example would be a situation in which someone who has checked out the first book of a series from a library is waiting until they check out the second book in the series before they begin reading the first. While another person has the second book in the series checked out and is waiting to read it until they get the first book. Oracle automatically detects deadlock situations like this and kills one of the connections after a wait period. Deadlocks can be resolved by increasing the speed of the server or by rewriting applications so that data is accessed by all users in the same direction.

Oracle has a great tool for detecting and monitoring locking contention called the Performance Monitor (specifically the Locking section), which is discussed later in this appendix.

Rollback Segment Issues

Oracle databases store changes to be committed in the rollback segments. Rollback segments can then be used to roll data changes back, if a Rollback statement is encountered before a Commit statement. The rule of thumb for the number of rollback segments needed is one rollback segment for every four concurrent transactions. For example, if you have 100 users adding transactions, you should have at least 25 rollback segments. Rollback segments are discussed in more detail in Chapters 5 and 7, "Creating and Managing Databases" and "Installing and Managing Applications," respectively.

You may have problems with rollback segments for one of three reasons:

- There is not enough room in the tablespace for rollback segments to expand.

- The maximum number of extents has been reached for existing rollback segments.

- The number of rollback segments is insufficient.

If you run out of room in the tablespace where you are storing rollback segments, you need to either manually increase the size of the files or set the files to automatically grow. Storage Manager can be used to increase the size of the tablespace files.

If you are at the maximum number of extents, you should increase the number of extents by using Storage Manager (see Figure B.2). You can also create new rollback segments with Storage Manager.

FIGURE B.2 Editing Rollback Segments

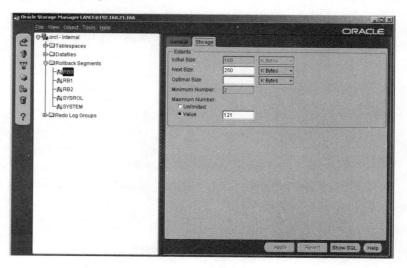

In Exercise B.1, you create a new rollback segment.

EXERCISE B.1

Creating Rollback Segments

1. Start Storage Manager.

2. Open the Rollback Segments folder.

3. Right-click the folder, and choose Create. You can also choose Object ➤ Create ➤ Rollback Segment from the menu or choose the Create icon from the left pane.

4. Enter a name for the rollback segment (such as RB2).

5. Change the tablespace to the rollback tablespace.

6. Set the segment to Online.

7. Go to the Storage tab. You should see something like that in Figure B.2.

8. Set the Initial Size to 100KB.

9. Set the Next Size to 250KB.

10. Set the Minimum Number to 2 and the Maximum Number to 121.

11. Choose Create to make the new rollback segment.

Redo Log File Issues

Redo log files hold copies of changes made to the database in case of a database crash. Remember that Oracle automatically rotates data between redo logs. The issues you might face when dealing with redo log problems are as follows:

- There must be at least two redo log files available.

- If Manual Archiving is set, a redo log file must be manually archived (by you) before Oracle can use it again.

Because Oracle switches back and forth between redo log files, it is a good idea to have the log files mirrored on two or more hard drives. Mirroring log files is done in the INIT<SID>.ORA file and is covered in Chapter 5, "Creating and Managing Databases."

Archiving redo log files is covered in Chapter 10, "Backups and Restorations." To add, modify, or delete redo log files, you can use Storage Manager. Simply highlight the Redo Log Groups folder to quickly tell which log file is the current one and what the number sequence and date are (see Figure B.3).

FIGURE B.3   Redo Log File summary

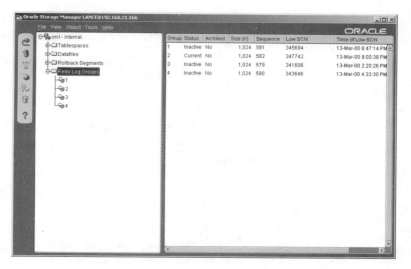

Parameter File Issues

When an instance is started, parameters are read from the INIT<SID>.ORA file. Parameters include the size of RAM that the instance will use, as well as how the RAM is divided by the instance. A common occurrence is for the parameter file not to get updated correctly when the hardware of the server changes. On a busy server, for example, you may decide to add 512MB more of RAM. If you don't go back and readjust the parameter file, the instance will use the same amount of RAM as before. Another common mistake is to forget that changing parameters only takes effect when the instance is restarted, not immediately.

The parameter file, and the various settings you need to pay attention to, are covered in Chapter 5, "Creating and Managing Databases," but the main parameters you need to be aware of are as follows:

Shared_pool_size   The size of the shared memory area

Db_block_buffers   The number of data blocks cached in RAM

Log_buffers   The number of bytes of RAM used by the redo log file

Performance Issues

When looking at performance issues, there are generally two scenarios:

- The hardware is insufficient to support the application and users.

- The application (for whatever reason) is not using the hardware to its full potential.

In other words, when looking at performance problems you need to decide whether it is a hardware or a software problem. In some ways, a hardware problem is easier to find and fix, because hardware speed (both maximum and current) can be readily found out. Software issues are harder to spot, as you first need to find which software piece is misconfigured (Oracle or the application) and then need to reconfigure it without breaking anything.

A common performance issue is hard drive performance. As shown in Chapter 5, "Creating and Managing Databases," hard drives and their configuration can have a tremendous impact on the performance of a database. RAID 5 drives, while efficient, are slow in write operations and are not recommended for large OLTP applications.

Oracle is also CPU and RAM intensive, which means that you may overwhelm slower servers, especially if the number of users climbs dramatically over a short period. Most operating systems allow you to watch CPU and RAM in use in order to determine if you have sufficient amounts for both the operating system and any applications you are running on the server. For example, Windows NT comes with Performance Monitor and Task Manager, while NetWare servers have the Monitor utility, all of which allow you to monitor CPU and RAM usage.

Applications can have performance problems due to the following issues:

- Poor table design

- Poor index design

- Too many indexes

- Not enough indexes

- Poorly written queries

Luckily, Oracle has a Diagnostics Pack add-on to Enterprise Manager that can be used to watch and analyze Oracle sessions.

The Diagnostics Pack

O racle has a utility called the Diagnostics Pack that allows you to monitor, capture, and analyze sessions against the Oracle server. The various pieces of the Diagnostics Pack allow you to set exactly what part of the instance and database you wish to monitor. Of course, the less items you monitor, the lower the overhead, although you don't want to monitor too few items in case you need the information for later analysis.

Installing the Diagnostics Pack

Before you run the Diagnostics Pack, you will need to install it. Exercise B.2 shows you how to install the Diagnostics Pack.

EXERCISE B.2

Installing the Diagnostics Pack

1. Choose a workstation that already has Enterprise Manager (or Enterprise Manager will be installed as well as the Diagnostics Pack).

2. Insert the Diagnostics Pack CD, and start the Setup program. You should see something like the following image.

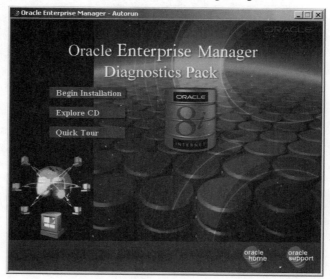

3. Click the Begin Installation button.

4. Choose Next, and the Welcome screen will appear.

EXERCISE B.2 *(continued)*

5. Choose Next again at the File Locations screen to take the default paths (you can change them if you wish, and then choose Next).

6. At the Available Products screen, choose Diagnostics Pack if you already have Enterprise Manager installed (the default) or choose Diagnostics Pack, Management Server, and Enterprise Manager Client if you haven't already installed Enterprise Manager. Select Next to continue.

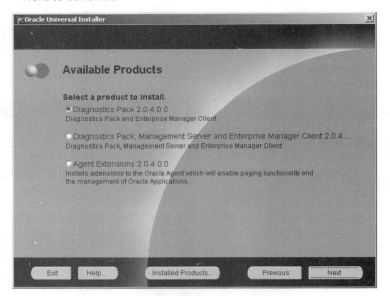

7. Choose Custom at the Installation Types screen to select and confirm what will be installed.

8. Once you have selected or deselected individual components (the defaults are suggested), choose Next.

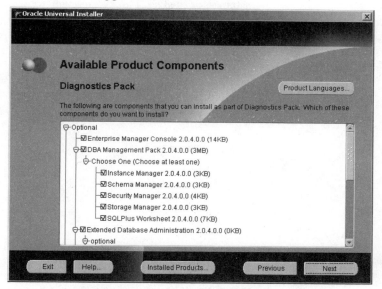

9. Select Install at the Summary screen.

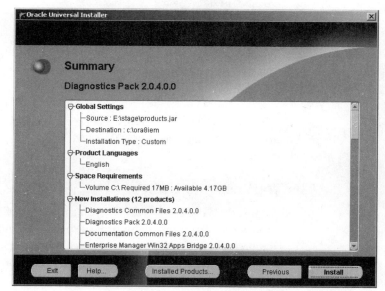

10. When the installation has completed, choose Exit and then Yes to close the Installer.

Running the Diagnostics Pack

The first time you run the Diagnostics Pack, you will be prompted to create additional tables in the repository, as shown in Figure B.4. Be sure to say OK to create the tables, or the Diagnostics Pack will not work. Once you choose to create the tables, you should see a Work in Progress screen like that in Figure B.5.

FIGURE B.4 Choosing to create the Diagnostics Pack system tables

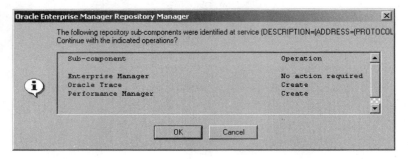

FIGURE B.5 Creating the Diagnostics Pack tables

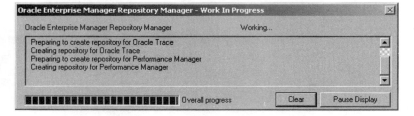

The Diagnostics Pack consists of several utilities. The utility you should be most concerned about is the Trace Manager, although the other utilities are also useful.

The TopSessions Utility

To start the TopSessions utility, you can choose Tools ➢ Diagnostics Pack ➢ TopSessions from the menu of Enterprise Manager, or you can go to the Diagnostics Pack program group and choose the TopSessions icon.

Once you log in to Oracle, you can see who is connected and their connection status (see Figure B.6).

FIGURE B.6   The TopSessions Utility

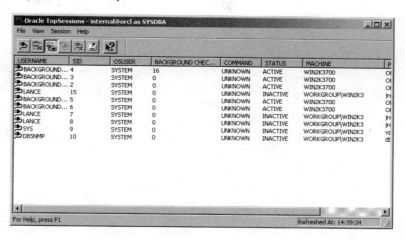

Items of note in the TopSessions utility include the Username (the name of the connected user), Background Checkpoints Completed (which gives you a feel for how much data the program is changing), Command (which lets you see the last command run), Machine (the name of the computer the connection came from), and Program (the name of the application that is connected to Oracle).

You may also want to go to the Session ➤ Options menu and select other items to monitor. Figure B.7 shows the Bytes Received via SQL*Net parameter selected for monitoring. Once you select OK, the new parameter is shown.

FIGURE B.7   Selecting parameters in TopSession

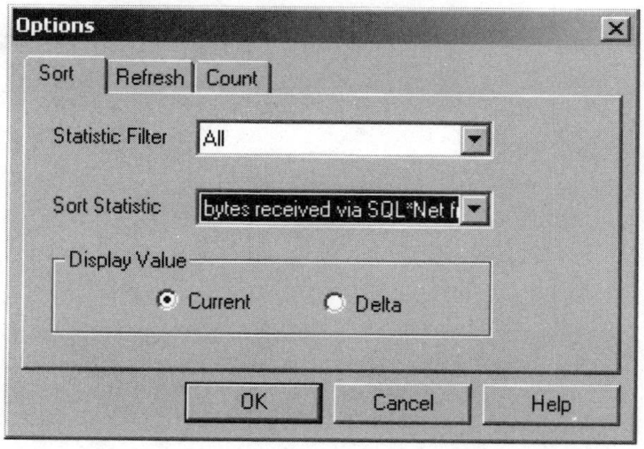

The Performance Monitor Utility

The Performance Monitor utility will be familiar with anyone who has run Windows NT's Performance Monitor program. You can choose to monitor various operating system parameters, as well as Oracle database parameters.

You can connect to the repository or directly to a database. Once connected, you can see live data from your database by opening the Databases folder and selecting the appropriate folder.

To view a particular chart, highlight the predefined display from the folder (such as the Locks Chart in Figure B.8) and choose Show Chart. You will see the chart you have selected (see Figure B.9).

FIGURE B.8 The Locks Manager Folder

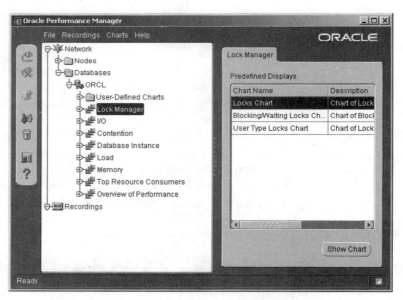

FIGURE B.9   The Locks Chart

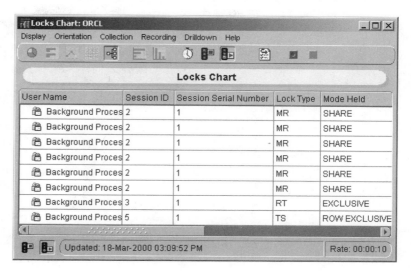

 You can change the update (automatic refresh) time by going to Collection ➤ Set Update Rate and the type of chart by choosing Display ➤ Pie, Bar, Strip, or Table.

Following is an explanation of the various folders in the User Defined Charts folder.

Lock Manager   You can see the current locks held in the database, as well as blocked and waiting locks. You can also see user locks as opposed to system locks.

I/O   From the I/O folder, you can choose charts that show you the overall as well as specific inputs and outputs of the instance. The instance-wide I/O Statistics Chart (the first one listed) shows overall activity in the database (see Figure B.10).

FIGURE B.10 The Instance-wide I/O Statistics Chart

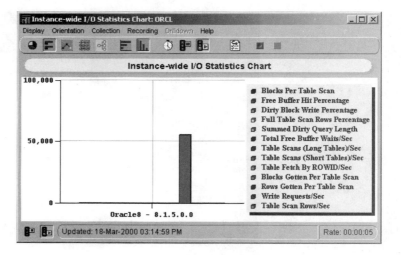

Contention The Contention folder allows you to monitor when and where contentions are happening. The Wait Statistics chart may be of use, as it breaks down various components of the instance and specifies how long each of them have been waiting.

Database Instance The Database Instance folder contains charts that allow you to look at various tablespace parameters such as status and size (see Figure B.11), free space (see Figure B.12), User Statistics (see Figure B.13), and initialization parameters. All in all, this folder contains some very useful charts and information.

FIGURE B.11 The Tablespace Chart

Tablespace Chart: ORCL

Display   Orientation   Collection   Recording   Drilldown   Help

Tablespace Chart

Oracle Server Instan...	Status	Total File Blocks	Total Quota Blocks
TEMP	ONLINE	25600	0
USERS	ONLINE	9951	9300
SYSTEM	ONLINE	65454	0
RBS	ONLINE	9101	0
DRSYS	ONLINE	40960	0
INDX	ONLINE	5120	0

Updated: 18-Mar-2000 03:28:04 PM   Rate: 00:00:05

FIGURE B.12 The Tablespace Free Space Chart

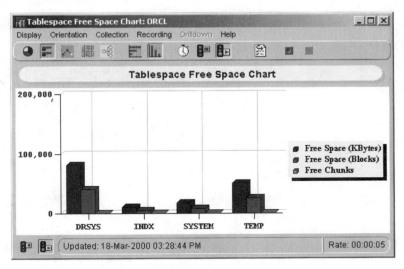

FIGURE B.13 The Users Statistics Chart

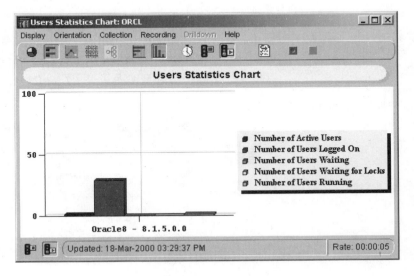

Load   The Load folder consists of charts that help you track session statistics (see Figure B.14), transaction statistics, redo statistics, throughput statistics, and recursive calls.

FIGURE B.14   The Session Statistics Chart

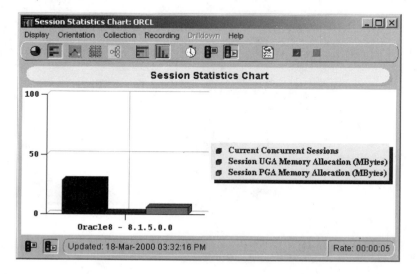

Memory   The Memory folder contains charts that allow you to see where Oracle has allocated the various memory types. There are many charts, but one of the more useful ones is memory statistics (see Figure B.15).

FIGURE B.15   The Memory Statistics Chart

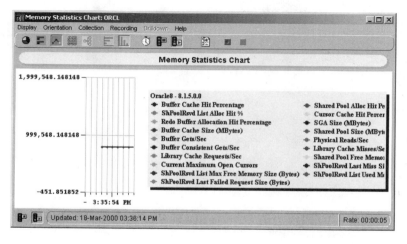

Top Resource Consumers The Top Resource Consumers folder contains various charts that can help you to determine who is using what resources in the database. The Top Sessions chart (see Figure B.16) is very similar to the TopSessions utility.

FIGURE B.16 The Top Sessions Chart

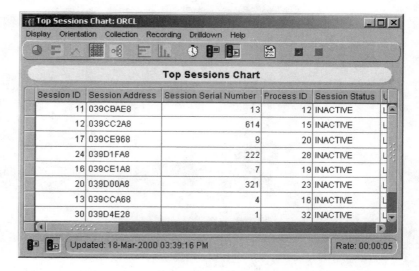

Overview of Performance The Overview of Performance folder contains two groups of charts, one is an overview of cache utilization and one is an overview of throughput.

While you can view the individual charts in the two groups of charts found in the Overview of Performance folder one at a time, viewing one or the other group of charts all at once lets you quickly compare many items at the same time.

The Capacity Planner Utility

You can look at existing loads on your Oracle server, as well as anticipate future loads using the Capacity Planner. To use the Capacity Planner, you must first connect to the repository or database and then set the options to be used when collecting data. To set options, highlight the service, and set the collection, storage, and purge options (see Figure B.17).

FIGURE B.17 Setting Capacity Planner data collection options

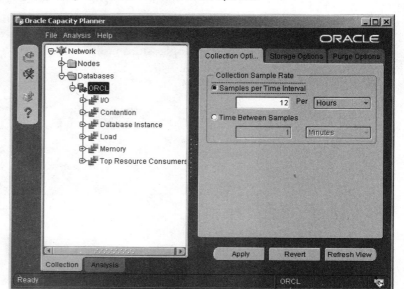

Once you have collected a sufficient amount of data to feel comfortable (only a few minutes for a busy, consistent server, but maybe a couple of hours for an inconsistent one), you can go to the Analysis screen. Once connected to the database where your historical data is stored, you can run the Capacity Analysis and look for future trends.

The Trace Manager Utility

The Trace Manager allows you to create traces of Oracle sessions for troubleshooting and/or performance tuning. Creating and viewing traces is beyond the scope of the role of database operators. For more information, please see *OCP: Oracle8i DBA Performance Tuning and Network Administration Study Guide* (Sybex, 2000).

The Trace Data Viewer

The Trace Data Viewer allows you to view stored trace data. To use the viewer, first create a trace with Trace Manager, save the trace, and then start Trace Data Viewer.

The Tuning Pack

Another set of utilities that Oracle has is the Tuning Pack. The Tuning Pack consists of utilities designed to help Oracle databases and queries run better. The utilities are Oracle Expert, Index Expert, SQL Analyze, and Tablespace Manager. To install the Tuning Pack, follow the instructions from Exercise B.2, substituting the Tuning Pack in place of the Diagnostics Pack.

The Tuning Pack will also require new repository tables to be created the first time you run the utilities (see Figures B.4 and B.5). Make sure you create the tables so that the Tuning Pack will work correctly.

Oracle Expert

The Oracle Expert is like having a high paid consultant come look at your database, instance, and application. The Expert can be used to create and analyze a session, which captures important information about the instance and how data is being used by Oracle. The Expert can then make recommendations, which you are free to modify, save, and execute.

As with many other diagnostics and tuning utilities, the Oracle Expert stores information in the repository, which means your management server must be available.

Once you start the Oracle Expert, you will need to create a tuning session. The Tuning Session Wizard will prompt you to load the sample tuning session (recommended for beginning administrators) or to create a new tuning session. In Exercise B.3, you load the default tuning session and look at the results.

EXERCISE B.3

Oracle Expert and Tuning Sessions

1. Start the Oracle Expert, and connect to the management server.

EXERCISE B.3 *(continued)*

2. When prompted, load the sample tuning session.

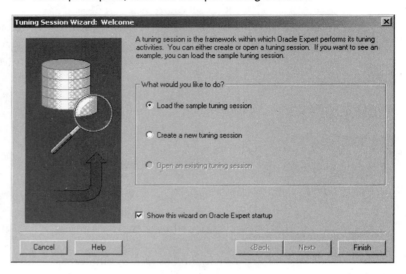

3. Choose Finish to load the sample tuning session.

4. Go to the Scope tab of the sample tuning session. Leave all of the defaults on.

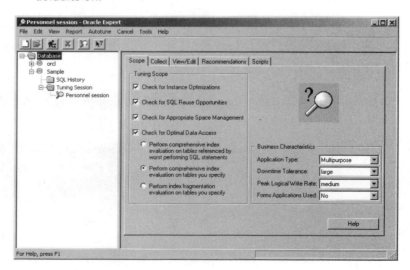

EXERCISE B.3 *(continued)*

5. Go to the Collect tab. Notice that all of the collection classes (types) are turned on.

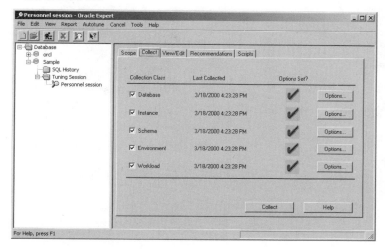

6. Click the Options button for the Database collection class. Notice the various options you can set for database collection. Leave the default settings by choosing Cancel.

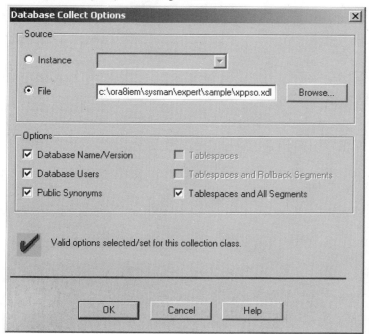

7. Click the Options button for the Instance collection class. Notice that you can collect instance statistics and options. Leave the default settings by choosing Cancel.

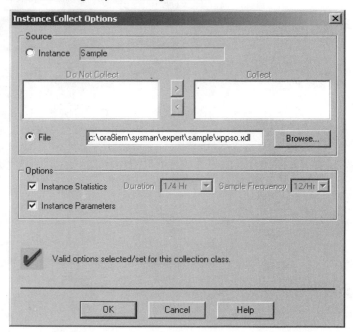

8. Click the Options button for the Schema collection class. Notice the various options you can set for schema collection. Leave the default settings by choosing Cancel.

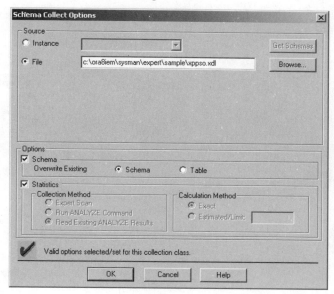

9. Click the Options button for the Environment collection class. Notice the various options you can set for environment collection. You may choose to collect less information if you know precisely what you need to monitor, but in many cases you will want to gather a lot of information and analyze it later. Leave the default settings by choosing Cancel.

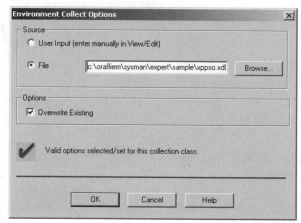

EXERCISE B.3 *(continued)*

10. Click the Options button for the Workload collection class. Notice the various options you can set for workload collection. Leave the default settings by choosing Cancel.

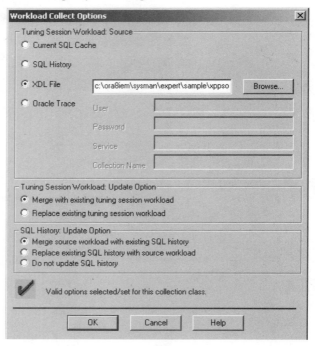

11. Go to the View/Edit tab. Note that you can expand various folders and change your settings for advanced tuning. For this exercise, leave the default settings.

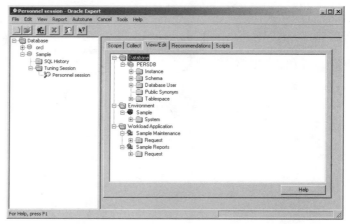

12. Go to the Recommendations tab. Choose Generate to generate recommendations (recommendations may take 5+ minutes to generate). You can open various recommendations after they are generated. You may see recommendations such as adding datafiles to tablespaces that are about full, adding or deleting indexes to improve performance, and changing passwords on users with no passwords.

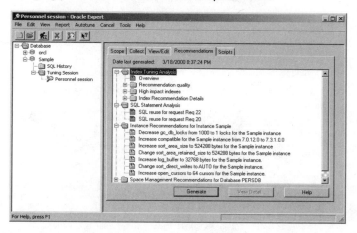

13. Go to the Scripts tab. Generate scripts for the recommended changes by choosing the Generate button.

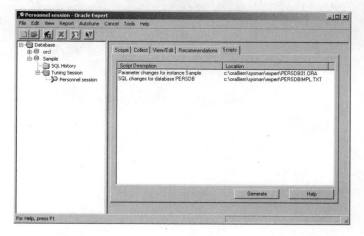

Index Tuning Expert

The Index Tuning Expert is run from Enterprise Manager and can look at and analyze indexes. In Exercise B.4, you run the Index Tuning Expert against the ORCL database.

EXERCISE B.4

The Index Tuning Expert

1. Start Enterprise Manager.

2. Choose Index Tuning Expert from the Database Tools menu.

3. The first page of the Index Tuning Wizard explains what it will look for and fix. Choose Next to continue.

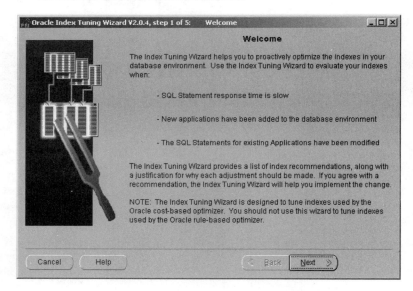

4. Choose the type of database you work with on page two of the Wizard. Leave the default setting if you are not sure. Choose Next to continue.

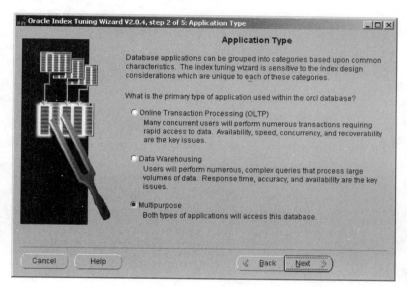

5. On page 3, you can choose which schemas to focus on. Leave the default setting, and choose Next.

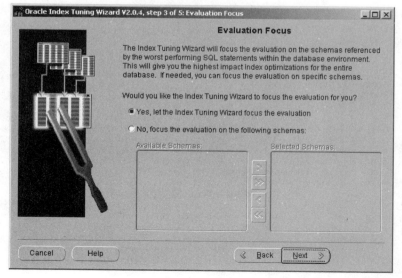

6. Choose Generate to generate recommendations. Note that you may not have any. Choose Next to continue.

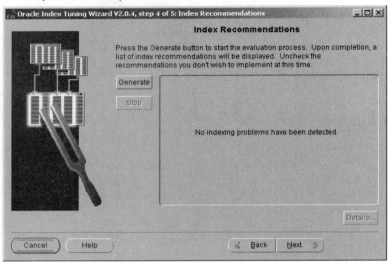

7. On the Implementation Summary screen, you can choose to run the recommendations immediately or save them for later analysis. Choose Finish when done.

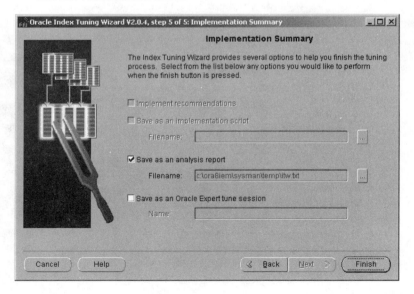

SQL Analyze

SQL Analyze can be used to look at SQL statements and code and determine if there is a better way to write code. To run SQL Analyze, you need to make your procedure first, then tell SQL Analyze where the procedure is that it needs to optimize. SQL Analyze is designed to be used more by developers than operators, which is why we will not cover it in detail here.

Tablespace Manager

Tablespace Manager allows you to quickly monitor and modify tablespace characteristics such as free space, datafiles, and extents. Schema Manager can do the functions of Tablespace Manager, although you may find Tablespace Manager easier to use. Tablespace Manager can also show you the fragmentation of objects within a tablespace, which is why this utility was introduced in Chapter 7, "Installing and Managing Applications."

Summary

Maintenance is an ongoing issue with Oracle databases. Common problems that may occur are running out of room in database files, not enough rollback segments, incorrect parameters in the initialization file, and general performance issues.

Oracle has many tools available to not only diagnose problems, but help you foresee problems before they happen. The Diagnostics Pack helps with current problems, while the Tuning Pack helps increase performance.

Lock contention happens when two or more users attempt to get at the same data at the same time, and a deadlock can occur when each has a resource the other is trying to gain access to.

Glossary

A

application   An application consists of one or more tables of data and usually other objects as well, including views, procedures, synonyms, and indexes.

ARCHIVELOG mode   The redo logs copy their contents out to archive files before they get overwritten. Production databases should be run in ARCHIVELOG mode.

C

Console   Another term for Enterprise Manager. See *Enterprise Manager*.

constraint   A method to enforce rules, defaults, and primary and foreign keys on tables.

control files   Binary files used by Oracle to manage the datafiles of a database. If the control files are unavailable, the database cannot be opened.

cross join   In a cross join, every row of one table is listed against every row of another table. A cross join is sometimes referred to as a Cartesian product, as every possible result is computed.

D

database   The complete set of objects, stored on physical files, that records data.

Database Configuration Assistant   The graphical Wizard used to create new databases.

datafiles   Files used to store Oracle databases. Datafiles can only be opened by an Oracle instance.

deadlock   A situation in which two connections are each trying to get resources the other has locked.

DELETE command   The DELETE command is used to delete rows of data.

DELETE permission   The permission that lets you delete rows.

Diagnostics Pack   The utility used to find common problems.

Disk Duplexing   RAID 1 with two hard drive controllers.

Disk Mirroring   Another term for RAID 1.

Disk Striping   Another term for RAID 0.

E

Enterprise Manager   The overall management tool also known as the Console or OEM. See *Console* and *OEM*.

event   A circumstance, such as whether the database is up or down, that is checked on a regular basis by Enterprise Manager using the Oracle Intelligent Agent.

Event Library   A set of events created for the server. Any of the events can be modified and resubmitted to the Oracle Intelligent Agent.

EXECUTE permission   The permission that lets you run procedures.

export   A function of OEM that saves Oracle data to a file.

F

fault tolerance   A method that tries to eliminate a single point of failure in your operation.

foreign key   A foreign key is used for referential integrity and points to an existing primary key.

foreign key constraint   A method to ensure there is a matching row in another table for a particular column.

I

import   To bring in data that was previously exported from an Oracle database.

Index   A storage structure used to speed up queries.

inner join   Inner joins only show results if rows from both tables have matching entries.

INSERT command   The INSERT command is used to add new rows of data.

INSERT permission   The permission that lets you add new data rows.

instance   The server memory and processes required to open a database.

Instance Manager   This graphical utility allows you to start and stop an Oracle instance.

J

job   A set of code or one or more actions scheduled to run at a certain time or under certain conditions; a scheduled action.

Job Library   A set of jobs created for the server. Any of the jobs can be modified and resubmitted to the Oracle Intelligent Agent.

L

Listener   A process that runs on the Oracle server that looks for new client connection requests.

LISTENER.ORA   This file holds all of the configuration information for the Listener. This file is only found on Oracle servers.

load   To bring in non-Oracle data.

N

Net8   The common language between Oracle clients and servers.

Net8 Configuration Assistant   This graphical utility helps you build database aliases, which means it creates and modifies the TNSNAMES.ORA file.

NOARCHIVELOG mode   The default mode of a database. Redo logs autowrap when they fill up, which means you can only perform full database backups, and you can only do them when the database is offline.

NULL   Null values represent data that could exist but doesn't for that particular person or thing.

O

OEM   Another term for (Oracle) Enterprise Manager. See *Enterprise Manager*.

OLAP   Online Analytical Processing, which emphasizes data that is mostly read-only.

OLTP   Online Transaction Processing, which emphasizes many writes to a database.

Oracle Intelligent Agent   The program in charge of jobs and scheduling. It acts as a middleman between Oracle and the operating system.

Oracle Universal Installer (OUI)   This is the program you run to install both servers and workstations. You will see a list of previously installed applications, as well as a list of applications that you can install.

outer join   Outer joins are useful for showing all of the rows from one table with any matching rows of a second table.

P

Parameter file   The ASCII file that the Oracle instance reads at startup. It contains various parameters for the instance.

Password file   The PWD file that contains the Internal, SYS, and other system administrators.

primary key   A column on a table used to track a row. Primary keys must be unique, in that no duplicate or NULL values are allowed.

primary key constraint   A method to ensure rows are unique in a given table.

procedure   SQL code that has been grouped together, given a name, and stored as part of the database.

Profile   A group of settings that can be assigned to more than one user and can control passwords and resource usage.

R

RAID 0   Another term for disk striping. It is the fastest access method, but it provides no fault tolerance.

RAID 1   Another term for disk mirroring. It provides moderate performance gains and fault tolerance, but it's expensive as you lose half of your drive space.

RAID 5   Disk striping with parity. It has good read, but slow write performance. Nonetheless, it's useful because it's very efficient. You lose $1/n$ where n is the number of drives in your array.

RAID 10   A mirrored, striped drive array. It's the fastest way to get fault tolerance, but the most expensive as well.

redo log files   Files used by Oracle to store changes to the database as they occur.

role   Another name for a database group—members of a role get all of the same rights as those assigned to the role.

rollback segments   Internal objects used to track data before and after transactions take place. They are used in case a transaction doesn't finish—the data will be rolled back to its original state.

S

schema   A group of related objects owned by the same account.

schema account   A schema account is simply a user account that owns one or more objects in the database.

Schema Manager   The graphical tool used to create, manage, and delete various database objects, and thus the schema.

Security Manager   The tool used to configure users, roles, and security.

SELECT permission   The permission that lets you read data.

SELECT statement   A SELECT statement can be used to retrieve specific rows and columns of information from one or more tables in one or more databases. There are three basic components to every SELECT statement: SELECT, FROM, and WHERE.

Server Manager   A command line program used to submit PL/SQL commands to the Oracle engine primarily from the server itself. Server Manager is started by running SVRMGR31 on NetWare servers, SVRMGRL on Windows NT, and SVRMGRL (or SVRMGRLO) on UNIX servers. This command prompt utility also lets you start and stop database instances.

SHUTDOWN ABORT   With this option, current transactions are immediately terminated, users are disconnected, and uncommitted transactions are not rolled back. After a SHUTDOWN ABORT, the next

time the database is started it will automatically begin an instance recovery. Completed transactions are not checkpointed into the database, which is why an instance recovery will be performed when the instance restarts.

SHUTDOWN IMMEDIATE   With this option, currently processing transactions are not completed, the transactions are rolled back, all users are disconnected, and the database and instance shut down. Completed transactions are checkpointed into the database before the shutdown.

SHUTDOWN NORMAL   With this option, Oracle will not allow any new connections and will wait for all users to log off. Once they have done so, Oracle closes and dismounts the database then shuts down the instance. This is the default SHUTDOWN mode.

SHUTDOWN TRANSACTIONAL   With this option, Oracle will not allow any new connections, and any connected clients will be disconnected as soon as they complete their current transactions. Once all transactions are finished, the database and instance are shut down.

SQL   Structured English Query Language, a database language that allows for interaction between the client and server and was designed to be easy to understand and use.

SQLNET.ORA   This configuration file is found on both servers and workstations and holds various configurations.

SQLPlus Worksheet   A more complex tool than SQL*Plus that allows you to send SQL code to Oracle. Commands are created in one screen, and the results appear in another.

SQL*Plus   A simple shell that allows you to write SQL commands to Oracle and have them immediately execute in the same screen. Server Manager is similar.

STARTUP MOUNT   This will start the instance and open the control file, but it will not open the database files. This is commonly used when doing a database recovery.

STARTUP NOMOUNT   This starts an instance without mounting any control or database files. This is commonly used when creating a new database.

STARTUP OPEN   This is the default option for starting Oracle. It starts the instance, and opens the control file and the database. If you only issue the STARTUP command, it is as if you issued the STARTUP OPEN command.

STARTUP RESTRICT   This will start the instance and open a database, but all users except those with the System DBA or the Restricted privilege will be unable to connect to the database.

Storage Manager   The graphical utility used to create and manage tablespaces, datafiles, redo files, and rollback segments.

synonym   A named object you can use to point to a different object in the database so that you only have to refer to the synonym object instead of the original object.

System Datafiles   Data that is kept and used by Oracle.

System ID (SID)   The 4–8 character label for an instance, as well as its database and files.

System Tablespaces   Tablespaces designed to hold system data.

T

table   The main storage structure of a relational database that holds the actual data. You will need to have at least one table for your application. Tables consist of a name for the table itself, as well as names and characteristics for each of the columns.

TNSNAMES.ORA   This file holds database alias names, as well as all connection information used to connect to a particular database instance.

Tuning Pack   Utility used to improve Oracle performance.

U

UNION   You can combine the results of two or more queries into a single result set by using the UNION operator. The UNION operator combines result sets and eliminates redundant results, while the UNION ALL operator shows all resulting rows.

UPDATE command   The UPDATE command is used to edit or update existing rows in the database.

UPDATE permission   The permission that lets you edit data rows.

user data   Data that is kept and used by people.

user tablespaces   Tablespaces designed to be used by people.

V

View   A storage structure that is basically a stored SQL query. Views don't contain any actual data. Views can contain columns from one or more tables and are very useful when the same query is being run over and over.

W

WebDB   A graphical, TCP/IP-based interface for the Oracle database that is used to manage objects and create Web sites.

WebDB Administrator   The main utility for WebDB. WebDB Administrator lets you manage and create objects, Web components, and Web sites.

With Grant option   The option that lets you grant your rights to others.

Index

Note to the reader: Throughout this index **boldfaced** page numbers indicate primary discussions of a topic. *Italicized* page numbers indicate illustrations.

Symbols

\ADMIN directory, 32–33
\ORACLE_HOME directory, 32–34, 71
\ORADATA directory, 32–33

A

accessibility for users, 13
activity logs, managing in WebDB, **377–378**, *377–378*
administrators. *See also* DBAs
    adding with Enterprise Manager, **97–98**, *97*
ALTER DATABASE command, 18, 184
application developers
    certification, xxii–xxiii
    responsiblities of, 6–7
applications, defined, 228
applications, installing and managing, 5, **227–250**
    creating and managing tablespaces, **234–236**, *234–236*
    database design, **229–233**
        instance parameters, **232**
        logical design, **229–230**
        overcoming bad design, 229

        physical database design, **233**
    database objects, creating and managing, **240–250**
        creating schemas, **240–250**
    database security, creating and managing, 250
    ensuring adequate resources, **233–234**
        determining CPU speed, 234
        determining network bandwidth, 234
        estimating amount of RAM, 234
        forecasting hard drive space, 233
    schema accounts, **237–239**
        creating and managing, **238–239**, *239*
        database accounts and, **237–238**
    summary, 250–251
    tablespaces, ensuring adequate sizing, 250
ARCHIVELOG mode, 327
    converting a database to, **330–335**, *331*, *333–335*
        editing the INIT.ORA file to support automatic archiving, 331, *331*
        editing the parameter file for automatic ARCHIVELOG mode, **330–331**, *331*

modifying the database to run in
ARCHIVELOG mode,
332–335, *333–335*
using Instance Manager, **332–335**,
333–335
summary, 345–346
vs. NOARCHIVELOG mode, **328–329**
arithmetic functions supported by SQL
(includes table), 135–136
Assessment Test, xxxi–xxxix
Autoextend properties of datafiles, 186, *186*

B

backing up databases, **324–342**
ARCHIVELOG mode
converting to, **330–335**, *331,*
333–335
vs. NOARCHIEVELOG mode, 328
backup scenarios, **327–328**
cold vs. warm backups, 328
instance failures vs. media
failures, 327
considerations for a backup plan, **325–326**
backup medium, 325–326
determining responsibility for, 326
expected frequency, 325
OS options, 326
verification method, 326
creating backup jobs, **335–338**, *336–338*
DBO and, 4, 345
immediate backups, **338–342**, *339–342*

NOARCHIVELOG mode
backing up in, **329–330**
vs. ARCHIVELOG mode, 328
reasons for backing up, 324–325
summary, 345–346
backup jobs, creating, **335–338**, *336–338*
Backup Manager, 113
Backup Wizard, 336–338, *337–338*, 339–342,
339–342
buffer cache, 15

C

Capacity Planner utility, 427–428, *428*
CD-ROM
downloading Oracle8i CD-ROM, 37
installing from, 37
that comes with this book, xxix–xxx
EdgeTek Learning Systems, xxix
electronic flashcards for exam
preparation, xxx
OCP: Oracle8i DBO Study Guide
Ebook, xxx
Certification Initiative for Enterprise Development, xxiii
character functions, 137–138
CHARACTER SET, 174
checkpoint (CKPT), 16
client preferences, storing, 35
client software installation, **63–69**, *63–69*
client/server
applications, **8–9**, *9*

communication, **16–17**

columns, 19, *19*, 214

communication between client and server, **16–17**

   the Listener, 17

   Net8, 16–17

components of databases (includes table),
   169–172

   control files, 171

   datafiles, **171–172**

      redo log files, 172

      rollback segments and, 172

      system datafiles, 172

      system tablespaces and, 172

      for user data, 171

      user tablespaces and, 171

   parameter files, 169–170

   password files (includes table), 170–171

components, building interface components, 367

configuration files and instances, 14, *14*

console. *See* Enterprise Manager

contentions

   avoiding with locks, 411–412

   monitoring with Performance Monitor, 424

control files, 18, **171**

   and non-Oracle data, 276–277

CONTROLFILE REUSE, 174

CPU

   determining speed, 234

   monitoring, 416

   speed and, 166

CREATE DATABASE, 173, 174

CREATE ROLLBACK SEGMENT, 174

Create Site Wizard, **383–385**, *383–385*

creating databases, **172–183**

   checking prerequisites, 172

   creating parameter files, 173

   creating password files, 173

   Database Configuration Assistant Wizard,
      175–183, *175–183*

   DBO and, 3

   exam objectives, 159

   instances, starting and restarting, 173

   preparation for, 172

   summary, 187

   using PL/SQL, 173–174

      CHARACTER SET, 174

      CONTROLFILE REUSE, 174

      CREATE ROLBACK SEGMENT, 174

      DATAFILE, 174

      LOGFILE GROUP1, 174

      LOGFILE GROUP2, 174

cross joins (Cartesian Products), 145, *145*

D

data

   control files and non-Oracle data, 276–277

   DBO and, 3

   exporting Oracle data, **264–269**,
      265–268, 282

   importing

      with INSERT statement, **260–263**,
         261–262

      summary of, 282

using Import Wizard, **269–274,** *269–274*

loading non-Oracle data, **274–276,** *275*

   constraints, enabling and disabling, **275–276**

   procedure for loading, **277–281,** *277, 279–281*

scheduling data jobs, **282**

Schema Manager for importing and exporting data, **264–276**

Database Access Descriptor (DAD), configuring in WebDB, 378–379, *379*

database administrators. *See* DBAs

database components, 17–20

   logical objects, **18–20,** *19,* 187

   physical objects, **17–18**

database design, **229–233**

   instance parameters, **232**

   logical design, **229–230**

      foreign keys, **231,** *231*

      indexes, **231–232**

      primary keys, **230–231,** *230*

      views, **232**

   overcoming bad design, 229

   physical database design, **233**

database files. *See also* rollback segments

   adding to database, 167

   control files, 18, **171**

      and non-Oracle data, 276–277

   fault tolerance, planning for, RAID 0, **161–162,** *162*

   increasing size of, 167

parameter files, **169–170**

   creating, 173

   editing for automatic ARCHIVELOG mode, **330–331,** *331*

   initialization parameter files (INIT.ORA), 34

   issues, 415–416

password files (PWD.ORA), 34–35, **170–171**

   creating, 173

   password file tools (table), 170

performance and placement of, **160–168**

   fault tolerance and reliability, planning for, **161–166**

   growth, planning for, **167**

   managing, **184–186**

   placement, **167–168**

   placement of databases, **167–168**

   speed, planning for, **166–167**

   summary, 187

   understanding, **168–172**

redo log files, 19, **172**

   adding, modifying and deleting, 415

   changing default settings for, 180

   defined, 414

   issues with, 414–415, *415*

   RAID 10 and, 166

Storage Manager, **184–186,** *184, 185, 186*

   Autoextend properties of datafiles, 186, *186*

   creating new datafiles, 185, *185*

system datafiles, 172

types of (table), 169

understanding, **168–172**

    physical components of databases
(includes tables), **169–172**

    System IDs (SIDs), 168–169

database objects, 19–20, *19*

browsing with WebDB, **363–366**, *364–366*

building with WebDB Administrator,
367–372, *368–372*

creating and managing, **240–250**

    indexes, **243–245**, *245*

    procedures, **247–248**, *248*

    synonyms, **248–249**, *249*

    tables, **240–243**, *242–243*

    views, **245–247**, *246*

database operators. *See* DBOs

databases. *See also* backing up databases;
creating databases; discovering databases;
managing databases; problems with databases; restoring databases

converting to ARCHIVELOG mode,
330–335, *331*, *333–335*

    editing the parameter file for
automatic ARCHIVELOG
mode, **330–331**, *331*

    modifying to run in
ARCHIVELOG mode,
332–335, *333–335*

creating groups, **98–99**, *99*

protection of, **324–346**

DATAFILE, 174

datafiles, 19. *See also* database files;
tablespaces

ALTERDATABASE command, 18, 184

creating new, 185, *185*

rollback segments and, 172

system datafiles, 172

system tablespaces and, 172

for user data, 171

user tablespaces and, 171

datatypes, 19

DBAs

adding to the management server, **97–98**, *97*

certification, xxii

privileges of, 237

responsibilities of, *5–6*

Sybex books for, 6

dbora_start file, 46–47

dbora_stop file, 46–47

DBOs

basic skills necessary, 124

certification, xxiii

    certification track (includes table), xxiv

    skills required for, xxv

privileges of, 237

responsibilities of, **2–5**, 21–22, 260, 345

DBWR (database writer), 15

deadlocks, 439

troubleshooting, 412, *412*

default objects, 20

452 default user passwords – exam

default user passwords, 125–126, *126*

Diagnostics Pack, 114, **417–428**, 439

    installing, 83–89, *83–89*, **417–419**, *417–419*

    running, 197, **420–428**, *420*

        Capacity Planner utility, 427–428, *428*

        Performance utility, 422–427, *422–427*

        TopSessions utility, 420–421, *421*

        Trace Data Viewer, 428

        Trace Manager utility, 428

directory mappings, configuring, 380–381, *381*

directory structure, **32–35**

    directories and contents table, 33

    initialization parameter files (INIT.ORA), 34

    ORACLE_BASE, 32–33

        \ADMIN, 32–33

        \ORACLE_HOME, 32–34

        \ORADATA, 32–33

    password files (PWD.ORA), 34–35

        adding users, 34–35

discovering databases, **93–95**, *94*, *95*

disk duplexing, **163**, *163*

disk mirroring, **162–163**, *163*

disk striping, **161–162**, *162*

DNS

    Intelligent Agent and, 301

    name resolution and, 61

DSS (decision support systems), 20

E

Easy Configuration utility, 72

EdgeTek Learning Systems, xxix

Ellison, Lawrence J., xxi

Enterprise Manager (OEM), 91

    administrators, adding, **97–98**, *97*

    for analyzing Oracle sessions, 416

    Configuration Assistant, 100, *100*

    connecting to the management server, 91–92, *92*

    creating jobs and events, **99**

    discovering databases, **93–95**, *94*, *95*

    exporting data with, 264–265

    groups, creating, **98–99**, *99*

    for implementing applications, 229

    installing, 82, **83–91**, *83–90*

    Oracle Intelligent Agent and, 296, 298–300

    preferences, configuring, **95–97**, *96*, *97*

    summary, 115

Event Library, 303, 305

events

    creating to automate common tasks, 99

    Event Library, 303, 305

    server management and, **302–306**

        creating, **303–305**, *304–305*

        modifying, **305–306**, *306*

    summary, 316

    using to detect problems with databases, 294

exam. *See also* exam objectives; exam review

    Assessment Test, xxxi–xxxix

CD-ROM that comes with this book and,
    xxix–xxx
cost of, xxvii
general preparation instructions, xxviii
locations, xxvii
practice exam, 394–407
registering for, xxvii
tips for taking, xxv
exam objectives
administration issues, anticipating, 291
applications
        creating objects to application
            data, 227
        creating objects to store application
            data, 227
        implementing logical and physical
            structure for new
            applications, 227
        implementing structure for new, 227
        securing application data
            manipulation, 197
        setting up users for new, 197
databases
        accessing, 81
        backing up, 323
        restoring, 323
        starting and stopping, 81
DBO duties, 1
finding Oracle files, 31
installing database software, 31, 81

loading non-Oracle data, 259
most current objectives, 1
Net8, 31
Oracle basics, 1
SQL
        data retrieval techniques, 123
        SELECT statements, 123
WebDB, 353
exam review, xxv
applications, installing and managing,
    251–258
databases
        backing up, 346–352
        creating and managing, 188–195
        restoring, 346–352
data, importing and exporting, 283–290
DBO duties, 22–29
Diagnostics Pack, 115–122
Enterprise Manager, 115–122
Instance Manager, 115–122
practice exam, 394–407
Oracle
        basics, 22–29
        installing and configuring, 72–79
server management, 316–322
SQL*Plus, 115–122
Tuning Pack, 115–122
WebDB, 386–392
exercises, table of, xix
Export Wizard, **265–268**, *265–268*

F

fault tolerance, planning for, **161–166**
    disk duplexing, **163**, *163*
    RAID 0, **161–162**, *162*
    RAID 1, **162–163**, *163*
    RAID 5, **164–165**, *164*, *165*
    RAID 10, **165–166**
files. *See* configuration files; database files;
    datafiles; system datafiles; tablespaces;
    trace files management
Financial Applications consultant
    certification, xxiv
flashcards (electronic) for exam preparation, xxx
flat-file databases, **10**, *10*
foreign keys, **231**, *231*, 241

G

Global Database Name, 52, *52*, 54, *54*
glossary, 442–445
Grant Manager, **373**, *374*
GROUP BY command, 140
GROUP command, 39
groups, creating, **98–99**, *99*
growth, planning for, **167**
    adding additional files to the database, 167
    making existing files larger, 167

H

hard drive, troubleshooting, 416
    forecasting hard drive space, 233
HAVING clause, 140
HOST files, and Oracle Intelligent Agent, 301
HP-UX, 7–8

I

Import Wizard, **269–274**, *269–274*
Index Tuning Expert, **436–438**, *436–438*
indexes, **231–232**, **243–245**, *245*
    index storage structure, 20
initialization parameter files (INIT.ORA), 34.
    See also parameter files
INIT.ORA files, 34. *See also* parameter files
    editing to support automatic archiving,
        331, *331*
inner joins (Equijoins), 142–143, *143*
INSERT statement, 146, **260–263**, *261–262*
installing and configuring Oracle8i, **31–72**
    DBOs and, 3
    directory structure (includes table), **32–35**
    installing client software, **63–69**, *63–69*
    installing on Linux, **35–48**
        hardware and software installation
            requirements, **36–37**
        Oracle 8.1.6 installation procedures,
            40–45, *41–44*
        post-installation tasks, **45–48**

user Oracle tasks, **39–40**

user root tasks, **37–39**

installing on Novell NetWare, **55–56**

    hardware requirements, *55*

    installation procedures, *56*

    software requirements, *55*

    tasks before installation, *55*

installing on Windows NT, **49–54**

    hardware requirements, *49*

    installation procedures, *50–54*, *50–54*

    software requirements, *49*

    tasks before installation, *49*

listener configuration, **60–63**

    starting and stopping the listener, *61–62*, *62*

managing trace files, **57**

Net8 configuration, **70–71**

start up with Server Manager, **57–58**

    STARTUP MOUNT, *58*

    STARTUP NOMOUNT, *58*

    STARTUP OPEN, *58*, *58*

    STARTUP RESTRICT, *58*

stopping with Server Manager, **59–60**

    SHUTDOWN ABORT, *60*

    SHUTDOWN IMMEDIATE, *59*, *59*

    SHUTDOWN NORMAL, *59*

storing client preferences, *35*

summary, *32*, *71–72*

instance parameters, **232**

instances, **13–16**, *13*

    components of, **13–16**, *14*

creating database files and, *173*

Diagnostics Pack and, *114*

I/O chart and, *423–424*, *424*

instance failures vs. media failures, *327*

Instance Manager, *57*, *63*, **100–109**, *102–108*

    converting databases to ARCHIVELOG mode using, **32–335**, *333–335*

    using to start and stop instances, **101–108**, *102–108*

opening databases and, *13*, *16*

pros and cons of using, *101*

starting, *100–101*

where to run from, *101*

interface components, building, *367*

Inventory Location screen, *42*, *42*

IPC, using to connect to databases, *67*, *67*

J

Java developer certification, *xxiii*

Job Library, *312*, *312*

jobs, **307–315**. *See also* backup jobs

    creating, *307–308*

        OS jobs, *308–310*, *308–310*

        SQL jobs, **310–312**, *311*

        to automate common tasks, *99*

    deleting, *315*

    Job Library, *312*, *312*

    job output, *281*, *281*, *313–315*, *342*, *342*

    modifying and running manually, **312**

    summary, *316*

using to respond to problems with
databases, 295
viewing job details, output, and history,
313–315, *313–315*

L

LGWR (log writer), 16
LIKE function, 137
Linux, **7–8**
 RAID 0 and, 161
 RAID 1 and, 162
 RAID 5 and, 164
Linux, installing Oracle8i on, **35–48**
 hardware and software installation
  requirements, **36–37**
 installation process, **40–45**, *41–44*
 post-installation tasks, **45–48**
 user Oracle tasks, **39–40**
 user root tasks, **37–39**
  creating Linux groups, 38
  creating the Linux user name, 38–39
  creating mount points, 38
  installing from CD-ROM, 37
  TCP/IP and, 37
LISTENER.ORA, 60–61, 71
Listeners, 17
 better control over, 62
 configuring, **60–63**
  automatically, *54*
  modifying, 61

starting and stopping the listener,
 61–62, *62*
creating groups, **98–99**, *99*
default preferences and, *95*
reserving a port for, 48
WebDB and
 changing settings, **379–382**, *380–382*
 configuring settings, **378–379**, *379*
Load Wizard, **279–281**, *279–280*
loads, conventional and direct, 274–275
locks
 issues, **411–412**
 managing with Performance Monitor,
  422–423, *422–423*, 439
log writer (LGWR), 16
LOGFILE GROUP1, 174
LOGFILE GROUP2, 174
logical objects, **18–20**, *19*, 187
logical operators, **139**
LSNRCTL for Listener control, 62, *62*

M

management servers, adding administrators to,
 97–98, *97*
managing databases. *See also* problems with
 databases; troubleshooting
 DBOs and, **4–5**
 events and, 302–303
 jobs and, 307
 Oracle Intelligent Agent and, 295
media, media failures vs. instance failures, 327

memory, monitoring, 426, *426*

MIME connections, configuring, 381–382, *382*

Mortensen, Lance, xxx

N

Net8, 16–17

    automatic configuration of, 53, *53*

    configuration of, **70–71**

    modification of, 61, 71

    Net8 Configuration Assistant, 65, *65*,
        68–69, *68, 69*

    NetWare Intelligent Agent and, 301

    Windows NT Intelligent Agent and, 296

NetWare, 7–8. *See also* Novell NetWare

    discovering databases and, 93

    integrating with Oracle, **216–217**, *217*

    loading the NetWare Intelligence Agent,
        300–302

    RAID 0 and, 161

    RAID 1 and, 162

network bandwidth, determining, 234

network operating systems for Oracle8i, **7–8**

NOARCHIVELOG mode

    backing up in, **329–330**

    summary, 345–346

    vs. ARCHIVELOG mode, **328–329**

nodes

    creating groups of, **98–99**, *99*

    default preferences and, *95*

NOMOUNT mode, 173

non-client/server database applications, 9, *9*

Novell NetWare

    installing, **55–56**

        hardware requirements, *55*

        installation procedures, *56*

        software requirements, *55*

        tasks before installation, *55*

NULL values, **138**

numeric columns, ordering, 133

O

object owners, 237–238

object permissions (includes table), **213–214**

object security and ownership, **198–216**, *199*

    creating new users, **200–206**, *201–205*

        assigning tablespaces, **203–205**, *204*

        changing tablespaces, **204–205**

        managing quotas for users,
            205–206, *205*

    database roles, **207–212**, *207–211*

        assigning to users, **211**, *211*

        creating, **207–209**, *207, 208*

        granting privileges and role mem-
            bership to, **209–211**, *209–210*

    default users (includes table), **199–200**

    object permissions (includes table), **213–214**

    profiles, **214–216**

        assigning, **216**, *216*

        creating and editing, **214–215**, *215*

    system privileges, **212–213**

objects. *See* database objects

OCP, xxi, xxv

    OCP: Oracle8i DBO Study Guide Ebook, xxx

OEM. *See* Enterprise Manager

OLAP (online analytical processing), 20, 177,
    410–411

OLTP (online transaction processing), 21, 177,
    410–411

online analytical processing. *See* OLAP

online transaction processing. *See* OLTP

OPEN mode, starting databases in, 58, *58*

opening databases and instances, 13

operating systems

    creating OS jobs, **308–310**, *308–310*

    protecting data with OS options, 326

Oracle. *See also* Oracle Expert; Oracle Intelligent
    Agent; Oracle Universal Installer; SIDs

    basics, **7–17**

        client/server applications, **8–9**, *9*

        communication with, **16–17**

        exam objectives, 1

        instances, **13–16**, *13*, *14*

        network operating systems for
            Oracle8i, **7–8**

        types of databases, **10–12**, *10*, *12*

    certifications, xxi, xxii–xxiv

    Oracle Certified Professioal certification
        (OCP), xxi

        certification track (includes table),
            xxiv–xxv

    Oracle Corporation, xxi, 7

    summary, 21–22

    tuning for optimal performance, 5

Web sites

    for certification information, xxiv

    for downloading Oracle8i, 37

    for downloading or ordering
        software, 8

    for exam preparation, xxix

    for training and certification
        information, 1

Oracle Expert, **429–435**, *430–435*

Oracle Intelligent Agent, 264, **295–302**

    about, 292

    loading the NetWare Agent, **300–302**

        configuring HOST file or DNS, 301

        configuring NET8 for NetWare, 301

        configuring SQLNET.ORA, 301

        procedures, 301–302

    loading Unix Agent, **302**

    loading Windows NT Agent, **296–300**

        changing Agent account
            password, 297

        configuring Agent account, 297

        configuring Agent in Enterprise
            Manager, 298

        configuring NET8, 296

        installing Agent, 296

        procedures for configuring and
            loading, **298–300**, *298–300*

        setting for automatic start, 297

Oracle System Identifer. *See* SID

Oracle Universal Installer, 32–33, 45

    configuring Listener and, 61

    configuring Net8 and, 62

for installing client software, **63–64**, *63*, *64*

Root Tasks screen, 43, *43*

starting within Windows Manager, 40

ORACLE_BASE, 32–33

\ORACLE_HOME directory, 32–34, 71

OS

  creating OS jobs, **308–310**, *308–310*

  protecting data with OS options, 326

OUI. *See* Oracle Universal Installer

outer joins, 144, *144*

owners, defined, 228

P

parameter files, **169–170**

  creating, 173

  editing for automatic ARCHIVELOG
    mode, **330–331**, *331*

  initialization parameter files (INIT.ORA), 34

  issues, 415–416

parameters when using PL/SQL to create
  databases, **174**

password files (PWD.ORA), 34–35, **170–171**

  creating, 173

  password file tools (table), 170

passwords

  changing for Oracle Intelligent Agent
    accounts, 297

  changing with WebDB, 375

  default users,' 125–126, *126*, 199–200

  SYS account, 54, *54*

  SYSTEM account, 54, *54*

performance

  issues, 416

  tuning, **409–439**

Performance Monitor, 422–427, *422–427*

  for dealing with locking contention, 412

  viewing charts and folders with

    Contention folder, 424

    I/O folder, 423, *423*

    Instance folder for viewing
      tablespace parameters, 424,
      424–425

    Load folder for tracking sessions
      statistics, 426, *426*

    Locks Manager folder, 422–423,
      422–423

    Top Resource Consumers folder,
      427, *427*

PGA (Program Global Area), 15

physical components of databases.
  See components of databases

physical objects, **17–18**

PL/SQL. *See also* PL/SQL tools

  adding comments to code, 145–146

  creating databases using, **173–174**

  summary, 148

PL/SQL tools, **126–130**. *See also* PL/SQL
Server Manager

    connecting to Oracle via,
      128–129, *129*

    starting, 128

  SQL*Plus, 129–130

    running a simple enquiry, 130, *130*

starting, 129–130, *130*

SQLPlus Worksheet, **127–128**

running a simple query, 128, *128*

starting, 127, *127*

practice exam, 394–407

preferences

configuring, **95–97**, *96–97*

storing, 35, 71

primary key contraints, 262

primary keys, **230–231**, *230*, 241

privileges

system, 212–213

users'

granting, **209–211**, *209–210*

granting privileges to with Grant
Manager, *373*, **374**

WebDB privileges, reporting, 375–377, *376*

problems with databases, **292–295**

complications of running OLAP and OLTP
functions simultaneously, 411

contention problems

avoiding with locks, 411–412

deadlocks, 412, *412*

detecting, **293–294**

with events, 294

manual detection, 293

responding to problems, **294–295**

manual response, 294

using jobs to respond to
problems, 295

summary, 316, 410

procedures, 19, *19*, **147–148**

creating, 147, **247–248**, *248*

profiles, **214–216**

assigning, 216, *216*

creating and editing, 214–215, *214*

protocols for connecting to databases, selecting,
67, *67*

PWD.ORA files, 34, 72

Q

quotas, managing, 205, *205*

R

RAID (Redundant Array of Inexpensive
Drives)

RAID 0, **161–162**, *162*, 167

RAID 1, **162–163**, *163*

RAID 5 (striping with parity), **164–165**,
164–165, 167

RAID 10, **165–166**, 167

RAM

estimating amount of, 234

monitoring, 416

RDBMS (relational database management
systems recovery), **11–12**, *12*

recovery scenarios, **327–328**

cold vs. warm backups, 328

instance failures vs. media failures, 327

redo log buffer, 15

redo log files, 18, **172**

    adding, modifying and deleting, 415

    changing default settings for, 180

    defined, 414

    issues with, 414–415, *415*

    RAID 10 and, 166

relational database management systems

    (RDBMS), **11–12**, *12*

repositories, creating, 87–89, *87–89*

resources, ensuring adequate, **233–234**

    monitoring use of, **427**, *427*

respositories

    creating and modifying, 100, *100*

    logging into, 91–93, *92–93*

restoring databases, **343–346**

    DBOs and, 4

    from a cold backup, 343

    from a full backup, **343–345**, *344–345*

    Recovery Wizard, 344–345, *344–345*

    summary, 345–346

Role Manager, 374, *374*

roles, **207–212**

    assigning to users, **211–212**, *211*

    creating, **207–209**, *207–208*

    granting privileges and role membership

        to, **209–211**, *209–210*

    Role Manager, 374, *374*

    system, 212

rollback segments, 172

    creating, 414

    editing, 413, *413*

    issues with, 412–413, *413*

root tasks at installation, **37–39**, *43*

rows, 19, *19*

    inserting, **146**

    updating, **146**

rules, 20

S

schema accounts, **237–239**

    creating and managing, **238–239**, *239*

    database accounts and, **237–238**

Schema Manager, 439

    creating schemas with, 240

    gathering information about tables, 261, *261*

    importing and exporting data with,

        264–274, *265–268*

schemas, 134, 251

    creating, **240–249**

    selecting tables from other schemas with

        SQL, **134–135**

Scheme Manager, 113

security, **197–219**. *See also* Security Manager

    creating and managing, 250

    database objects management and, 5

    integrating NetWare and, **216–217**

    integrating Unix and, **218**

    integrating Windows NT and, **218**

object security and ownership, **198–216,** *199*

    creating new users, **200–206,**
        201–205

    database roles, **207–212,** *207–211*

    default users (includes table),
        199–200

    object permissions (includes
        table), **213–214**

    profiles, **214–216**

    system privileges, **212–213**

password files (PWD.ORA), 34–35, **170–171**

    creating, 173

    password file tools (table), 170

passwords

    changing for Oracle Intelligent
        Agent accounts, 297

    changing with WebDB, 375

    default users,' 125–126, *126,*
        199–200

    SYS account, 54, *54*

    SYSTEM account, 54, *54*

summary, 218–219

Security Manager, 113

    creating and assigning database roles with,
        208–209, *208,* 211

    creating new users with, **201–203,** *201–203*

    profiles and, 214–216

    setting quotas and, 206

SELECT statements, **130–146**

    adding comments to SQL code, **145–146**

    arithmetic functions (includes table), 135–136

    character functions, 137–138

    components of, 130

    joining tables, **142–145,** *143–145*

        cross joins (Cartesian Products),
            145, *145*

        inner joins (Equijoins),
            142–143, *143*

        outer joins, 144, *144*

    logical operators, **139**

    NULL values, **138**

    ordering numeric columns, 133

    renaming columns, 134

    selecting tables from other schemas, **134–135**

    summarizing data, **139–140**

        GROUP BY command, 140

        HAVING clause, 140

    UNION operator, 140–142

    uses of, 130

Server Manager

    connecting to Oracle via, **128–129,** *129*

    shut down with, **59–60**

        SHUTDOWN ABORT, 60

        SHUTDOWN IMMEDIATE, *59, 59*

        SHUTDOWN NORMAL, *59*

    similarity to SQL*Plus, 112

    start up with, **57–58**

        STARTUP MOUNT, *58*

        STARTUP NOMOUNT, *58*

        STARTUP OPEN, *58, 58*

        STARTUP RESTRICT, *58*

servers

    connecting to the management server with
        Enterprise Manager, 91–92, *92*

management of

    common problems, **292–295**

    DBOs and, **4–5**

    events and, **302–306**

    jobs and, **307–315**

    Oracle Intelligent Agent and, **295–302**

    summary, 316

  processes, 15, 16

sessions

  analyzing with Enterprise Manager, 416

  tracking, 426, *426*, 427, *427*

  using Performance Monitor for tracking

    sessions statistics, 426, *426*

SGA (System Global Area), 14, 181

shared pools, 15

shut down, automating, 45–48

SHUTDOWN ABORT, 60

SHUTDOWN IMMEDIATE, *59*, *59*

SHUTDOWN NORMAL, *59*

SHUTDOWN TRANSACTIONAL, *59*

SIDs (system IDs), 40, 52, *52*, **168–169**

SNMP, 93

speed, planning for, **166–167**

SQL*Plus, 34–35, 126, 129–130

  running a simple enquiry, 130, *130*

  similarity to Server Manager, 112

  starting, **129–130**, *130*

  using to run SQL commands, **110–111**, *111*

SQL. *See also* PL/SQL; SQL*Plus; SQLPlus

  Worksheet

  about, 124–126, *124*, *126*

  codes, 19

    adding comments to, 145–146

    creating new users with, **202–203**, *203*

  commands

    using SQL*Plus to run, **110–111**, *111*

    using SQLPlus Worksheet to run,

      109–110, *110*

  creating SQL jobs, **310–312**, *311*

  procedures, **147–148**

  rows

    inserting, 146

    updating, 146

  SELECT statements, **130–146**

    adding comments to code, **145–146**

    arithmetic functions (includes

      table), **135–136**

    character functions, **137–138**

    components of, 130

    joining tables, **142–145**, *143–145*

    logical operators, **139**

    NULL values, **138**

    ordering numeric columns, 133

    renaming columns, 134

    selecting tables from other

      schemas, **134–135**

    summarizing data, **139–140**

    UNION operator, **140–142**

    uses of, 130

  statements, analyzing, 439

  summary, 148

syntax
  creating roles with, 207, 209
  creating schemas with, 240
SQL Analyze, 439
SQLNET.ORA
  Oracle Intelligent and, 301
  for storing client preferences, 35, 71
SQLPlus Worksheet, **109–110**, *110*, 126, **127–128**
  adding comments to SQL code, 145–146
  running a simple query, 128, *128*
  starting, 127, *127*
start up
  automating, **45–48**
  with Server Manager, **57–58**
STARTUP MOUNT, *58*
STARTUP NOMOUNT, *58*
STARTUP OPEN, 58, *58*
STARTUP RESTRICT, *58*
Storage Manager, 112, **184–186**, *184*, 413
  adding, modifying and deleting redo log files, 415, *415*
  Autoextend properties of datafiles and, 186, *186*
  creating a new datafile with, 185, *185*
striping with parity (RAID 5), **164–165**, *164*, *165*
summarizing data, **139–140**
  GROUP BY command, 140
  HAVING clause, 140
Sun Solaris, **7–8**
Sybex books for DBAs, 6
Sylvan Prometric Authorized Testing Centers, xxvii

synonyms, 248–249, *249*
SYS account passwords, 54, *54*
Sysdbas, 170. *See also* DBAs
Sysop. *See* DBOs
SYSTEM account password, 54, *54*
system datafiles, 172. *See also* tablespaces
System DBA. *See* DBA
system files, 234. *See also* tablespaces
System IDs. *See* SIDs
system privileges, 212–213

T

tables, 19, *19*
  creating, **240–243**, *242–243*
  inserting data into, **260–263**, *261–262*
  joining, **142–145**, *143–145*
    cross joins (Cartesian Products), 145, *145*
    inner joins (Equijoins), 142–143, *143*
    outer joins, 144, *144*
  using Schema Manager to gather information about, 261, *261*
Tablespace Manager, 439
tablespaces
  creating, 184, **234–236**, *235–236*
  defined, 234
  ensuring adequate sizing, 250
  expanding, 184
  implementing, DBOs and, 3

monitoring and modifying characteristics, 439

paramaters, 424, *424–425*

Storage Manager and, 112, 184

system tablespaces, 172, 203

Tablespace Manager and, 439

users and, 171, **203–205**, *204*

tasks, using events to automate common tasks, 99

TCP/IP, connection to databases, 67, *67*

TNSNAMES.ORA, 61, 70, 71

TopSessions utility, 420–421, *421*

Trace Data Viewer, 428

trace files management, 57, 182

Trace Manager utility, 428

transaction processing vs. warehousing, **20–21**

triggers, 20

troubleshooting, 5. *See also* problems with
databases

applications, 416

deadlocks, 412, *412*

Diagnostics Pack and, 114, **420–429**

events, using to detect problems, 294

hard drive, 416

Index Tuning Expert, 436

installation, 45

Oracle Intelligent Agent, 295

Oracle Universal Installer, 70

parameter files, 415–416

redo log files, 414–415, *415*

rollback segments, 412–413, *413*

Trace Manager utility and, 428

using jobs, 295

tuning for optimal performance, *5*

Tuning Pack, 114, **429–439**

Index Tuning Expert, **436–438**, *436–438*

installing, 90, *90*

Oracle Expert, **429–435**, *430–435*

SQL Analyze, 439

Tablespace Manager, 439

Tuning Session Wizard, 429–430, *430*

types of databases, **10–12**

flat-file databases, **10**, *10*

relational database management systems
(RDBMS), **11–12**, *12*

U

UNION operator, **140–142**, 140–142

Unix, **7–8**

integrating with Oracle, **216–217**, *217*

loading Unix Intelligent Agent, **302**

Unix Group Name screen, 42, *42*

UNMASK command, 39

UPDATE command, 146

UPS power systems, 161

User. *See also* users

accounts, 251

DBOs and setup and management
of, 4

types, 237

data storage, 171

security, **197–219**

users. *See also* user
    accessibility and, 13
    creating new, **200–206**, *201–205*
        with Security Manager, **201–203**,
            201–203
        using SQL code, **202–203**, *203*
    default passwords (table), 199–200
    granting privileges to with Grant Manager,
        373, 374
    managing quotas, **205–206**
    managing rights of, 113
    passwords, 125–126, *126*
    summary, 218–219
    tablespaces and, 171, **203–205**, *204*
    tracking with locks, 411
    User Manager and WebDB, **373**, *373*

V

views, 20, **232**, **245–247**, *246*

W

warehousing
    vs. transaction processing, **20–21**
    and the Web, 21
Web sites
    for downloading Oracle8i, 37
    for exam preparation, xxix
    for registering for exams, xxviii

    for sophisticated configuration setup
        information, 45
    for Sybex books for DBAs, 6
    for training and certification information, 1
    WebDB Web site, 361
WebDB, **354–385**
    accessing, 354
    Administer options, **373–382**
        changing Listener settings,
            379–382, *380–382*
        changing passwords, *375*, *375*
        configuring Listener settings,
            378–379, *379*
        Grant Manager, **373–374**, *374*
        Role Manager, **374**, *374*
        User Manager, **373**, *373*
        WebDB Activity Logs, configuring,
            377–378, *377–378*
        WebDB privileges, reporting,
            375–377, *376*
    building sites, **383–385**, *383–385*
    connecting to, **361–362**, *361–362*
        Web address for WebDB, 361
    installing, **355–360**, *356–360*
    key features, **354–355**
    monitoring, **382–383**, *382*
    summary, 385
    WebDB Administration program, 362, *362*
    WebDb Administrator, 355
        browsing database objects with,
            362–366, *363–366*

building database objects with, 367–372, *368–372*

building interface components with, 367

WHERE clause, 132, 139

Windows NT, **7–8**

    installing Oracle8i on, **49–54**

        hardware requirements, 49

        installation procedures, 50–54, *50–54*

        software requirements, 49

        tasks before installation, 49

    integrating with Oracle, **216–217**, *217*

    RAID 0 and, 161

    RAID 1 and, 162

    RAID 5 and, 164

    stopping and starting WebDB manually and, 361

    Windows NT servers

        configuring and loading Windows NT Intelligent Agent, **296–300**

        discovering databases and, 93

Wizards

    Backup Wizard, 336–338, *337–338*, **339–342**, *339–342*

    Create Site Wizard, **383–385**, *383–385*

    Database Configuration Assistant Wizard, **175–183**, *175–183*

    Export Wizard, **265–268**, *265–268*

Import Wizard, **269–274**, *269–274*

Load Wizard, **279–281**, *279–280*

Recovery Wizard, **344–345**, *344–345*

Tuning Session Wizard, **429–430**, *430*

Oracle Software License Agreement